For three wise men who passed
on in the last year: Yashvantrai Naik,
Mohamed Bouazizi and Athiraman
Kannan. We learn from their
(unnecessarily short) lives each and
every day.

Responses

to *Critical Cities Volume 1* and *Volume 2*

"Let me make this clear right from the start: I recommend you read *Critical Cities Volume 2*. I predict you will find many of the pieces gathered together within it interesting, informative, passionate, thought-provoking, and ultimately enriching. It is also quite possible that you will find the book infuriating and throw it down in exasperation once or twice, but then let me clarify: I think you should read this book because it will be good for you to do so." DOMINIC CHURCH, *Architectural Review*

"*Critical Cities Volume 2* is a fascinating, challenging and insightful critique of contemporary urbanism and gives a voice to many who are often overlooked and bypassed in development processes. It is an essential counterweight to the glib assertions of many urban commentators." JULIAN DOBSON, co-founder of *New Start Magazine* and author of *Living With Rats Blog*

"Cities are turbulent masses of contradictions, in which exhilaration can turn to frustration at the turn of a corner. So if I say that this book also has these traits, I mean it as the highest compliment, because in that it reflects the urban condition. A typical academic response to cities is to iron out the mess in order to control the contradictions under the guise of reasoned argument, be it in the commonplaces of 'placemaking' or the doctrines of new urbanism. In contrast, this book dismisses any notion of control or single viewpoint, and instead allows voices from outside and underneath to bubble up." PROFESSOR JEREMY TILL, author of *Architecture Depends*

Published in 2012 by Myrdle Court Press, London, UK
in association with This Is Not A Gateway

ISBN 978-0-9563539-3-1

Myrdle Court Press is an independent
publishing company that advances critical ideas
generated by emerging urbanists.

Unit 24 Myrdle Court, Myrdle Street, London E1 1HP
www.myrdlecourtpress.net

Designed by Karolin Schnoor
www.karolinschnoor.co.uk

Printed and bound by Imprint Digital, Exeter, UK

CRITICAL CITIES

IDEAS, KNOWLEDGE AND AGITATION
——— *from* ———
EMERGING URBANISTS

VOLUME 3

edited by
DEEPA NAIK *&* TRENTON OLDFIELD
THIS IS NOT A GATEWAY

Contents

5

STRATIFICATION

INTRODUCTION

City As Inequality

DEEPA NAIK & TRENTON OLDFIELD

Cities are lauded, particularly by the Urban Industry[1], as being unrivalled fonts of creativity, trade and financial might, as well as the 'natural' landscape for democracy – city as progress and modernity. However, despite the intense 'bread and circuses' regime[2] running since at least 2008, this heavily sponsored proposition seems not to be holding together quite like before. Even month-long government–funded events with themes such as 'The Playful City'[3] are failing to disguise that cities are also the sites, and perhaps more importantly, the producers of increasing inequalities.

The contributions to this book, from various corners of the planet, draw out many of the compelling characteristics of cities. At the same time the authors' research and experiences suggest quite vigorously that it is crucial to consider 'cities' as spaces and sets of social relations that result from, produce and perpetuate inequalities. This goes against commonly held views and beliefs and it seems timely to re-propose 'city' as inequality. Doing so enables us to re-focus a critical lens on past, current and future urban lives. Taking a starting point that cities are a result of inequalities, and forge and maintain these inequalities, one can re-interrogate urban histories and many of the fundamental assumptions of our contemporary lives. At the same time this lens of inequality might generate new perspectives on better ways to live in post–capitalist possibilities.

Two of the characteristics of the accelerated drive of neoliberal capitalism in the late 20th and early 21st centuries are the ever–increasing rural–to–urban migration and densification of urban areas, both often projected as inevitable for 'progress' and hence desirable. Working through the lens 'City As Inequality' assists in raising questions about how people have been encouraged or forced to migrate to cities and who it is that owns the vast tracts of the world's countryside? What are the political ramifications of close to five billion people potentially having no direct agency or access to essential resources such as food and water? What role does the Urban Industry play in this mass migration? What class exploitation is at work and what might future class conflicts look like? Analysis of who benefits from the de-population of the countryside and the consequent crowding of the world's population into a few huge conurbations has become essential in comprehending current contexts and trends.

What elements of contemporary urban planning, architecture and 'regeneration' are exacerbating inequalities and providing indications of what cities might look like in the future? With so many people living together on a small percentage of land surface, questions no doubt arise around the already-increasing reappearance of divisive architecture, city gates, barriers and walls – be they vertical, dormant or digital.

Is it the 'planned' and constructed embodiment of the status quo – the disparity between the majority of urban citizens' poverty and the minority's ostentatious wealth and exclusive zones – that makes cities such a long-standing subject of philosophical debate? Might this lens of inequality be a tool to finally focus academics, currently busy flying around the world networking with one another[4], onto the urgent concerns of the people they feel so comfortable writing about without making the effort to ever actually meet them or offer them a platform?

As the contributions to this book reveal, many of the world's cities, *despite* breathtaking technological advancements, universal suffrage, local democracy, scores of think tanks[5], countless 'urban labs' and urban festivals, are as unequal today as they were in the 1850s in heat of the industrial revolution and the malignancy of European imperialism. The essays published here start to draw out some of the reasons why these inequalities not only remain but are resurgent following a brief respite in the wake of the inhumanity witnessed in World War II. They call for an urgent reappraisal of the motives and logic driving contemporary societies and suggest alternative possibilities. What might our lives be like if our individual and collective decisions were based on the rigorous pursuit of equality, equal opportunity and the pursuit of happiness[6] for all? This opens an optimistic and critical path towards post-capitalist thought and comprehensive regime change – in opposition to those who simply wish to make capitalism a little more 'comfortable' and ask politely for it to be more gentle or 'playful'.[7]

Everything is different

The content of this volume relates to the TINAG festival that focused on the subject of financial districts. Festival participants came from cities across the planet to share their interrogations of spaces such as the City of London, Canary Wharf, Dubai, Hong Kong, Wall Street, Chile's San Isidro, Silom in Bangkok, Seoul's Teheranno, La Défense in Paris and Mumbai's Dalal Street. As the essays are particularly powerful, propositional and rigorous, we have written a detailed text introducing each of the four chapters – Erase, Stretch, Relinquish; Archipelago; Agency; Stratification – and kept this general introduction brief.

This book was published a year later than first envisaged – the TINAG festival it relates to was held in 2010. The delay in publishing was due, firstly, to our urgent relocation to Vancouver, Canada. We swapped our computer screens, books and meetings for doctors' appointments, hospital stays, family gatherings and in the end a cremation.[8] Then secondly, since returning to London, an act of protest at the entirely unnecessary and unacceptable inequalities in the UK resulted in significant time engaged in defence against intimidation and the threat of a long custodial sentence.[9]

These two separate acts and the ensuing lessening of our work are the antithesis of everything that is expected of 21st–century companies, organisations, workers and 'patriotic' subjects. The work ethic and capitalist notions of professionalism that so powerfully permeate most aspects of contemporary lives means that prioritising family and ideals is interpreted as borderline, if not totally, barmy. There is no doubt we would have been voted off Dragon's Den or whatever television or internet competition.

It was clear to us that if we chose the work ethic over family then running This Is Not A Gateway, organising the festival for critical voices and publishing propositional books would be meaningless – we would be standing on hollow ground and clearly supporting the tenets of capitalism.[10] Nurturing the extended family, giving love and support to others and 'making do' economically are considered utterly worthless actions and ideas in capitalist regimes, but, in their own small way, they are revolutionary acts in the current context, as are idling[11] and non-participation[12]. Furthermore, an act of political conscience, civil disobedience and protest, which nowadays almost always results in criminalisation and extremist 'media' attacks that may somehow, we are told, result in possible 'brand devaluing' or 'brand contamination'[13], is something akin to suicide in the capitalistic mind-set.

Everyone alive today knows it is possible to overthrow regimes

Remarkable, breathtaking and persistent courage by tens of millions of people across the planet, particularly since early in 2011, is changing everything. As a result of the desperate act of an individual fruit seller, the people of Tunisia chased the brutal tyrant Ben Ali and his entrenched regime from their shores. Strikes by Egyptian workers spearheaded a momentum that brought hundreds of thousands onto the crossroads of the nation's main cities and led to the eventual removal of Mubarak and his rapacious regime. Libyans, through armed struggle strategically assisted by NATO, overthrew Gaddafi and one of the world's longest continuous dictatorships. All three nations have subsequently held elections and have written post-dictatorship democratic constitutions. Of course there are problems, in some cases, significant problems, as the 'axis of evil' – capitalists, the military and religious leaders – remain mutually supportive even if on the surface they seem to have different agendas. Nonetheless, the overthrow of each of these three tyrannical regimes was shared with hundreds of millions not only via broadcast television but through direct interaction with revolutionaries via their user-created media. The revolutionaries have given a tremendous energy boost and sense of solidarity to tens of millions of people around the world who are going on the streets to seek greater agency, register their indignation at injustices and declare their determination to work for equality in our interconnected lives. The revolutions will continue. Everyone alive today knows it is possible to overthrow regimes – they have seen it with their own eyes.

Whether instigated by striking factory workers, student protestors, displaced farmers or anti-capitalist 'occupiers', these revolutions take place in cities as they are the causative centres – the location of governments, corporation headquarters and financial districts. The essays published in this edition of *Critical Cities: Ideas, Knowledge and Agitation from Emerging Urbanists* spur us on. Everything is different (and so much stays the same) to just a few years ago. Two of the most important aspects apparent from the crisis are: the revealing of a previously opaque (also possibly happily ignored?) corruption in most institutions, and the willingness and determination of millions upon millions around the world to take to the streets (and other public spaces) in order to defend themselves and assert control over the mechanisms that will contribute to shaping their future. There seems to be a shared sixth sense that the next few years will make the difference between cities, now fully integrated through globalisation, becoming more and more like open prisons, or cities and citizens changing up a gear and working towards being locations where ideas of justice, equality and critical knowledge can be worked on. What will matter is tactics and the willingness to use them.

1. For more information see our introduction to *Critical Cities: Volume 2* titled 'The Urban Industry and its Post–Critical Condition' (Myrdle Court Press: London, 2010) pp. 3–27. In the paper we analyse how academia alongside the fields of architecture, property development, real estate investment, planning, design, urban regeneration, conservation management, the creative industries and visual cultures (along with their related foundations, festivals, media and PR) have assisted in attempts to assemble the many in subservience to capitalist interests.

2. 'Bread and Circuses' is understood to have been coined by Roman Empire poet Juvenal (circa 100 CE) who patronisingly saw Roman 'citizens' easily politically distracted by free wheat and elaborate spectacles – often extremely violent 'games' – now a classic strategy for mollifying the repressed masses. In present times we have Papal visits, Royal weddings, national jubilees, hyped celebrity scandals, large sporting events like the summer and winter Olympic 'games', world cups and even regular fixture professional sports as well as government or corporate sponsored festivals, blockbuster exhibitions and mega concerts. Recently the phrase was used as the name of an organization (http://breadandcircuses.org. uk/) set up to problematise the 2012 Summer Olympics in London: "Grand spectacles are being used by the government and corporations to take our minds off austerity measures, the global economic crisis and the commodification of everything, even art."

3. The thematic for the 2012 London Festival of Architecture was 'The Playful City'. In the words of the organisers, "The theme of the 2012 Festival –'The Playful City' – responds to the presence in London of the Olympic and Paralympic Games." The festival is organised jointly by the Royal Institute of British Architects, the Architecture Foundation, New London Architecture and the British Council. It is difficult to understand how these organisations could possibly not acknowledge and be unaware of the fact that London is the most unequal city in the 'western world'. In some London boroughs over 50% of children live in poverty.

4. For example, the recently announced joint initiative by the UCL Urban Laboratory London, Techniche Universitat Berlin, École Polytechnique Fédérale de Lausanne Switzerland, Università della Calabria Italy, Pontificia Universidad Catolica de Chile, Kamla Rehaja Vidyanidhi Institute for Architectural and Environmental Studies India, University of the Witwatersrand South Africa, and the Chinese University of Hong Kong. Funding

of €473,372 was awarded for the network to run from 2013 to 2015 under the Erasmus Mundus Programme. "This investment will support the participating Urban Laboratories in expanding and developing their work through international partnerships. Activities will focus on enhancing urban teaching and research, and will include joint symposia, workshops, faculty exchange and hands-on projects. These are structured around three clusters; interdisciplinarity, global education, and exchanges between academic researchers and built environment professionals." The Urban Industry once more reinforcing its own closed and isolated position within a highly subsidised and post-critical network. See http://www.ucl.ac.uk/urbanlab/en2/index.php?page=1.3.0&getlistarticle=179&listrange=current.

5. Interestingly the winner of the 2012 Venice Biennale was an architectural company that has secured a global registration for its very name Urban Think Tank®.

6. The pursuit of happiness in this context is not in reference to the American Declaration of Independence but instead to more subtle ideas around dignity, fraternity, equality and a good quality of life for everyone, all 7 billion of us.

7. Nothing is quite as optimistic as this, particularly in Britain where we write this – a nation devastated by corruption, authoritarianism and class war and distracted by global sporting events and royalist bread and circuses.

8. We received news that Deepa's father was diagnosed with stage-four terminal cancer. We had three days to decide if we would press ahead with the 2011 festival in London, due to go into production the following week, or relocate to Canada. One week later we were in Vancouver and stayed with him till his death on 11 January 2012.

9. On 7 April 2012 Trenton undertook an act of civil disobedience by swimming into the antiquated pageant that is the Oxford and Cambridge Boat Race held on London's River Thames. Trenton was protesting the crippling and increasing, though entirely unnecessary, stark inequalities in the UK. In the few days preceding the Boat Race the coalition government signed the bill to privatise the NHS and introduced the bill to gain access to private digital information and the Olympics' minister called on people to report neighbours they suspected might protest at the Olympics. Over 70% of the coalition government ministers were at the time Oxbridge educated. Trenton was charged with Public Nuisance, a common law charge. He faces a longer prison term than Pussy Riot's sentence in Russia. His trial starts on the 24 September 2012.

10. Max Weber, *The Protestant Ethic and the Spirit of Capitalism*, new translation of the 1920 classic study revised and introduced by Stephen Kalberg (OUP: New York, 2010).

11. Idling confronts the Protestant and capitalist work ethic head on, challenging the notion that work in and of itself is a good thing. To theoretical idlers, work distracts people from the true pleasures and focus of living while at the same time giving over their bodies, minds and time to make money for others. It is well known that, in one of cruellest of lies, the sign on the gate of the Auschwitz 1 concentration camp read 'Work sets you free'.

12. Withdrawing participation can be a powerful act of resistance. The general expectation is that people will 'join in', thereby acknowledging and condoning whatever the proposed activity or idea is. On an international level, non-participation might include nations declaring themselves 'neutral' or 'non-aligned'. On a personal level, refusing to do military national service or refusing to fight in a war would be a potent form of non-participation. Not voting can also be seen as withdrawing agreement with the status of a political system.

13. See http://iammybrand.eventbrite.com/.

Contributors' Biographies

Ana Kutleša graduated in art history and philosophy from the University of Zagreb. Her work with the association [BLOK] began in 2008, and since 2009 she has been a member of the curatorial team for UrbanFestival, a yearly festival of contemporary art in public spaces. Since the end of 2007 she has worked in Gallery Miroslav Kraljević, producing socially engaged projects and curating several exhibitions by younger generation artists. As the author of forewords, reviews and interviews she has collaborated with the Gallery SC, Secret Exhibitions project, Gallery VN, web magazine Kulturpunkt, *Journal Kontura*, the magazine of art history students *Kontrapunkt*, the bi-weekly paper *Zarez* (*Comma*) and the magazine *Život Umjetnosti*. She lives and works in Zagreb.

Ana Povoas trained as an architect at the University of Porto and worked in London as a master planner, experiencing the drift of the malleable semantics of urban regeneration discourses and agendas. She is currently a PhD candidate at the Ecole Polytechnique Fédérale de Lausanne. Rooted in the concept of spatial justice, she is challenging the physical dimension of space as the primary matter of urban planning. In parallel, she is developing participatory cartographies in the context of the Porto Festival she co-presented at the TINAG festival 2009. The ideal space of the inhabitants and the soft physicality of the public space are the resources of this urban investment. Spirit of '68 is her anchor to London's excesses, abuses, seductions and resistant energies.

Ashley L. Wong is an artist, cultural worker and researcher based in London. Originally from Canada, she completed an MA at Goldsmiths, University of London. She has lived in Hong Kong where she worked on a number of cultural projects and for media arts organisations. She is the founder of independent arts platform LOUDSPKR and co-founder of international research collective DOXA along with Yuk Hui. Her work has been presented in the Hong Kong and Shenzhen Biennale of Urbanism and Architecture (Hong Kong, 2009), Urban Nomad Festival (Taipei, 2009), Rencontre Internationale (Paris/Madrid/Berlin, 2009), New York (Asian Cultural Council, 2009), ARTe SONoro (Madrid, 2010), Clandestino Festival (Gothenburg, 2010), Sound@ Media (Seoul, 2010), and This is Not a Gateway Festival (London, 2010). (www.loudspkr.org, www.doxacollective.org)

Bojan Mucko is a student of philosophy, ethnology and cultural anthropology at the University of Zagreb. His work deals with cultural anthropological theories of identity and anthropology of space, and he is interested in methodological cross–sections of humanistic disciplines and contemporary arts. He works as a freelance writer, researcher and visual artist.

Cristina Garrido Sánchez has an MA in urban sociology (Goldsmiths College, University of London) and a BA in visual arts (University of Barcelona). Her research is the intersection of art with social, cultural and political issues, especially how creativity can be a tool for questioning and eventually changing dominant contemporary realities. She has worked as a freelance researcher and curator for different projects and organisations in various international contexts, such as Post It City, Occasional Urbanities (CCCB, Barcelona 2008); Skill Exchange (Serpentine Gallery, London 2010) and the Franklin Furnace Archive (New York). She is currently working at the Centre for Urban and Community Research (CUCR), Goldsmiths, University of London, where she is undertaking research and evaluation of community art projects. She also works as a projects co–ordinator at Idensitat, a non–profit organisation based in Barcelona which commissions socially and politically engaged art projects. She has written for several catalogues and magazines and writes periodically about art and society in the magazine *Encuentros*.

Clare Burnett is a painter, sculptor and site–specific artist, based in London. She makes pared–down, abstract artworks which encourage people to engage visually, philosophically and creatively with their environment. In partnership with Clare Odgers, she devised and ran a film and art project about the 1908 White City Olympics, working with local schools and residents, to mark the centenary. (www.greatwhitecity.com, www.clareburnett.net)

Clare Odgers is a documentary filmmaker who helps young people use digital technology to give themselves a voice and express what they feel about the world. She has made films with schools across London, working most recently for local councils, Building Schools for the Future and the Victoria and Albert Museum. In partnership with Clare Burnett, she devised and ran a film and art project about the 1908 White City Olympics, working with local schools and residents, to mark the centenary. (www.greatwhitecity.com)

Claudia Loueiro graduated as an architect in 1974 at the Federal University of Pernambuco and completed her PhD in architecture and urbanism at the Faculdade de Arquitetura da Universidade de São Paulo in 2000. She is a retired lecturer from the Federal University of Pernambuco. Her interests lie in architectural design, architectural morphology and architectural theory.

David Boulogne is a French artist photographer, based in London, who documents and questions social issues and the medium of photography itself. (http://www.davidboulogne.com)

David Rosenberg is a writer, teacher, educationalist and tour guide (www. eastendwalks.com). He is the author of *Battle for the East End: Jewish responses to fascism in the 1930s*, published by Five Leaves Publications, and part of the Organising Committee of Cable Street75.

Deepa Naik has worked with Art for Change, public works and the Serpentine Gallery, while co-ordinating projects with Irit Rogoff (Goldsmiths) including: De-Regulation (MuHKA 2006, Herzliya Museum of Contemporary Art 2007); A.C.A.D.E.M.Y: Learning from the Museum (Van Abbemuseum 2006); SUMMIT: non-aligned initiatives in education culture (Multitude e.V. 2007); and Eye Witness (Birkbeck School of Law 2008). She continues to explore a set of questions that have resulted from her interest in post-colonial theory, the intersection of cultural movements and legal systems, critical art practice and alternative pedagogies. She teaches aesthetics and criticism in the Faculty of Design and Architecture at Dar Al Hekma in Jeddah. In 2007, together with Trenton Oldfield, Deepa Naik formally established This Is Not A Gateway, a not-for-profit organisation that creates platforms for critical investigations into cities. (www.thisisnotagateway.net)

Demetris Taliotis is a conjectural theorist, a transdisciplinary artist and impromptu restauranteur. He is also the Director of APOTHEKE Contemporary Arts, Nicosia, Cyprus.

Evanthia Tselika is a researcher, visual producer and educator, currently undertaking research at Birkbeck, University of London, on social engagement and the arts–development in the divided centre of Nicosia. She has worked, exhibited and collaborated with various galleries and museums in London, El Salvador, Cyprus, Greece and Brazil.

Fadi Shayya is a practicing urban planner and critical urbanist, living and working between Beirut and Arab countries. He is interested in public space as the spatial manifestation of power struggles and in landscape as the platform of post–modern urban planning. Fadi is the editor of *At the Edge of the City* and the co–ordinator of DISCURSIVE FORMATIONS, a Beirut–based critical think tank and research platform. (http://www.discursiveformations.net/)

Fouad Asfour is a freelance writer and editor, living and working between Vienna and Johannesburg. He has worked with various art institutions and was part of the editorial team of documenta 12 magazines, Kassel. Experiencing the production of contemporary art and culture, he has critically distanced himself from various forms of cultural hegemony, and he is currently examining ways to apply critical discourse analysis to conditions of production and teaching of contemporary art as part of his PhD thesis.

Hassan Mahamdallie is a senior officer at Arts Council England. He has a background in radical theatre and for many years was a campaigning journalist. He is the author of *Crossing the river of fire: the socialism of William Morris* (London: Redwords, 2008). He contributed to the publication *Beyond Cultural Diversity: The Case for Creativity* (*Third Text*, 2010). Hassan is the editor of *Defending Multiculturalism: A Guide for the Movement* (Bookmarks 2011) and is on the editorial board of the new journal *Critical Muslim*.

Henrietta Williams is based between the UK and Ireland. Using still photography and multimedia, her practice examines the built environment exploring ideas around regeneration, liminal spaces, borders and fortress urbanism. Alongside commissions her personal work has been exhibited widely in the UK and Ireland and featured in documentaries in the UK, Germany and Switzerland. (www.henriettawilliams.com)

Ivana Hanaček graduated from the University of Zagreb with a degree in history and art history. She has been working in the association [BLOK] since 2010 and, as a member of the curatorial team of UrbanFestival, she has been exploring aspects of contemporary art in public space. She has been actively engaged in curating since 2005 as a student member of the curatorial association Katapult 6, curating the programme of the photo gallery KIC. During 2006–07 she worked as a curatorial assistant in the Zagreb gallery Križić Roban. In cooperation with Klaudio Stefančić she initiatied Interzone, an international exhibition programme within Gallery Galženica (2009). At the end of 2009 she initiated the interdisciplinary research platform Secret Exhibitions, which does research on the mechanisms of censorship in the context of visual arts, and which received the Chancellor's Award and the award of the Croatian Designers Society in 2010. She has published reviews, critical art pieces and interviews in several Croatian magazines and newspapers. She works with the Croatian Photo Association on the Conceptual Photos in Croatia project. From 2010 she has also been engaged in pedagogical work and teaching art.

Jhon Arias (Bogota, 1979) is a Colombia artist, interested in the implementation, dissemination and teaching of arts from a modern, diverse and multimedia perspective.

Jo Anne Butler is an Irish artist and designer. Holding a first class joint honours degree from NCAD (National College of Art and Design, Dublin, and the Academy of Humanities and Economics, Lodz, Poland) she has worked across a variety of public art disciplines. She began studying architecture at UCD (University College Dublin) in 2007 and currently studies at Arkitektskolen Aarhus, Denmark. This route from art towards architecture then became the starting point for Culturstruction, a collaborative art/design practice with Tara Kennedy. Recent work includes Polyvalency (2011) at the Irish Museum of Modern Art as part of an invited research residency and Conquested at Temple Bar Galleries, Dublin (2011). Jo Anne Butler has also worked as an arts project manager with Breaking Ground, the Ballymun Regeneration Limited per cent for art programme in Dublin, and is co-curator of Commonage, an architectural research project in Callan, Kilkenny, Ireland. (www. culturstruction.com, www.commonagecallan.com)

Juan delGado was born in Cartagena, Spain, and has lived and worked in London since 1994. His work explores urban territory, especially the physical and psychological impact it has on us. Focusing on traumatic experience such as violence, displacement and alienation, delGado has developed a body of work that includes *The Wounded Image* (1997–2003), *Don't Look Under the Bed* (2001), *Who Are You Entertaining To ?* (2002), *Suspended Reverie* (2006) and *Le Rêve de Newton* (2010). He produced *The Flickering Darkness* following a three-month residency at the Universidad de los Andes, Bogota, as part of the 2009 Visiting Arts Colombia–UK artist residency programme.

Judith Ryser, qualified as an architect and urbanist with an MSc in social sciences, is dedicating her cosmopolitan professional life to the built environment, its sustainability and its contribution to the knowledge society. Her activities in Paris, Berlin, Stockholm, Geneva (United Nations), Madrid and London in public sector posts, private practice and universities are focused on cities and development strategies with emphasis on Europe. Based in London, she researches, edits and writes books and articles, produces reports for international organisations and works on regeneration projects also with community groups. She speaks at international professional conferences, carries out consultancies and has published many books and articles. She was vice-president of Isocarp, led one of its urban advisory planning teams and is joint editor of the *International Manual of Planning Practice*. She is a member of the Chartered Institute of Journalists, the Urban Design Group and its editorial board, and the International Advisory Council of the Fundacion Metropoli for which she writes and co-operates in projects.

Lahary Pittman is a New York visual artist and photojournalist working in gelatin silver prints, film/video and pastels. His films and photographs have been screened and exhibited in New York and internationally including Britain, France, Australia and the Netherlands. Works from his series The Shifting Boundaries & Culture of Manhattan's Lower East Side were exhibited at the 2010 TINAG festival. In the Delaware Art Museum's Gordon Parks

Arts Competition 2008–09, his film *Rhythm and Pain* won Best In Show in the film category and his gelatin silver print *Succos on the Bowery* was a jury winner in the photography category. He is a published photographer with works at auction and in public and private collections. Lahary Pittman has a background of social activism. He was formerly president of a United Nations NGO dedicated to using acupuncture for chronic health conditions worldwide, including Native American Indian reservations, and has received awards and recognition for this work in Spain and Austria.

Lana Salman is a researcher and consultant on urban development and economics, living and working in Beirut. She co–ordinated the Research Advocacy & Public Policy Program at the Issam Fares Institute of the American University of Beirut and has consulted for the United Nations and the World Bank. Lana is currently writing her thesis in urban planning on actors and masterplans in post–conflict societies.

Luiz Amorim is an architect and urban designer (PhD University College London) and Associate Professor at the Federal University of Pernambuco, where he co–ordinates the Advanced Architectural Studies Laboratory – lA2. His work is focused on the relationship between space configuration and behaviour, particularly regarding housing. He was a visiting Professor at the Taubman College of Architecture and Urban Planning, University of Michigan (2004), has published widely, lectured in Brazilian and European universities and participated in conferences internationally.

Marijana Rimanić (Pula, 1985) graduated from the University of Zagreb with a degree in comparative literature and art history. Since 2010 she has been working within the association [BLOK], as a member of the authorial team for the UrbanFestival and as a collaborator on the project of Lala Raščić, Damn Dam. In 2007 she co–initiated the curatorial association Wo_kolektiv, aimed at asserting critical and innovative curatorial practices. As part of the Wo_kolektiv she has curated several exhibitions: Visible and Invisible – Fragments of the City (Gallery Pravi Put, Zagreb, 2007), ALUdiranje (Touch On) (VN Gallery, Zagreb, 2008), Am I That Name? (SC Gallery, Zagreb, 2009). She participated in the realisation of the festivals Queer Zagreb in 2008 and Perforacije in 2009 and worked on the project Secret Exhibitions.

She has worked on the realisation of the exhibition A Different Motovun in 2009 in Gallery 5 Tower in Motovun, organised by the Filip Trade Collection. From 2008 to 2010 she worked as a journalist in HRT's programme, Transfer, dedicated to contemporary art and the urban scene. Her articles have been published in the arts publications *Zarez* and *Život Umjetnosti* (*The Life of Art*). She has written prefaces for exhibition catalogues of the younger generation artists. She lives and works in Zagreb.

Marisa Gonzalez is a photographer and video artist from Bilbao, Spain. She lives and works between Madrid and London. She graduated in music in Bilbao and in fine arts at the University Complutense, Madrid, and holds an MFA from the School Art Institute of Chicago. Her research focus in the last decade is the city, its memory and transformations, abandoned industrial architecture and its inherent concerns. She has done extensive work on Bilbao's nuclear plant and the migrant transformation of Hong Kong. She has had more than 50 solo and 170 group exhibitions all over the world including Spain, Beijing, Bogota, Bamako, Hong Kong, New York, London, Germany, Prague, Vienna etc. (www.marisagonzalez.com)

Martin Slavin has lived in Hackney for over 20 years. He has worked with photography in journalism for most of that time. When London won the vote for the Olympics he thought this would make an interesting subject for publication. He joined with others to report on these developments. They set up the GamesMonitor website in 2006 to publish the results of their research. (www.gamesmonitor.org.uk/)

Miriam Metliss is learning officer at the University of Essex Collection of Latin American Art. A joint honours graduate in art history and hispanic studies (University of Nottingham, 2007), she has worked as client liaison for Christie's Auction House, London (2008–10); at Visiting Arts, London (2007–08); and as education facilitator for the Other Worlds Project, Universidade Estadual de Londrina, Paraná, Brazil (2006). Since 2007, Miriam has worked with the Latin American migrant community in Southwark, Lambeth and Islington, and currently sits on the management committee of the Indo–American Refugee and Migrant Organization (IRMO). She has worked as alliances and education co-ordinator for Colombiage festival of contemporary arts (2008–10).

Mital Patel is a volunteer community campaigner based in North London. On finishing a degree in biochemistry in 2007 she became involved in the Wards Corner Community Coalition and has spent the last four years challenging the hierarchy of the planning system and inequalities of urban development. She has been a key organiser in many of the campaign's successes including a precedent-setting win in the Court of Appeal.

Nanna Nielsen is a visual anthropologist. She makes films mainly for exhibitions and humanitarian organisations. Over the last few years she has made filmic explorations on various forms of urban development and their effects on people living in the city.

Richard Carter is in two minds: a professional architect and an amateur social theorist. By day, he tailors the bursting seams of contemporary citymaking, by night he is troubled by the cultural consequences of the commercialised sustainable regeneration industry. Raised in the Far West and graduating from the University of East London in 2002, following a deep draught of Danish social materialism and Polish emotional irrationalism, he strongly believes a proper resolution for the specificity of place can be found at the intersection of art with commerce, language, politics and the shared environment.

Robin Bale is an artist and writer from London. He makes improvised spoken word pieces. He studied sculpture at the Royal College of Art and has recently received a scholarship to study for a doctorate in fine art at Middlesex University, with the working title of 'The Performer and the Polity'. (http://www.purgeglut.blogger.com, http://www.robinbale.blogger.com)

Romeo delaCruz has spent most of his life working with the cultural communities, governmental agencies, non-governmental organisations and academic institutions in the Philippines on culture and development. A former commissioner of the National Commission for Culture and the Arts, the Philippine's highest policymaking body on culture and arts, he has an interest in cultural empowerment, indigenous peoples, tourism and cultural policy. He taught culture and tourism at the University of the Philippines and chaired the arts management programme of an arts and design college in Manila. After earning an MA in cultural and creative industries from

King's College London as a Chevening Scholar, he has decided to pursue a PhD on cultural regeneration and cultural industries at the University of Northampton.

Ruth Allen is a resident of Tottenham, North London, and has been involved in public speaking, organising and developing strategy for the Wards Corner campaign since it started in 2007. She is a social work practitioner, leader, educator and writer, mostly in the field of mental health. She is particularly active in professional leadership development, ethics and the links between British and international social work. Her focus is also on developing social work's role in community empowerment. She is personally involved in a range of local community activities including being part of the residents' associations movement in the London Borough of Haringey.

Siraj Izhar: My works are active social processes, generators of activity, which cut in and out of multiple aspects of contemporary life often involving intervention and activism, creating spaces for multiple and complex forms of participation. They are about the making of new structures for experience, not representation, the making of forms or formats for engagement. In particular these forms create a working space for a series of contestations: legal versus illegal, autonomous versus mass culture, individual versus collective. The concept of ecology is central to these engagements, which are based on a creative picturing of different social, cultural or political situations as visual ecologies. These entwine in real and virtual space to create hybrid ecologies differentiated for different aspects of contemporary life in the digital age. Mainstream society may be pictured as state-based consumer monoculture flowing in a uni-direction; autonomous realities more like concentric circles, creating complex eddies and ripples in the cultural landscape.

Tijana Stevanovic is an independent researcher who, after being a Chevening Scholar at UCL 2009-10, is neither based in London, nor in Belgrade. She takes off from the notion of being displaced and not-belonging to concentrate her research on the political dimension of participation in public space, its representational value as well as the agency of subjectivity within community action. Previously, she has assisted teaching both MA and BA courses at the

Faculty of Architecture, University of Belgrade, and exhibited internationally, including Venice Architecture Biennale 2008. She assisted the research and preparation for TINAG 2010 festival, London.

Trenton Oldfield has worked for over a decade in non–governmental organisations specialising in urban renewal, cultural and environmental programmes. He was Coordinator of the Thames Strategy – Kew to Chelsea, Strategic Project Manager at Cityside Regeneration, and a Community Development Worker in North Kensington. Alongside his formal work he has continued to explore questions about cities via personal projects, including installations in the public realm, film, guest editing and guest lecturing, and has been active on the boards of the Westway Development Trust, London Citizens and Subtext. Current projects include research for a book that unearths the socio–political history of fences/railings in London, part of an attempt to find a way beyond the existing conventions around ownership, specifically land ownership in the 21st century. Trenton Oldfield formally established the not–for–profit organisation This Is Not A Gateway with Deepa Naik in 2007. (www.thisisnotagateway.net)

Vicky Casia–Cabantac defends the rights and welfare of migrant Filipinos as deputy secretary general of United Filipinos in Hong Kong. She was born in the Philippines but left her country in October 1992. She was a teacher and at the time a teacher's salary was one–third of what she could earn as a domestic helper in Hong Kong. She sacrificed her family life to make a decent living for her children and her family in the Philippines. She was vice chairperson of the Migrants Sectoral Party in 2004. She is a member of the International Migrants' Alliance and a member of the Gabriela Women's Party. She participates in many congresses and conferences with immigrant workers and labour movements all over the world.

Wing Shing Tang is currently Professor at the Department of Geography, Hong Kong Baptist University and Chair of the Hong Kong Critical Geography Group. His research interest is on the interrogation of Lefebvre, Foucault, Gramsci and others, and with local history, in order to construct a better informed understanding of urban (re)development in Hong Kong and other Chinese cities.

Yuk Hui is a PhD researcher for the Metadata Project (Leverhulme Trust) at the Centre for Cultural Studies, Goldsmiths, University of London. His research centres on the philosophy of technology and phenomenology, especially concerning the web and digital objects. He is the co-founder of DOXA, which is currently developing a research project on creative space and generating critical discourse on cultural industries in cities like London and Hong Kong. (www.doxacollective.org)

Acknowledgements

The successful production of each volume of *Critical Cities* feels like something of a marvel, something miraculous. We are indebted to many individuals, including all those, past and present, who have demanded popular agency over 'the printing press' or who have forged new techniques and approaches to democratise knowledge production, availability, circulation and reunderstandings of 'education'. Digital technology has enabled us, a small-scale, micro-funded, not-for-profit organisation, to establish an independent imprint to produce critical publications.

We celebrate and thank the 28 authors who have come together to create a book that aims to inject new ideas and knowledge into disciplines concerned with cities and the Urban Industry. Arguably the most suitable though imperfect format for collectively sharing diverse voices and arguments, this anthology presents contributions from a number of cities including Beirut, Bogota, Hong Kong, London, San Paulo, Zagreb and New York. We have had the good fortune of collaborating with architects, activists, artists, planners, filmmakers, academics, writers and students – all of whom are working on concerns that are both urgent to their own cities and often shared by citizens in quite distant regions of the world. We thank them for the opportunity to learn and for the challenges they offer in their research, arguments and propositions.

Critical Cities has been described by reviewers as "the street–meets community centre–meets the academy" and this is due in large part to Barbara Murray's expert copy–editing skills and wider political knowledge and experiences. We thank Barbara for her essential contribution and also for her consistent counsel on matters related to publishing as well as broader political concerns.

To ensure the material within the volume is best understood and thus able to circulate and be referenced widely, readability is a key design requirement. It was no mean feat for Karolin Schnoor, illustrator and designer, to strip back the excesses of 'the noughties', cohere divergent materials and formats, and create a handsome contemporary book. Thank you, Karolin!

As this volume is in part a result of the annual This Is Not A Gateway festival, salons and year round activities, there are also hundreds of individuals and a number of organisations we wish to acknowledge and thank.

Hassan Mahamdallie and Tony Panayiotou of Arts Council England immediately understood what we were trying to do with the festival project, and along with the Norman Melburn Trust they ensured it remained a free platform for diverse practitioners and theorists.

We are immensely grateful to Anisa Johnny, at Christ Church Spitalfields, who suggested that we 'finish what we started' in 2009 by restoring the upper floors of Hanbury Hall. The festival would not have happened without Anisa championing our work and acting as a conduit with the landlords.

Refurbishing the entirety of the building – within two weeks – proved to be a significant undertaking. We are indebted to those who munificently bestowed their time, energy and toil as volunteers. This includes: Henrietta Williams, George Gingell, Marc Martines, Steve Hignall, Alexi, Katie, Nico and Lola, Rachael Davidson, Wards Corner Community Coalition (James, Mital and Danny), Hyemin Park, Simon Brackenborough and the 30+ volunteers Nick Hart brought with him from Turner. Working together, using over 100 litres of white paint and seemingly endless cleaning products, they transformed Hanbury Hall into a venue fit to support and host over 160 contributors and more than 2,000 participants.

A few days before the festival, Andrey Vrabchev arrived at our flat wearing a three-piece suit and carrying a small tool box. We first met Andrey at the 2009 festival and have referred to him since then as the 'Renaissance-man' due to his truly remarkable catalogue of skills, his ingenuity, his sincerity, and his interest and knowledge on just about everything. Despite not sharing sympathies on political concerns, there isn't anyone else as enjoyable and demanding to debate them with. In just a few days, Andrey helped to install the 25+ exhibitions, two cinemas, several multi-screen installations, four 'lecture halls', new wiring systems and lights. It is no exaggeration to say that without Andrey we would not have been able to open the doors of Hanbury Hall.

With multiple events occurring at the same time it was essential Hanbury Hall was able to accommodate the many people converging and crisscrossing at any one moment. We are grateful to Maximilian Joel Steckelmacher for ensuring the programme ran as smoothly as possible. He not only took us in hand – guiding us on ways we could use emerging technologies and spreadsheets – but also communicated methodically and thoughtfully with the festival contributors. Thank you to Maria Isabel Botero for her excellent logistical organisation and warm welcoming of participants and contributors. Students from the LSE's Cities Programme and UCL's UrbanLab were also great hosts, guides and bookshop tellers.

We are enormously grateful to Eva Kostelidou and Dominic Rich, who provided an inviting space for people to recharge and kept festival–goers fueled with home–made cakes, pastries and teas, and also to the Spanish Cultural Ministry and Wines from Spain, who provided superb wine for the launch.

We would like to thank Valentina Floris and Ben Foot of SDNA for their support with audio–visual equipment and Cockpit Arts who kindly lent us their projectors.

At the first TINAG festival, seeing us fumble, tumble and sometimes fail to restart projectors, speaker systems and the like, Tom Flynn jumped up from his seat to rescue us and he has been the master of digital technology at our events ever since. For the 2010 festival, Tom put together a formidable team that included Thomas Wasley and Scott Stannard. Somehow these three young men managed to not only be in more than one place at the same time but they resolved any technical complications that arose, anywhere. Anyone who has run or participated in an event like the festival will know that this was quite a triumph.

It is fair to say, that until the potent though poorly named 'Occupy Wall Street' protests got under way in late 2011, there was little focus or readily available literature on the geographies of finance and corporations. Financial districts were, for reasons we are yet to entirely understand, by and large perceived as benign and not of interest, except perhaps for their signature skyscraper architecture. In the months leading up to the festival Tijana Stevanonic established 'Blog the Corporation' to pull together critical news stories, web references and opinion in order to generate a body of current perspectives on the theme of the festival. We wish to thank Tijana for creating a most splendid and useful site.

Throughout our endeavours, we have been fortunate in working alongside remarkable individuals and organisations that are engaged and invested in challenging current practices, policies and understandings of cities. We would like to thank the many audience participants who have contributed to the festival and salon discussions, some of whom are organising their own events in the forthcoming festival.

And finally, we are wholeheartedly grateful to our working group members: Ana Kutlesa, Cristiana Bottigella, Ellen O'Hara, Fadi Shayya and Fiona Whitty. They have been and remain brilliant at challenging our thinking, informing the practical aspects of the organisation and generously investing their time and expertise in the pursuit of independent, rigorous and critical practice.

ERASE,STRETCH, RELINQUISH

Introduction

DEEPA NAIK & TRENTON OLDFIELD

We first introduced the concept of 'Erase, Stretch, Relinquish'[1] in 2008, as the integrated globalised economies started to openly suggest their economic and theoretical presumptions were disintegrating around them. The widely accepted pivotal moment or the key protagonist for the first major financial calamity of the 21st century was the sanctioned sacrifice of Lehman Brothers.[2] It was suggested that Lehman Brothers' failure was due to its heavy exposure to the largely suburban phenomenon of 'toxic debts' resulting from the re-packing and selling on of high–risk mortgages. This time around, the urban condition, or the shift to an urban age[3], was designated the responsibility for capitalism's most recent crisis. The ensuing melodrama has been having profound implications ever since for the agency citizens have over their own lives. Week by week, and quite possibly hour by hour, since 2008, the burdens on the poorest have been increasing while the very wealthiest people and corporations have in consequence seen their fortunes increase by a magnitude not witnessed since the period of European imperial expansion.[4] Unsurprisingly, today's inequalities between citizens reflect the inequalities of that earlier predatory period. London, for example, is the most unequal city in the 'western world' – the income difference between its richest and its poorest is an astounding 236 times.[5]

'Erase, Stretch, Relinquish' was proposed as a way of understanding the processes of late–capitalist urban development and finance. Our focus at the time was the then under–construction Olympic 'park' and Dalston Junction, but it is a mode of operating that is endemic in cities across the globe. In short, *Erase* is the process that enables governments and developers to call an area/ site a 'wasteland' - emptying and demolishing buildings, fogging memories, side–lining alternative proposals and ignoring opposition. *Stretch* is the process of maximising every inch of the site to gain the greatest ideological and financial accumulation - increasing building density, imposing cultural signifiers and branding, importing spectacles. And *Relinquish* is the process of making people let go – governments handing all over to the private sector, instituting and formalising public access rather than public space, and despite years of protest and resistance, dissenters are forced to acknowledge 'there goes the neighbourhood', as part of the city is surrendered to private interests.

In a manner not dissimilar to the by–and–large 'spontaneous combustion' of the decades–long anti–globalisation protests and the Reclaim the Streets activities in the days following the 9/11 melodramas, resistance to the capitalist–led erasure and stretching of urban space has either largely evaporated and/or been criminalised. Just as a number of long–term anti–war and civil rights activists supported the invasions of Afghanistan and Iraq,[6] unlikely people and organisations have been calling for 'growth', and often 'growth at any cost'. Unemployment is at unprecedented levels in much of the world, particularly for young people, along with significant overall reduction in wages for lower–income earners and the exponentially growing debt burden, making it an entirely unsurprising reflex reaction to call for something, anything, to help address the inevitable destruction of the social contract that results. If there is to be a return to growth, what matters is how it is achieved, its source and process, and who controls the mechanisms, the distribution of newly generated gross domestic product and the enactment of equality. Despite a good handful of democratic revolutions, there is no indication of democratic control or distribution and no pursuit of equality anywhere. The Urban Industry – land ownership, along with the constant re–building and management of cities – remains one of the most profitable industries for corporations despite, and perhaps because of, the crisis.[7]

This chapter takes us across four continents and into the intimate lives of five cities. We learn that, rather than retreating as a result of the storm of the 'global financial crisis', the corporate–led Urban Industry is taking advantage of low–paid and sometimes unpaid labour, government subsidies, and 'states of exception'[8] driven by mega–events and pro–growth–at–all–costs planning policies.

Brazil, the focus of the opening essay by Luiz Amorim and Claudia Loureiro, has been selected to host the next mega–event of the International Olympic Committee (IOC) – the 2016 Olympic Games. As they did in London in 2012, the demands of the IOC are spearheading significant urban, cultural and political changes in Brazil. One little–known fact about this immense and compelling country is that most of the land is owned by a small number of families, descendents of the earliest colonialists.[9] Its population is one of the most culturally diverse and mixed, largely a result of trans–Atlantic slavery, transported indentured labour, periodic migration from Europe and elsewhere, and the ongoing survival of a number of the indigenous populations. Since its colonisation by Europeans, Brazil has been, and to this day remains, one of the most unequal societies anywhere, at any time.[10]

This is communicated nowhere more poignantly than in the film *High-rise (Um Lugar ao Sol)* directed by Gabriel Mascaro.[11] The documentary is composed of a series of interviews with people who live in penthouses in high–rise buildings. Their candour in regard to how they see themselves and their lives can be summed up in the footage of one woman who, while warmly smiling with her husband, explains how she enjoys watching the gun fights in the *favelas* they look over: "They are beautiful! A free daily fireworks display! From the *favela* to the cemetery." It is these buildings and these apartments Amorim and Loureiro critically study in their essay 'Tall and Enclosed: Housing Form and Social Use in Brazilian Apartment Buildings'.

Tall apartment blocks were the most–built architectural form of the 20th century and, according to a Canadian documentary also called *Highrise,* the most ubiquitous building type on planet earth[12]. Rather than the stereotypes of alienation resulting from neglected social housing or tower blocks in places like Europe, it is quickly apparent in both Mascaro's film and Amorim and Loureiro's essay that in Brazil vertical living is associated with social prestige. The authors suggest a combination of contributory factors for this, which include the nudging of urban planners who favour density (with its increased tax revenue per plot) over sprawl, the greater profit margins in high rises for property developers, and social perceptions that the limited entrances and exits to high rises make them appear, rightly or wrongly, as less vulnerable and easier to defend (enclose) than detached houses.

Taking the city of Recife in northeast Brazil as their case study, Amorim and Loueiro chart the socio–political history, or the acceptance of and then manufactured desire for these buildings. The most potent insights into the construction of people's desire for height and status come through the authors' exposure of two elements. First, the role of the picture, shown in particular through a detailed investigation of advertising imagery, which could be described as the picturing of place in aspirational and divided societies. And second, the impact of branding through the deployment of names, predominantly of well–known European families or places, stretching the value. We learn about real and perceived aspects of a housing format not valued previously and apparently derided almost everywhere else.

On the other side of the planet, over 7,687 high–rise buildings huddle on a very slender strip of land along the edge of Hong Kong Island's harbour, and within the greater Hong Kong area it's understood that 52 buildings reach over the height of 200 metres and 272 buildings reach 150 metres above ground.[13] Yuk Hui and Ashley Wong[14] interview Professor Wing Shing Tang and share important insights on this context in 'Hong Kong: The Property Regime'. The paper argues the pre–dominant force in Hong Kong is not the financial services industries, as commonly suggested, but the real estate industry or what Wing Shing Tang calls the 'land (re)development regime'. This is embedded not only across the island's economy but also in the process of generating a rational, conformist hegemony among citizens – the argument being, 'follow these steps and we all can get rich quick'. It is this status quo and this alluring promise made to people across all levels of society that according to Wing Shing Tang means property development happens almost at any cost. The erasure of 'traditional or historic neighbourhoods' has happened on a significant scale, and Tang warns us not to read the resistance to these demolitions from the perspective of western–style 'historic conservation' protests. Rather he suggests they should be seen as a response to the public–private partnerships started in the 1980s via the newly established Land Development Corporation. In order to continue the system, more and more complex development sites needed to be configured; the value of the development sites had to be continually stretched further and further. Residents had little enough say in this structure but no say at all when Compulsory Land Purchases were introduced with the establishment of the Urban Renewal Authority that only reported direct to the Hong Kong government.

What Tang reveals next is perhaps the most important aspect for those interested in power relations in cities and how those with capital and motivation to maintain the status quo can quickly and easily co–opt, colonise and re–package the aims and the language of activists and the general public in order to carry on without any fundamental changes or compromises. Tang reveals several examples of token, historified and community–centred gestures through which "the general public has, somehow, believed this rhetoric and has been side-tracked from the real issue". He highlights how activists are often wrong-footed by developers and state officials as they focus not on the regime itself but on specific topics, such as housing for the poor. In regards to Wedding Card Street (Lee Tung Street), activists focused on their aspiration for 'diversity' (poor and rich living side by side) but failed to address the regime, and thus ended up legitimising and praising the development in the process of securing their single-issue aim. Tang also suggests that cultural districts for so-called creative industries are little more than a distraction and colourful rhetoric as "everything in Hong Kong ... is all about property, property, property". Using a number of cases, including cultural districts, Tang suggests that until the people of Hong Kong focus on the land (re)development regime itself the same patterns will continue.

Tang's argument comes into stark relief when we are confronted, in the next presentation, with postcards of an entirely erased landscape – the site of the London 1908 Olympic Games. In their visual essay 'The Lost Legacies and Lagoons of the First British Olympics', Clare Burnett and Clare Odgers force us to consider what might happen to the London 2012 Olympic Park if 'the regime' is not confronted, if people end up being distracted by specific issues. Is it possible, despite the continuous public announcements of a legacy resulting from the 2012 Olympic Games, that all that might be left in Stratford is promises and postcards?

Burnett and Odgers place the promises made by the 2012 Olympic Games officials under images of what were beautiful buildings and waterways. Grand, ornate and carefully planned, it's hard to imagine they could ever have been erased from London's landscape, let alone when linked with what we are led to believe is such an important public event. Their research and essay ask us to question what will happen "once this generation of dream-building politicians has moved on". It is a highly significant question, and demands even more attention when there is persistent talk of a 'legacy plan' which is being calibrated not by the people but by extra-legal companies dominated by private interests and with politicians in tow. Perhaps it is a matter of taste but if these compelling 1908 Olympic buildings and spaces could be erased from the city with such ease, it would seem even more probable the Meccano-and-tarpaulin-style 'buildings' of the 2012 games will vanish too, possibly more quickly – perhaps as a direct result of the existence of a legacy company. Who will benefit from the 'stretching' of the historic site? How will East

Londoners be encouraged to finally relinquish their memories, associations and businesses? And what will be the final event or methodology employed to embed a new narrative for this part of London?

Lahary Pittman's black and white photographs, *Double Jeopardy, Liberation Goddess* and *Hostile Takeover,* from a series entitled Shifting Boundaries and Culture of Manhattan's Lower East Side (LES), document the actions of people claiming their space through street art. Such works are often temporary. Some are erased not long after their application. Others, like the images in this contribution, have been added too; their meaning and role transformed over time by other people and also by changes in the environment around them.

In his accompanying essay 'The Seduction of Capitalism, Crime and the American Way of Life', Pittman offers critical insights into the changes resulting from determined neoliberal globalisation in New York in particular and across the country generally – where the cranes keep increasing the height of corporate America and more and more people join queues for food and shelter.

The European settlement of New York City never pretended to have socialist aspirations, its very existence built on the brutal erasure of the native populations and its development achieved through the use of indentured labour and laissez–faire governance where those who dared often won[15]. The violence of New York City was and continues to be well documented and available through archives, films and regular breaking–news events.

In contrast, New Belgrade, the locus of Tijana Stevanovic's essay was a city built with explicit modernist and socialist ambitions. The modernist architecture, though adulterated, remains, while the socialist ambitions evaporated during a decade of civil war, and Tijana Stevanovic argues this is creating the possibility for new types of urban development, particularly in regard to being beyond inflexible social, architectural and planning structures.

Most of the contributors to this chapter are writing about the place they have grown up in; a place they know intimately. This lived knowledge is apparent alongside their academic arguments and of immeasurable benefit to us. Tijana Stevanovic's own lived experience of New Belgrade provides us with first–hand knowledge of a retreating state and the little–by–little erasure of an ideological ambition. We are asked to question "the potential of the city's unfinished past, rather than provide models for resisting the global homogenisation of urban settlements".

We learn that New Belgrade was built on a marshland in–between the Sava and Danube Rivers and picturesquely on the 'no man's land' that existed between the Ottoman and Austro–Hungarian empires. "Built for and by the people after World War II, its aim was building a city for the socialism to come" but we discover that, unlike other socialist cities built during this time, it was not subject to a specific plan or development methodology. It was, though, subject to the succession of different fads including the shift from mega structures to more domestic scales that was popular in the 1980s. Stevanovic reveals the greatest changes took place in the 1990s – the decade of war – and it wasn't long before New Belgrade started to be called 'Cardboard City'. The urgency to address daily needs (fuel, food, services and income generation), along with the evaporation of the state as it focused on war, resulted in colonisation by private interests of a previously public sphere. The social was gradually erased and the new spaces began to be stretched and maximised – from individuals colonising shared areas to supermarkets replacing community centres. Post–war, the privatisation accelerated with the erasure of the social property laws and their replacement with legislation in support of private property.

The transformation of society through the re–introduction of private property continues to reconfigure spaces and social relations in former socialist states. Not far from New Belgrade, Zagreb, which was also previously part of the former Yugoslavia, is experiencing a different condition as a result of the transformation of socialist state to 'capitalist economy'. Bojan Mucko's essay, 'Zagreb's Empty Shop Windows and Transition *Flâneurs*: A True Story', enables us to stare through rain splattered and carbon stained windows into the dusty interiors of over 50 empty shops on just two kilometres of Zagreb's old city. The author helps us to decipher the often-faded signs placed in the windows inviting interested people to contact the City of Zagreb's Department of Business Premises. Why do these shops, often in prominent locations, remain empty? It is not, Bojan Mucko points out, a result of the global recession but due to the post–partition government's Act on Compensation for the Property Confiscated during the Communist Regime of Yugoslavia. This is a poignant essay to close the 'Erase, Stretch and Relinquish' chapter as it confuses and problematises all the issues raised in the preceding texts. Nothing about these empty shops is as expected. Here in Zagreb the post–socialist neoliberalism ushered in in the 1990s tangles itself into knots and forges itself into still lifes and forced reflections through dirty windows on past and present contradictions.

1. Deepa Naik and Trenton Oldfield (eds), *Critical Cities: Ideas, Knowledge and Agitation from Emerging Urbanists Volume 1* (Myrdle Court Press: London, 2009) p. 15.
2. John Gapper, 'Paulson made the right sacrifice', *Financial Times*, 15 September 2010.
3. For more information see, Ricky Burdett and Deyan Sudjic (eds), *The Endless City* (Phaidon: London, 2008).
4. For more information see, The Organisation for Economic Co-operation and Development (OECD), *Divided We Stand: Why Inequality Keeps Rising* (OECD: Paris, 2011).
5. For more information see, Guy Palmer, 'Income Inequalities in the United Kingdom', http://www.poverty.org.uk/09/index.shtml (accessed 26/08/12).
6. See for example, Christopher Hitchens, *A Long Short War: The Postponed Liberation of Iraq* (Plume: USA, 2003); Martin Amis, *The Second Plane* (Jonathan Cape: London, 2008).
7. David Harvey, The *Enigma of Capital and the Crises of Capitalism,* 2nd edition (Oxford University Press: New York, 2011).
8. Giorgio Agamben, *State of Exception* (University of Chicago Press: Chicago, 2005).
9. Mike Davies and Daniel Bertrand Monk (eds), *Evil Paradises: Dreamworlds of Neoliberalism* (The New Press: New York, 2007).
10. Emir Sader, 'The most unjust country in the world' in *ibid.*, Davies and Monk (2007).
11. Mascaro screened *High-rise* at the 2010 TINAG Festival.
12. For more information see, *Highrise*, directed by Katerina Cizek, National Film Board, Canada, 2011.
13. For more information see, Emporis, a website that collects data on tall buildings, http://www.emporis.com/statistics/most-skyscrapers (accessed 26/08/12).
14. Ashley Wong and Nicolas Sauret (directors) screened their documentary *Non-space* (2009) at the 2010 TINAG festival.
15. 'Who Dares Wins' (*Qui audit adipiscitur*) is the motto for at least nine Special Forces, including the British SAS, American Marines and Israel's Sayerat Matkal. In *Critical Cities Volume 2* (Myrdle Court Press: London, 2010) pp. 31–37, we introduced this term in relation to the Urban Industry. 'Who Dares Wins' advances notions of opportunism, expedience, realpolitik, advantage, risk and even recklessness and a cut-throat attitude. We argued that these behaviours, these propositions and their economic motivations are erroneously understudied and remain 'undiagnosed' in the conception, production and administration of cities.

Tall and Enclosed

*Housing Form and Social Use
in Brazilian Apartment Buildings*

LUIZ AMORIM *&* CLAUDIA LOUREIRO

The private housing market in Brazil is largely constituted by high–rise apartment buildings – an urban phenomenon that has its origins in the introduction of vertical collective modernist housing in major Brazilian cities in the first quarter of the 20th century, but which has taken on different characteristics since then. The most recent characteristic is based on the mobility of the upper and middle social classes from individual housing units to vertical condominiums, with significant increase observed as of the 1970s. Many factors contribute to this phenomenon, but the most relevant are: (a) from the urban planners' point of view, the urban density of vertical structures is desirable; (b) from the development industry's point of view, permissive urban legislation generates a market that seeks higher profits; and (c) from the citizens' point of view, organised condominiums offer, or at least appear to offer, better protection in a society of greater social inequalities and the resulting violence against individuals.[1] Regarding the latter, collective protection achieved by means of an organised condominium structure has replaced the individual detached house as the symbol of protection and safety for the modern family. Indeed, flats have achieved the status of the ideal contemporary home that is safe and practical, and the housing marketing people seem to know that, as they offer products that promise to meet the ever–changing immediate needs, from enclosure to leisure, technology, sustainability and so on.

In this market, developers and builders are the key actors in the urban housing industry and, by and large, they get the majority of the generated profits. City Hall also gets a generous portion with the augmentation of housing units per plot (from one to eighty in a single tower block, for example) increasing the profits accruing to the municipality from compulsory collection of urban, territorial and building taxes.

The market is fed by the constant re-creation of the ideal way of living through the continuous introduction of new products, which may meet consumers' expectations and which keep the housing industry fully profitable. And advertising plays a fundamental role in keeping alive this constant desire to acquire the perfect place for living.

This study[2] presents an analysis of the different prototypical lifestyles used by housing developers in Recife, Brazil, to sell you the 'house of your dreams' through newspaper advertisements and promotional materials in which certain contemporary life attributes are associated with the architectural distinctiveness of the housing properties. These model lifestyles represent marketing strategies that offer the potential owner a phenomenology for the future, i.e. an ideal world where all expectations are fulfilled. The model functions like a mirror that not only reflects and reproduces the ideal home for an individual, but also feeds the construction and growth of the dream.[3] Within this context, understanding which elements or forces have shaped the middle social classes in the past decades is of fundamental interest, and particularly the basis on which the collective dream of acquiring a home is constructed by marketing agencies through their advertising campaigns.

The research milestone for this study is the 1970s, when marketing strategies took on a fundamental role in the local housing market. The main sources of information used are the advertisements published in Sunday newspapers in order to reach the typical weekend housing hunters, and the range of promotional materials including leaflets, brochures, buildings' catalogues and developers' promotional magazines distributed at traffic lights and at stands in shopping centres and supermarkets, as well as at the seaside and at sports and music events. The advertisements were analysed in order to identify the concepts, keywords and key images that helped establish the image of the ideal home. These main attributes were described, classified and grouped into four categories: (a) the property's location, especially highlighting the qualities of the neighbourhood and access to the services offered at that location; (b) the architectural programme for the housing complex (individual units, services and common facilities); (c) the title of the building and housing complex, highlighting social and cultural symbolism; and (d) the height of the apartment building, also described by the number of storeys.

These are the kinds of attributes that seem to interact according to social and cultural variables to induce a new living experience – living in the heights, apart from city life and sharing a safe community. In fact, several patterns co-exist in time and space; however, the dominance of certain patterns, particularly those adopted by the wealthy social classes, guide consumption in a cross-cutting pattern. For example, there are programmatic and morphological elements, such as high walls and sentry boxes, which are pervasive in rich and poor neighbourhoods, even in social housing situations, and not limited to major cities but also observed in small and middle-sized cities. This is the face of the recent kind of Brazilian urbanism that has transformed Brazilian cities into a succession of housing enclaves dispersed along blind streets that were previously used for vehicle circulation.

Apartment buildings in Recife, northeast Brazil

Historically, co-habitation was not seen as a positive social attribute. As revealed in the testimony of 19th-century travellers,[4] co-habitation denoted a family's low social status, and it remained a strong social index in the following century. Apartment buildings were first introduced in Recife in the 1930s to provide hygienic and comfortable housing for social security companies' clients. It was only in the late 1940s and early 50s that a private market started to emerge. At that time, the location of the buildings seemed to be an important factor to seduce middle-class families because proximity to work or services, which were mostly centralised in the historical centre, was key in offering this new product. This new lifestyle was not immediately grasped by the local middle class because private houses were not only desirable but also affordable and sustainable due to the cheap domestic labour at hand. It took another two decades and the pressure to produce new housing units for a growing population, which led to government investments to boost the housing market, to suppress the remaining negative connotations associated with co-habitation.

It is evident, however, that changes in the local social structures and social relations backed up the acceptance and proliferation of apartments. At the end of the 19th century, families were structured under a rigorous semi-patriarchal regime and safely guarded at the heart of their homes. The urbanisation of Brazilian society slowly freed women and children from the strong patriarchal ties, giving rise to the modern family, which was still centred around the father but open enough to allow women's independence and their effective presence in the labour market. Contemporary urban society in Brazil reflects the complexity of our age; it is multifaceted and comprises a diversity of family arrangements, such as single parents, childless couples, extended families generated by multiple marriages and divorces, and families headed by parents of the same gender. It is also characterised by high levels of urban violence. The combination of these factors has contributed to giving the apartment building the status of the ideal form of housing.

Up to the mid-1970s, the production of apartment buildings marginally exceeded the production of single houses in Recife.[5] It was only after the second half of the 1970s that the housing market in the metropolitan area of Recife (RMR) turned towards the upper middle class, initiating the process of verticalisation of the city in areas of higher income concentration. The production of apartments in the form of tall buildings was supported, to a large extent, by a permissive urban regulation that favoured the increase in urban density at the expense of the dispersed and low-density urban fabric that had characterised Recife in the mid-20th century.

The urban regulation that defines the use and occupation of private and public land in the municipality of Recife, known as the Land Use and Occupation Law (LUOS), was promulgated in 1997. The two main fundaments of the LUOS are: (a) to promote urban density and (b) to create undifferentiated urban territories by generalising urban indices in the municipal territory. The latter concept contradicts the local 20th-century tradition of urban regulation, which was based on the concept of zoning, severe use restrictions and/or limitations, and different urban indices for different zones. The indices that regulated building height according to a zone location were, therefore, suppressed, and height became a function of the plot size and of the development profile – clientele, type of the apartment etc. As a result, some neighbourhoods went through an intense process of verticalisation.

With the replacement of individual houses by collective housing structures hosting, in some cases, more than 80 families in a single tower block, the huge impact on the urban infrastructure and on the former social tissue became clear. Nevertheless, the housing market in Recife remains strong, and with several world records for tall structures[6], it is responsible for feeding the pride of some sections of its citizens.

Advertisements: Building a dream

Publicity played a central role in this context, conveying and reinforcing people's perceptions of their needs and introducing new forms of living. But to understand how marketing strategies helped change people's preferences and notions of their ideal home, it is necessary to describe the mechanisms that advertising campaigns used to achieve their goals.

Advertising campaigns encourage consumption, stimulating the desire to acquire new products, either to fulfil basic needs or simply to satisfy a compulsive desire to buy. In order to influence consumption, the promotional materials exhibit the product in a particular manner, distinguishing it, making it different from others of the same class. As exemplified in Hanson's study on housing market and space form in Milton Keynes, UK,[7] the content of the promotional message offers not only available alternatives, but also interpretative commentaries, in order to assist the potential consumer to recognise the merits of the new home. They offer the advantages of an ideal world to consumers who are enticed to consume.[8]

The publicity materials operate through images and messages to reinforce necessity, aiming to act at the level of the decision to buy. They are based on surveys of potential consumers that enable developers to be aware of consumers' needs. These surveys identify the images and messages that could be used to achieve sales. The messages that are communicated present the dreamland of a contemporary life, nobility and tradition, shaping the preferences of the new middle class, offering both a fantasy life and a set of cultural cues.

In the last decades of the 20th century, new forms of dreaming up the domestic world were facilitated by the use of new information technologies. Virtual 3D models and e-commerce are some of the marketing tools used to reach middle-class consumers, who are offered an almost real experience of the future living space; something like a frame you can go through to visit the ideal world. As highlighted by Dovey, these models offer a phenomenology of the future.[9] They allow developers to shape consumers' dreams.

In Recife, the advertising campaigns released since the 1970s explore attributes of social differentiation observed at three different environmental levels: the neighbourhood, the building and the apartment. As social differentiation is an issue to distinguish the product in the marketing, there are strong elements of social classification present in the attributes of the advertisements.

Location: 'Tell me where you live and I will tell you who you are'

The first differentiating attribute of housing is related to the location – following the traditional commerce logic of "location, location, location". According to Ribeiro, buildings tend to be differentiated by their location not only in terms of volume (number of units to be sold), but also in terms of price (certain areas allow luxury developments, others do not) and transaction type (mortgage, direct sale).[10]

Ribeiro affirms that the merchandise – the building – is not determined by its architectural qualities, but fundamentally by its location in the urban territory, because the housing development could incorporate its qualitative and quantitative properties offered by the means of production and collective consumption.[11] This process is regulated by the following rules of thumb: (a) landscape factors, such as proximity to beaches, rivers or mountains; (b) immediacy of a large supply of public services and facilities, such as schools, supermarkets and public transport; (c) distance to the business centre; and (d) symbolic values that distinguish citizens socially according to the place they have chosen to live.

Symbolic values, or the symbolic division of the urban territory, were explored by Velho, an eminent Brazilian anthropologist, in his 1970s study, in the internationally famous Copacabana neighbourhood in Rio de Janeiro, aiming to establish a relationship among social division, housing and ideology. His argument is that the society, rather than simply presenting a differentiation between rich and poor citizens, takes the neighbourhood where people live as a reference. In this sense, it is the neighbourhood where you live that will establish your social prestige and status.[12]

In this 'social map', as defined by Velho, territorial boundaries can be either clear or fuzzy. The advertisements for housing in Recife show neighbourhood frontiers as elastic in order to incorporate positive values found in the vicinity of a housing development. There are two main strategies. The first consists of extending the limits of a more distinguished neighbourhood, so that a development in a stigmatised neighbourhood appears in the media with a name borrowed from an adjacent and more affluent area. Perhaps the expectation is that, with time, boundaries will be extended, as new families move in and the old families move out. The second strategy is the use of adjectives to distinguish certain areas. Locations carrying certain social stigmas can be renamed. In Recife, there are notorious cases. *Nova Torre* (New Tower), for example, was used to identify a neighbourhood emerging after the dissolution of textile industries in the 1980s and the subsequent speculation on the land for housing projects. The parcels and apartment buildings being constructed needed to be identified with a 'new' piece of the urban territory, not with the old industrial area. In this context, a gentrification process caused by the expansion of noble areas has also been observed. This is what Smith[13] named the new urban frontiers, a phenomenon consisting of a sort of differentiation of parts of the already established urban territory, adding quality to the area and smoothing any social class connotations associated with it.

Apart from these social attributes, proximity to public services can qualify an area as a 'good neighbourhood', as well as offering practical benefits to its inhabitants by reducing, for example, tiresome and stressful urban travel for shopping, recreation or to take children to school. Another aspect that significantly increases the value of a development is proximity to natural sites and landmarks. In both cases, symbolic values are aggregated to the advantages of the housing development, even if some of these values and advantages are imaginary or fuzzy. It is common to find key phrases such as 'close to …' and 'a few metres from …' used in the advertisements to capture the intrinsic value of a natural site/landmark, even if these 'metres' are not exactly a few. And to make these messages more effective, it is common for advertisements to show distorted images of the surrounding areas to induce potential clients to believe that the desired services or sites of interest are closer than they are in reality.

Architectural programme: The building and its insertion in the city

At building level, the promotional campaigns express the pragmatic side of the architectural programme, but also its glamour, which is often synthesised in its name. The advertisements normally highlight the diversity of services and equipment offered. More and more developments offer collective services that extend the limits or domains of the housing units. Playgrounds and recreational areas become more sophisticated with the inclusion of gyms, swimming pools, football pitches and playrooms with a full range of facilities, such as fully fitted kitchens, toilets etc. The other side of the coin is that these larger common areas are used as justification for the reduction of private areas, i.e. flat sizes.

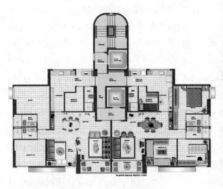

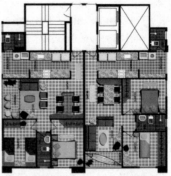

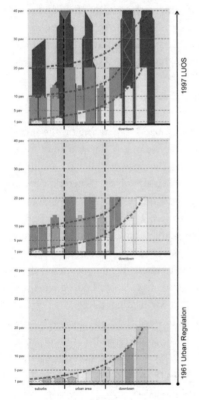

TOP – Plans of typical flats, 2011,
CRISTIANA GRIZ

LEFT – Evolution of urban regulation in
Recife, Brazil, 2010, CLAUDIA LOUREIRO

RIGHT – Luxury flats at Boa Viagem Beach,
Recife, Brazil, 2008, LUIZ AMORIM

Recent trends take this sort of all–inclusive housing programme to another level of sophistication and independence in the urban club residence. Built on large urban parcels either resulting from recent landfill or grey–field lands, this new modality invests in leisure to counterbalance the lack of urbanity (curiously promoted by the market itself) and high technology, implying security and advanced infrastructure.

Regardless of size, complexity or sophistication, housing developments are all based on the principle of enclosure, i.e. restricted access and limited visual interface with urban life at street level, which contributes to and emphasises the social inequalities that still characterise contemporary Brazilian society. One of the more evident consequences of the rapidly accelerating process of replacing the old housing forms, which enhanced the quality of urban life by generating intense interaction between public and private spheres, with the *no touch, no see, no talk* housing model, is the emergence of blind and unconstituted streets (i.e. with few accesses to buildings) that suit anti–social behaviour.

Architectural programme: The apartment and space organisation

The architectural programme for the flats is varied, depending on the social class that is supposed to acquire them. The size of the flat and the design programme always go together: the larger the size of the flat, the more complex the architectural programme. This rule is also observed in recent developments that had the flat sizes reduced to adapt to recent financial constraints, particularly after the 1990s. For example, a three–bedroom flat advertised in the 1970s would have had an area of approximately 160 square metres, whereas the latest products can be found with an area of 80 square metres.

The market offers a great variety of flat types, from simple one–space units, to complex maisonettes equipped with five or six bedrooms, three or four reception areas, large terraces and swimming pools. The typical three–bedroom flats for middle–class families are the most common type. In all cases, the flats are carefully divided into zones or sectors that organise domestic activities in a particular manner. This sectors' structure organises the potential interactions of inhabitants, visitors and strangers, making them predictable and replete with social meaning.[14] This type of domestic space organisation has been socially reproduced, and is also inculcated by means of the promotional materials, acquiring the character of a normative housing model to be replicated. The model is defined by the classification and grouping of domestic activities into three sectors: social, private and service. It is designed to put the social sector at the core of the flat, but also to give easy access to the service sector and proper isolation to the private sector.

This general pattern is present in housing units (houses or flats) of different sizes and offered to different social classes. The distinction made between social classes is identified by the complexity of the architectural programme: the higher the social status is, the longer the prescriptive text. In this sense, the sectors are immutable, but the text, which establishes the requirements of each flat, is altered. In the social sector, for example, the multifunctional living room, normally found in social housing and middle–class flats, has its area increased for the higher classes with the 'spatialisation' of specific activities in proportion to the social status of the dwellers. These distinguishing programmatic elements, such as the reception room, the dining room, the playroom and the TV room – recently renamed the 'home theatre' – are then advertised. The increase in the number of labels is a sign of higher classification and greater complexity in the attributes of the architectural programme.

This phenomenon is highly significant in the private sector of the flat. In middle–class flats, new adjectives and labels (for example, 'en–suite') emerge as strategies to highlight rooms with a more specialised function. In reality, a single room, with the introduction of new commodities, becomes a spatial complex. The en–suite bedroom, with the addition of a dressing area, gym or office, becomes a 'master suite'. At this most intimate level, strong spatial classification marks gender differentiation in some upper middle–class apartments, as is the case with separate toilets and dressing areas for husbands and wives.

Service activities stand out significantly in advertising campaigns, particularly to highlight their number and the uniqueness of the architectural programme. The service sector, for example, may be a single kitchen–service space in small flats, or may include one to two servants' bedrooms, a servants' bathroom and a store room in larger ones.

But the most distinguishing programmatic element, which is largely advertised in middle–class flats, is the 'reversible room'; an ingenious solution that allows the use of the servants' bedroom as either a private or a service space. Its origin is related to the regulation of the servants' profession and the consequent rise in their wages, the economic recession that hit Brazilian society in the 1980s, and the emergence of new family arrangements. The reversible bedroom is designed to meet the needs of families that cannot afford to have a permanent servant, or those who simply need more space but cannot afford it.

Recently, developers realised that a significant number of the flats offered to the market were altered before being inhabited. The need to adapt flats is so common that in some buildings 100% of the flats have undergone important transformations.[15] Recent research[16] based on a larger sample of upper middle–class developments confirmed this trend and revealed interesting space arrangement patterns, either keeping pre–existing category differentiation, for example between servants and inhabitants, or suggesting new modes of living, made clear by the increase in the social area compared to the original plan for the apartment and by the introduction of novel activities in the domestic ambience, such as home offices and home theatres.

As a result, and in order to avoid or reduce the number of refurbishments, developers and architects started offering different potential spatial arrangements for the apartments. This opportunity to choose a particular floor plan has become an important attribute featured in promotional materials. One consequence of this trend is the emergence of studios and lofts (used here to describe a certain spatial arrangement where visual continuity replaces the traditional segregation and division of space) offered to a new sub–culture identified within certain young professional classes.

In summary, the advertising campaigns appeal to three aspects of the potential buyer's dream through three features of the architectural programme for the flats in three different forms: (a) they express conformity with social norms in the traditional domestic spatial organisation of the plan, the segregation of the service area, the isolation of the private spaces, etc.; (b) they emphasise social status by calling the attention to the number of rooms ('4 en–suite bedrooms') or particular spaces ('home theatre'); and (c) they highlight individuality in the flexibility of the floor plan and the possibility to select different arrangements.

On height: 'Tall buildings – because Recife thinks big ...'

In the Brazilian housing marketing, living in the heights is perceived as one of the most desired attributes, at least for a certain social class. In general, the higher the apartment units are, the higher their prices will be, with values being 15 to 25% higher than those on the lower floors. This is the price to pay to be more separate and distinguished from fellow members of the condominium.

Penthouses are a special chapter of this social stratification. The symbol of maximum status in local society and the jewel in the crown of any local developer, they were launched during the conceptualisation of the early luxury developments in the late 1960s as the necessary product to attract members of the higher ranks of society to this new housing form and to convince them to leave behind the old-fashioned secular suburban villas. *High-rise*, a recent film by Mascaro,[17] depicts the symbolism behind the penthouse in Brazilian society with rare sensitivity by revealing the feelings and arguments of their occupants. The formal attributes (height, isolation, visual privacy) and the social attributes (distinctiveness, social segregation, power) are beautifully perceived in the owners' testimonies, sometimes showing some ingenuity, but in other cases giving clear expression of arrogance and social prejudice.

In fact, a tall building is an icon of power, social status, progress, wealth and technological expertise; the greater the social and technological development, the greater the capacity to build more and higher. Societies and cities compete in an international ranking of the tallest buildings on earth, and Recife is in on the game. However, the acceptance of tall buildings in the city seems to have faced some initial resistance by the clientele, motivating the association of local developers (ADEMI-PE) to launch a public campaign in 2003. Its main slogan was "There is something bigger than the tall buildings of Recife..." and it argued that the newspaper readers and TV watchers could link tall buildings to any aspect supposedly relevant to the social and urban development of Recife.

In the campaign's first advertisement, some advantages drawn from the building process were shown. It suggested that approximately 30,000 new jobs and 150,000 indirect job positions would be created, as well as education, qualification and health assistance being offered to the work force. In brief, constructing tall buildings would promote the introduction of a considerable part of the local population into the realm of legality and social justice. The theme explored in the second advertisement was the preservation of green areas, and consequently the preservation of the quality of city life. According to the promoters, urban regulation restricts taller buildings to a smaller footprint compared to lower buildings, thereby not only ensuring the preservation of existing green areas, but also extending them. The third and final advertisement of the campaign appealed to the citizens' self-esteem, tradition and pride. It focused on Recife's long tradition of quality in architecture and engineering, always associated with the boldness

of erecting high buildings and symbolised by the Malakoff Tower, part of a 19th–century navy yard and, for many decades, the tallest building in Recife.

It is important to state that some of the arguments used in the campaign were fallacious. For example, the smaller footprint refers to a tower building but is not applicable to a parking building, and therefore the preservation of the green area, in some cases, is limited. Nevertheless, the campaign was highly successful, and the skyline of Recife is the expression of this fine–tuning of marketing, capital, pride, tradition and social inequalities.

On names: Romancing developments

Status, social identity and traditional values, particularly those related to the local oligarchy, are used by the property market to create a cyclical interest in their products. Another key element in this game of illusion and seduction is the name given to the product. Names can convey social and cultural messages as well as be symbols for self–promotion, and advertising companies explore them with a particular sense of creativity, even though limited to certain themes.[18]

Archetypal imagery is fundamental in this context, establishing what Dovey has interpreted as the "province of meanings"[19]. Perhaps the most notable in Recife is the evocation of nobility, power and tradition through the use of the names of castles, kings and queens: Queen Mary, Baronesa de Gurjahu, Barão do Rio Branco, Versailles. Tradition is also associated with the local sugarcane oligarchy, displayed in the names of sugar mills (Banguê, Engenho Monjope), and with local personalities, such as painters, writers and historical figures. Native themes, mainly represented by the names of indigenous tribes (Acaiaca, Tupy, Tamoyo, Kamayurá), evoking the imagery of an ideal home found in distant places or past times, were quite popular until the 1980s.

In the competitive Recife housing market, the name of the property is so important that developers have created identifying themes that function as a 'griffe' to be assigned and looked for. One company, for example, is identified

TOP – "Find your treasure at Graças neighbourhood. The ark of the treasure: swimming pool, sauna, playroom, gym, cable TV. The treasure: 4 bedrooms, 2 en–suites, dressing area, living room with 3 living spaces, kitchen and scullery, 2 garages, facing East, 152,00m². Cap Ferrat Building: a treasure for a lifetime." Promotional leaflet for the Cap Ferrat Building, 2002, Exata Engenharia (translated by the authors)

BELOW – Still from *High-rise*, Recife, 2009, GABRIEL MASCARO by personal names initiated by 'Maria' (Maria Norma, Maria Eduarda), while another produces the series 'Villa …', in an effort to relate its buildings to the distant Italian villas or to the more modest eclectic suburban villas in Recife. Others use foreign languages to name their buildings, conveying a certain distinctiveness; after all, we live in a global era. Apart from 'villa', it is also common to use the English word 'residence' to avoid any association with '*residencial*' in Portuguese, which carries a connotation of popular, low–income housing. Developers and advertising companies try to avoid names that give any negative sense of co–habitation or collective housing, even if an apartment building is essentially that.

Other thematic groups are names of the local flora (Jacarandá, Samambaia) or natural sites (Golden Garden, Golden River, Golden Lake). Also common are naval motives (Atlântico, Jangadeiro, Catamarã, Jangada) and seaside resorts, particularly those carrying a sense of glamour and wealthy lifestyle (Nice, Biarritz, Saint Tropez, Cannes, Estoril).

Finally, the most recent fashion is either baptising the development in the name of the family that originally owned the site, or paying homage to someone closely related to the developer. In the first case, the old proprietor's name creates an identity linking the development with the history of the place and tries to seduce the old neighbours to accept the significant transformations in their vicinity. In the second, the effect is the creation of a new tradition, as the building and its name are now urban references.

This trend is more evident in developments originated from a municipal regulation, commonly known as Buildings of Preservation Interest, which allows housing development within the confines of a listed building as long as it is preserved. In this case, buildings of historical, architectural, cultural and artistic interest aggregate distinction to the housing development, even if the qualities of the original building are not entirely preserved.

The myth of tradition is reinforced through the marketing strategies. Attributes such as nobility, social distinction and glamour are sustained by the selected names and synthesised in the advertisement by a key image. The building's architectural form, however, neither evokes these images and names, nor carries the archetypal elements that are, somehow, announced.

As highlighted by Bonta,[20] forms acquire meaning not only by contrast with other forms, but also through similarities with other forms that carry the same meaning. But this is not what is found in the housing marketing. In some advertisements, the promise is to bring back the suburban lifestyle that was brought to

Recife by British travellers and immigrants in the 19th century. The desire to acquire and live a specific lifestyle is what is sold, but what is actually bought is a dream.

Marketing and architecture

In Recife, advertising campaigns were powerful instruments in the introduction and establishment of a strong housing market that is founded on, and dependent on, a continuous recreation of certain lifestyle expectations. Advertisements were, and still are, both the representation of people's desires and the origin of those desires. In the specific case of Recife, they are effectively used to evoke popular images that suggest a safe and comfortable life, reminiscent of the stability, tradition and wealth, presumably real, in our recent past. Nothing is more evident of this process than the collection of architectural imagery explored in the campaigns; the architectural attributes of the housing developments (style, proportion, decoration) seldom bear any relation to the images evoked by their names.

The particular market for tall buildings explores the same attributes but introduces height and the symbolic attributes attached to it as the most relevant aspects of the development. As tall buildings are generally associated with larger plots, leisure and green areas are extensively explored in the promotional advertisements.

All these constituted attributes are exhibited by means of four conceptual strategies: (a) imitation, by translating foreign lifestyles, as seen in the use of key images and keywords that evoke a sort of lifestyle never to be experienced locally, such as that of ski resorts and royal palaces; (b) simulation, by inducing and reinforcing non-existent attributes through digitally created 3D imaging; (c) representation, by using symbolic references to past times and places; and (d) identification, by exploring cultural aspects of the local society, particularly the current focus on getting closer to the higher ranks of the society. These marketing strategies are constantly observed in gentrification processes.

However, the gentrification processes that occur in Recife and its metropolitan region are particular as they are based on the local culture. By dealing with the social representation of the middle class, these strategies are successful in influencing the decision–making process that is based on traditional relations, even though tradition, sometimes, has to be invented.

1. T. Caldeira, *Cidade de muros: crime, segregação e cidadania em São Paulo* (São Paulo: Ed. 34 / Edusp, 2000); V. Del Rio, 'Historical background', in V. del Rio (ed.), *Contemporary Urbanism in Brazil: Beyond Brasilia* (Gainesville: University Press of Florida, 2009); L. Leitão, *Quando o ambiente é hostil: uma leitura urbanística da violência à luz de Sobrados e Mocambos* (Recife: Edufepe, 2009).

2. The authors thank the Conselho Nacional de Desenvolvimento Científico e Tecnológico (CNPq) and the Fundação de Amparo à Ciência e Tecnologia do Estado de Pernambuco (FACEPE) for supporting this investigation.

3. K. Dovey, *Framing Places: Mediating Power in Built Form* (London: Routledge, 1991).

4. M. Graham, *Journal of a Voyage to Brazil and Residence There During Part of the Years 1821, 1822, 1823* (London: Longman, Hurst, Rees, Orme, Brown, and Green, 1984); L. L. Vauthier, 'Casas de residência no Brasil', in *Arquitetura Civil I* (São Paulo: FAU-USP / MEC-IPHAN, 1975) pp.1–94.

5. M. A. Melo, 'O estado e a promoção imobiliária formal na RMR 1964-1988', 37pp texto para discussão, MDU, Recife, 1989.

6. 'Uma Cidade verticalizada', *Diário de Pernambuco*, Recife, 06/02/2011, Caderno Vida Urbana, pp. C4–C5.

7. J. Hanson, *Decoding Homes and Houses* (Cambridge: Cambridge University Press, 1998) pp. 134–154.

8. *ibid.*, Dovey (1991) p. 139.

9. *ibid.*, Dovey (1991).

10. L. Ribeiro, *Dos cortiços aos condomínios fechados: as formas de produção da moradia na cidade do Rio de Janeiro* (Rio de Janeiro: Civilização Brasileira, IPPUR/UFRJ-FASE, 1997) p. 114.

11. *ibid.*, Ribeiro (1997) p. 115.

12. G. Velho, *A utopia urbana: um estudo de antropologia social* (Rio de Janeiro: Zahar Editores, 1975) p. 81.

13. N. Smith, *The New Urban Frontier: Gentrification and the revanchist city* (London: Routledge, 1996).

14. L. Amorim, 'The sectors paradigm: understanding modern functionalism in domestic space', in M. Major, L. Amorim and F. Dufaux (eds), *Proceedings of First International Space Syntax Symposium* (London: University College London, 1997) pp. 18.1–18.4; L. Amorim, 'The Sectors' Paradigm: a study of the spatial and functional nature of modernist housing in Northeast Brazil', unpublished PhD thesis, University College London, 1999.

15. A. Cavendish, 'Arrumando a casa: investigando transformações no espaço doméstico', unpublished diploma dissertation, Universidade Federal de Pernambuco, 2000.

16. L. Amorim, C. Loureiro and C. Griz, 'A casa deles, a casa minha ...', in *Novos padrões de acumulação urbana na produção do habitat: olhares cruzados Brasil–França* (Recife: EdUFPE, 2011) pp. 179–214.

17. Gabriel Mascaro (director and producer), *High-rise*, Recife, 2009.

18. C. Loureiro and L. Amorim, 'A Moradia dos sonhos – onde e como morar', in *Proceedings of the IX ENTAC* (Foz do Iguaçu: ANTAC, 2002) pp. 819–827.

19. *ibid.*, Dovey (1991) p. 148.

20. J. P. Bonta, *Architecture and its interpretation: a study of expressive systems in architecture* (London: Lund Humphries, 1979).

Hong Kong

The Property Regime

WING SHING TANG IN CONVERSATION[1]
WITH ASHLEY WONG *&* YUK HUI

AW & YH: Hong Kong is widely known as a financial city and trading hub. However, looking back at history in the 1970s and 80s it appears as though Hong Kong's economy was mainly sustained by manufacturing. From the 1990s up to the present, Hong Kong moved towards becoming a global financial centre and new industries, including high technology, logistics, and creative industries have been introduced to broaden the city's economic base. These industries draw mainly from the process of financialisation and their final goal is to be listed on the stock market. According to critics such as Leung Man Tao, this demonstrates certain features of colonial modernity which results in the development of a single economic culture. The consequence is that the culture becomes too homogenous to produce a heterogeneity. What is your view on this?

WST: I find the statement that attributes the current development in culture to financialisation imprecise. Yes, from economic statistics, we have seen the growing importance of the financial industry. But in the case of Hong Kong, that growth must be understood together with the growth of the real estate sector. A land (re)development regime has been evolving since the late 1960s, when Chinese real estate developers started to become more influential in the economy and society than their British counterparts, and it gained further momentum from 1979, when the British realised that Hong Kong was to be returned to China. The growing dominance of Chinese capital was premised on the financialisation of the real estate market in the late 1960s. Since then, the boom and bust of the two markets of real estate and stock equities have been intertwined. At the private level, when people gained money from the stock market they re-invested in the real estate market, and vice versa. At the urban societal level, while the real estate market can obtain the indispensable capital for expansion from the stock market, the former must raise the profit margin recorded in the company's annual ledger prepared for the latter. This can best be achieved by increasing the level of commodification of the real estate market, the sales volume of flats in particular. The dominance of exchange value over use value has constructed the ideology that economic prosperity – property development in particular – is the norm, and the government is meant to pursue it on behalf of the people. Once the government has implemented relevant actions, the latter form the 'rational' practice of the society and it is expected that the society and the economy should not deviate from this 'rational' course. Any course other than the designated procedures is dismissed as irrational and

therefore slated to be rejected out of hand. People in all walks of life, including government, private entrepreneurs, town planners, architects, engineers, housing managers, legal experts, social workers, community organisers, local and legislative councillors, the middle class and a considerable part of the working class, should support it. All tend to favour the status quo, meaning property development almost at any cost. The dominance of the land (re) development regime is the root cause of the homogeneous culture.

AW & YH: In recent years we've seen more and more resistance emerging to contest the misuse and mis–regeneration of space in Hong Kong, for example the Lee Tung Street, Star Ferry and Queens Pier[2], and Tsoi Yuen Chuen movements[3]. These movements resonate with what happens in the west, especially the notion of conservation based largely on a specific conception of history. As we can see, each of these movements proposes to preserve either historical sites or rural villages, which already establishes its own tradition and communities. In the film *Nønspace* (2009)[4], architect

Alvin Yip suggests that perhaps Hong Kong shouldn't follow the same conception of history and preservation. What are your thoughts on this? And how do you approach the significance of such an understanding of space?

WST: I don't know the argument of the architect Alvin Yip. My understanding, however, is that the concept of historical conservation has very little to do with the discernible resistance to urban redevelopment in recent years. If the point I made above is valid, the resistance has a lot to do with the magnitude and mode of redevelopment taking place in Hong Kong. Regarding the particular mode of redevelopment, the requirements of the land (re)development regime are detrimental. The latter requires land availability at low cost. But, given the complexity of ownership in high-rise buildings, land assembly is always a big problem to resolve. As a result, in order to expedite land assembly, the Hong Kong government initiated the mode of public-private partnership for redevelopment by establishing the Land Development Corporation in 1988. This corporation assembled land

and sold it to the developer for redevelopment while the affected residents had little say in this partnership model. As the land (re)development regime developed further in the 1990s, it became apparent that the corporation had failed to expedite land assembly. The government then introduced the Urban Renewal Authority, whose function of compulsory land purchase is only responsible to the Lands Development Branch of the Hong Kong government (not, as in the past, to the Executive Council). To minimise objections at the stage of ordinance enactment, the government promised that urban renewal would be 'people-centred'. As experience in the late 1990s and the early 2000s informs us, the partnership model still places emphasis on exchange value at the expense of the people. It is this sad experience that has urged people to resist urban redevelopment. Of course, in the process of deliberation and resistance, people did raise their concern for the treasure of their community network and the prevailing way of life. But, as explained above, labelling this development as being induced by the concept of historical conservation completely misses the point. Nevertheless, the government has seized on this – emphasising the rhetoric of collective memory and historical preservation – as an opportune way to divert the resistance. I am hesitant to say that, unluckily, the general public has, somehow, believed this rhetoric and has been side-tracked from the real issue.

AW & YH: In your investigation on what you call 'Shatin value', you are trying to develop a theory on the construction of subjectivity, which we can say also refers to a certain type of governmentality, in the terminology of Michel Foucault. To Foucault, governmentality entails a set of management techniques that correspond to a specific historical development, for example the control of populations.[5] Can you tell us more about how the creation of 'Shatin value' becomes a technique in your analysis? And, as Shatin is a new town where middle-class professionals gather, what is the significance of the middle-class 'Shatin value' compared with the mainstream discourse of the 'Central value'[6]?

WST: I am against the employment of spatial metaphors in many

cultural analyses of Hong Kong. My concept of 'Shatin value' is a confrontation of the once popular concept of 'Central value'. The latter employs the spatial metaphor of a district – Central District in particular – to portray the dominant culture in Hong Kong as developed from the colonial past. In doing so, it has naturalised the development of the colonial past. I employ the concept 'Shatin value' to argue that the dominant culture, which emphasises technicality, rationality and procedure, has its tempo-spatial root. It is related to the massive governmental programme created in response to the 1967 riots. The government had to take measures to regain legitimacy and to ensure the functioning of its authority. In particular, I argue that cultural transformation was somehow achieved through the development of the new towns in Hong Kong. In contrast to the 'old' way of life in the inner city, everyday life in the new towns is comparably legible and can easily be moulded and transformed in the way that the government would like. By placing houses here, offices and community facilities there, in designated zones, the government has incorporated the everyday life and desires of people into its desires and representations. Accordingly, hegemony can be achieved.

To push my point even further, if one is interested in grasping the development in Hong Kong, I would like to claim that the concept of the middle class is dead as it lacks a tempo–spatial root and, therefore, the power of explanation.

AW & YH : You speak of a cultural transformation from the 'old' way of life that was introduced by the development of these new towns. Could you describe this transformation from your personal understanding and experience of the history and culture of Hong Kong?

WST: I think in the case of Hong Kong, if we go back to the 19th century, the development that happened was very Chinese, in the sense that they had their own way of doing things. At that time, Hong Kong had not gone through what we call in the west, the 'modern' revolution. It was in that process of development in the 1950s, when we saw the slow introduction of the modern factory and that started to change things. Nevertheless, a lot of things still remained. For example, we know that when

the factories started a lot of the workers came from mainland China and as a result, we would argue, a lot of the 'peasant' way of life still prevailed. That changed a little bit over time, in the 1950s and 60s. It was in the 1970s that we started to see specific kinds of changes. What were some of the changes we started to see? In the past, people were more varied, and people didn't consider exchange value so important in their fortunes. As time proceeded they began to see exchange value as more important. The people started to narrow down, and all or most differences became really dominated by this particular one.

AW & YH: What is this 'old', 'peasant' way of life? Was there more sense of community or sense of civic life as opposed to now?

WST: In the past, from the Chinese perspective, we were very much concerned about family and people's lives revolved around their family. People didn't have notions of 'rationality' in mind, for instance things like: if it fits the family, then it's OK. People didn't do things in a calculated way, not in the way that what we would call the 'modern man' would do it in western society. Even so, back in the 1950s and 60s people lived in the so-called 'inner city', where there were buildings and buildings, and where there were simply crowds of people. I wouldn't speak of it as a community network or a feeling like that. It was simply that people cared about each other more, and people would know what other people were doing as a whole. This is not the case now, a result of the development in the 1970s.

What I am arguing, and what I think is more important, is the dominance of one particular value system in Hong Kong. Hong Kong is now very much dominated by the notion of 'exchange value'. People are very concerned about the exchange value of their flat, and related to this, people have started to do whatever they can to try to ensure that the exchange value really counts. We then begin to see the value of other things – that are not related to exchange value – starts to decline. Recently there have been a lot of debates about Hong Kong's financial budget. In many cases, people like to talk about financial budgets. For example, young people in their 20s start to wonder how they can manage to buy a flat? In a meeting with an official of the Bureau of Housing and Transport, one boy said, "I couldn't get married because I couldn't buy a flat." This sort of logic is now really dominant in Hong Kong. Everyone only cares about that logic and the valuation of their flat. This was not the case in the past. We started to see this change basically at the end of the 1970s, accelerating in the 80s, and then even more so in the 90s. Life has become very much focused on the *right to property*, and not so much on the *right to live*. Everyone cares about property and all their discussions centre around it. For example, people are valued by whether they can afford to buy a flat, and then by how much the flat is worth. And because of this whole culture of exchange value, when we talk about anything it is very much related to that. So Hong Kong society has become, so to speak, and to put it in quotes, "so simple".

AW & YH: You say this is changing now? How is it changing?

WST: It has started to change. I think some people have started to reflect on it. The numbers have been growing, but not to the extent that we would see a qualitative change in society. This is how I interpret it. Hong Kong has not yet reached such a stage of qualitative change.

AW & YH: There has been more reaction against the privatisation of space. For example, in Times Square, where artists such as Luke Ching have been occupying and hi-jacking[7] the space. The authorities have started to put benches there now, and they have fewer rules on the use of the space. Do you see things changing towards the development of green spaces and more public spaces?

WST: I don't know, maybe I'm too pessimistic. Until now I haven't seen this. We might get qualitative change but only when we start to see the careful articulation of spatial representation by the people. Once we start to see spatial contradiction, then we will start to see change.

Right now, what is prevalent in Hong Kong society is an emphasis on diversity. For example, on Wedding Card Street (Lee Tung Street)[8] people have dramatised the case. What they have been arguing for is diversity. But what they are doing is not challenging the regime. They are asking for diversity, and then they keep on making proposals and following

the technical rationality. They still go through the stipulated planning application procedures, and try to do things. In the case of Shun Ning Road[9], the proposal of the concerned group was to build houses for the poor. Then the government authority emphasised that the developers need to be allowed to make a profit. So then the group changed the proposal to accommodate the making of profit by the developers. In doing so, the concerned group praised the proposal as the one that has upheld diversity.

What's really important is that we need to change the whole attitude of the society. That's why the regime has to be changed. That's why I use the concept of the regime.

AW & YH: Where do you see the points of resistance?

WST: We need to articulate the social issues together and form a social question, in Henri Lefebvre's term, from minimal to maximal difference.[10] The problem with numerous previous attempts by other social movements is that they have concentrated on a single issue. For the homeless issue, for example, we should not concentrate on housing alone. In that way, the technical rationality behind the land (re)development regime cannot be uprooted. The homeless problem requires us to tackle social insurance, right of citizenship, health, jobs, public transport, etc., together with housing. In the Shun Ning Road redevelopment project, there are people fighting for the right of abode for new immigrants in Hong Kong who so far have not been allowed to stay as citizens. If we can unite all these fronts and then try to formulate ideas, we might be able to do something. If we simply stick to diversity as a concern, I don't think it can work. The Hong Kong government's response to the people fighting for diversity is: "Yes, you love collective memory, you love historical preservation? I'll give it to you." That's why recently we have all these projects on historical preservation. That simply dilutes the resistance, and as a result we see that whereas originally there were a lot more people fighting against the regime, now some have stopped resisting because they say that the government has already done something. If we fall into that trap, then we are in trouble. We shouldn't take all this rhetoric. I think the problem is the

hegemony of the regime – a regime that all the people participate in: the developers, the government and individuals. The regime has done a lot of things to stop all these differences from developing into what I would like to call 'counter–hegemonic actions'.

AW & YH: How do you see the changes in Hong Kong in the past 14 years since the handover? There have been many changes during this time, particularly the rise of the Chinese economy, and now there are new developments around the Pearl River Delta Economic Zone that attempt to unite the region of South China economically. How will this development shape Hong Kong?

WST: In the first few years following the handover, basically Hong Kong was alright. I would argue that things only really changed after the resignation of the first Chief Executive. The administration of the first Chief Executive started promoting the integration of Hong Kong into mainland China. He did a lot work trying to promote Hong Kong as a part of China, but he did not succeed in achieving much integration. As a result of his failure and all the activities accumulated to 2003, he was finally forced to step down in 2005. Following that we started to see a lot more integration. First of all it was only in economics, not real integration. If we talk about people, in 1997 the hostility towards the mainland was greater. If you do a survey now, the degree of hostility has declined. Economically there is a lot of integration through the numerous measures supporting Hong Kong capital to build their manufacturing, their services and their producers and personal services to do business in China. As a result of this integration a lot more people who were originally hostile to China are now more sympathetic. Nevertheless, a lot of people are trying to promote resistance to integration as well. A lot of them have been putting forward what they call 'locality'. They say you need to think from the perspective of Hong Kong locally. For example, some people resisted the construction of the express train last year, and then this year, just after Chinese New Year, there was a movement against China's plans with regard to the development of the Pearl River Delta Bay Area, together with Shenzhen, Guangzhou and some

areas around it. There are all these things happening. The Hong Kong environment is changing. More people are integrating and hostility has been reduced. Although recently, because of that, we have started to see some kind of reaction that is trying to promote seeing everything from the perspective of Hong Kong, and then whatever is promoted jointly by the Hong Kong government together with the Guangdong government is considered a hostile project.

AW & YH: It is interesting to see the different economic forces operating in Hong Kong, from its rapid modernisation and susceptibility towards globalisation, a result of its former colonial relationship with Britain, and now, the return to China just as it rises as a major global economic power. With Hong Kong's unique history and geopolitical position, how do you envision the city developing in the future?

WST: I think Hong Kong has a great future. It takes full advantage of its 'one country, two systems' position. And China wants Hong Kong to retain its 'one country, two systems' so that it can do a lot of things that would not be possible if Hong Kong was completely integrated into the mainland. I see a lot of people giving in before they have fully explored the advantages of Hong Kong. I think what Hong Kong should be doing is developing stronger connections with the outside world. The connection to mainland China will be there anyway. If we want to promote Hong Kong, I consider connection with the outside world best for its future.

AW & YH: In many ways Hong Kong is very much connected to the outside world because of its colonial past and its development as a global financial trading hub. We see a lot of highly qualified foreigners, such as bankers, who stay in the city for a short period of time to make lots of money and then leave. This creates a very transient culture, where the city can be easily abandoned and investment quickly withdrawn (as mentioned by Alvin Yip in the case of SARS in 2001 when many of the elite escaped the city). Hong Kong consistently sits in this place in–between its relationship with China and the global financial market. In your opinion, what effect has globalisation and global capital had on the city and society?

WST: As long as it remains the base for international capital to invest in the mainland, Hong Kong will attract the in–flow of highly qualified foreigners. As long as international capital maintains a high degree of mobility, these foreigners will come and go. One real issue is whether these foreigners will consider Hong Kong their home. Another is whether Hong Kongers consider Hong Kong their home. In the recent past many have deserted Hong Kong for other cities in the mainland, showing the lack of confidence in Hong Kong, but developments in the last few years have shown that they are wrong.

As I mentioned before, when the first Chief Executive took office he tried to integrate Hong Kong into the mainland, and the second Chief Executive tried even more. If we are not doing anything to integrate into the mainland, we are warned that we are being marginalised. As a result, what is starting to dominate in local thinking is that our most important concern is to integrate with mainland China, while the connection to the outside world can be ignored. I think it's going to be like that in terms of thinking. I want to reverse it. There is danger in the dominance of that kind of thinking, which is growing, and growing to such an extent that we can start to worry about it.

AW & YH: It seems there is a movement in Hong Kong towards the cultural and creative industries as a new model for economic and urban development, such as in the development of the West Kowloon Cultural District[11] and other large-scale projects like the Victoria Prison/Central Police Station[12]. As Hong Kong strives to become a 'world class' city, it must develop culturally, often taking the UK as a benchmark. However, as you mentioned previously, the local culture and community has been homogenised as a result of the emphasis on property and financialisation. People's lives revolve around the need to acquire individual wealth and own property, resulting in a very materialist culture that reflects very little independent, critical or creative thinking beyond working long hours to become financially successful and participating in a highly accelerated shopping culture and buying luxury goods to reflect one's wealth, which is where the value of never 'losing

face' becomes so important. What are your thoughts on this?

WST: The way I see the development of West Kowloon, and places like the cultural district of Fo Tan,[13] is that they are artists working very hard from the perspective of the Hong Kong government. From the viewpoint of a lot of people, all these are property development projects, including West Kowloon. The thing is we have never promoted culture in Hong Kong. In the past, a lot of people and families were very pragmatic, and if one of their kids wanted to do music or art, the parents would deter them from doing so. Now a lot of parents in Hong Kong are sending their kids to learn piano or take art and drawing classes. What is in their mind is not necessarily to develop their kids' critical thinking or creativity, but to enable them to have another qualification to excel in the future, something that might place them in a better position to enter a leading university, for example.

AW & YH: To prove they participate in extra-curricular activities?

WST: We have a lot of kids learning

how to play the piano, and there are a lot of kids who have written the exams for the Royal Conservatory of Music. All these exams seldom really reflect an appreciation for music or for art. I think, because of that, the society has not reached the threshold to really develop culture and cultural districts. The government has not really encouraged or promoted it. The percent of GDP we spend on research on culture is minimal in comparison to a lot of other cities. The government has no intention to develop culture. I think it is all rhetoric.

In terms of the development of West Kowloon, the government has to do something to show that they are doing something for the good of the public. The West Kowloon Cultural District (WKCD) project was stopped almost 10 years ago because it was a property development project and not a cultural project. We have never had a cultural policy. The only thing the Hong Kong government did was, after the 1967 riot, when they felt that the youth problems were serious, they started to build libraries, exhibition halls and music halls, and still that was only minimal. Then, in 1997, the Hong Kong government, through the first Chief Executive, gave a whole

tract of land to a developer to build the Cyberport[14], and because other developers were not equally privileged they tried to air their objection to the government. When the West Kowloon project came up, instead of giving it to one developer, the government divided it and gave it to three developers. Then others started to ask how come that was the case, and they could not settle it so the project was stopped. All this talk, saying that they're trying to develop the site for culture, it's all rhetoric. Everything in Hong Kong, it's all about property, property, property.

A student of mine is doing a project on Fo Tan to see how the artists are working and looking at their relationship to the community. Basically, there is no connection at all. The artists in the Fo Tan area are just working on their own and they have no effect on the community. In the west there is talk about culture and creativity, and using culture to stimulate development and all that, but I don't see it in Hong Kong. It's really pessimistic, but it's the reality.

AW & YH: Is there hope for Hong Kong? Do you have any new visions and alternatives to propose?

WST: I think what we have been doing in Hong Kong is to provide the incubator for youngsters to develop more alternative thinking and then alternative practices. In my case, I have been advocating not just the right to property but the right to housing and the right to learning. Even when I was asked to do a future development study for Wanchai that involved Wedding Card Street, in my recommendation I proposed to build public housing. Once you say something sensible, people start to trust you. Your trust starts to change the whole way of thinking, and then that will start to affect the whole practice in daily life. People start to think differently. Basically, what we have been trying to do is increase the number of people adopting more alternative ways of thinking, and thereby people will start to put forward their ideas in different domains and different areas. Slowly we will then build up a better understanding and better practices that would be able to change the everyday life of the people.

And, indeed a lot of people are doing things. Really small actions. All these efforts have to accumulate to a threshold, reach a certain extent, then we would be able to see possible changes. I don't want to exaggerate, but maybe in 10 years we might be able to see something. People are starting to resist what I call the 'land (re)development regime' but the numbers nowadays are small, so it will take time. The thing is, we must recognise the crux of the problem, then we will be able to deal with it.

There are always hopes for Hong Kong. The must–do option for the city's urban future is to resume the construction of public housing, preferably not in the periphery but somewhere in the centre of the city.

1. This conversation took place in response to the film *Nønspace* (co–directed by Nicolas Sauret and Ashley L. Wong 2009) screened during the 2010 TINAG festival.
2. A movement in 2006 and 2007 against the demolition of the Star Ferry and Queen's Pier and for heritage conservation in resistance to the constant rapid redevelopment of the city with a disregard to older cultures and histories – relating to the issue of memory and the problem of forgetting its colonial past in exchange for a rootless and amorphous modern culture. The Queen's Pier was demolished and rebuilt in 2008 several hundred metres onto the harbour as part of the Central Reclamation Project.

3. A movement that peaked in 2009 and early 2010 lead by media activists and the 'Post-80s Generation' against the development of the Guangzhou–Hong Kong Express Rail Link, a high-speed train that links South China and Hong Kong that has been criticised for the displacement of village communities, disruption of the environment and being extremely costly.

4. A film produced by Ashley Wong and Nicolas Sauret featuring interviews with artists, architects and academics on the notion of 'space' in Hong Kong as an exploration of its complex history, culture and identity. View the full film at http://vimeo.com/19287551?ab.

5. Michel Foucault, *Security, Territory, Population* (London: Palgrave Macmillan, 2007).

6. Shatin is a new town in the New Territories of Hong Kong; Central is a financial district in Hong Kong Island. 'Central value' refers to an elite culture, which is nevertheless based on economic values. The 'Central value' has been credited as the core value of Hong Kong, and to which it also attributes its economic success.

7. In 2008, there was a movement against the privatisation and over-control of space in Hong Kong that resulted in a series of performances by artists and activists in the hijacking of Times Square in an attempt to reclaim public space. Since then, there have been efforts to include a regular programme of public artworks in the space to pacify reactions against the lack of truly public spaces in the city. See http://hijackpublicspace.wordpress.com/.

8. A street located in Wanchai on Hong Kong Island that has been under redevelopment plans since 2003, where small local businesses, namely print shops for items such as wedding cards, are being pushed out by rising rents and larger commercial businesses.

9. A road in the Sham Shui Po area on the Kowloon side that is undergoing redevelopment. What makes it notorious is that many landlords or sub-landlords have evicted tenants from their properties so that they can obtain a bigger monetary compensation from the Urban Renewal Authority. To facilitate resistance, a concerned group was formed. See http://www.hkhs.com/eng/business/21.asp?contentid=1&estid=21.

10. Henri Lefebvre, *The Urban Revolution* (Minneapolis: University of Minnesota Press, 2003).

11. A highly debated government-led multi-billion dollar development project, which in March 2011 selected Fosters + Partners' City Park design as the masterplan out of three proposals, in competition with Rem Koolhaas' OMA and Hong Kong-based Rocco Design Architects. The site is a prime location along the Kowloon waterfront and aims to become the equivalent, in the Asia–Pacific region, of London's Southbank Centre. The project has experienced many criticisms and pitfalls including the resignation of Graham Sheffield (former Artistic Director of the Barbican who was elected Chief Executive of the project in 2010) after five months in the post (the second to resign from the position due to suspected government bureaucracy). The project is expected to open in 2015. See http://www.wkcda.hk.

12. Another major development project in the guise of 'cultural development' in Hong Kong. The project is located in Central Hong Kong at the site of a historical police station that was built in colonial times and is to be converted into theatres and cultural space. See http://www.centralpolicestation.org.hk/.

13. An industrial district on the Kowloon side of Hong Kong that is occupied by a number of artists' studios and has gained increasing attention through the annual Fotanian festival, which features open studios and tours of the area. See http://www.fotanian.com/.

14. Created as a hub for creative digital organisations and media start-ups, Cyberport is located in Telegraph Bay in the Southern District of Hong Kong. See http://www.cyberport.hk/.

The Lost Legacies and Lagoons of the First British Olympics

CLARE BURNETT & CLARE ODGERS

In 100 years will the residents of Stratford remember they were the hosts of the 2012 Olympics or will all be forgotten as the next generation attempts to build bigger and better things?

The rhetoric and the infrastructure of the 1908 White City Olympics in Shepherd's Bush, West London, were similar to what we hear now of London 2012. New transport links were created, great art was shown, cutting–edge building methods were used, and 8 million visitors came. But all that is left is a name, a transport system and the length of the modern marathon, none of which most people link to the first British Olympics.

The potential to build on and remember West London's sporting and cultural heritage has been all but forgotten in the desire to create a brave new world in the East. Yet even initial conversations with residents who inhabit the 1908 site show the benefits of being linked to it. They feel part of the Olympic timeline and that they, as a community, are important in terms of the city's history.

We juxtapose the rhetoric of both and ask you to question whether there is a value in leaving collective memory as well as infrastructure, and if so, how this will happen once this generation of dream–building politicians has moved on.

The Stadium, Franco-British Exhibition, London, 1908

fig.01

*fig.*02
OVER: *fig.*03

299

Algerian Pavilion, Franco-British Exhibition, London, 1908

fig.04

All postcards from White City 1908,
Hammersmith and Fulham Archives and Local
History Centre, and private collections

*fig.*01
"'Team Stadium' have done a fantastic job
against a challenging brief – their innovative,
ground-breaking design will ensure that the
Olympic Stadium will not only be a fantastic
arena for a summer of sport in 2012 but also
ensure a sustainable legacy for the community
who will live around it." John Armitt, Chairman,
Olympic Delivery Authority, at the unveiling of
the design for the flagship stadium, 7 November
2007, www.london2012.com

*fig.*02
"May the Franco–British Exhibition [the Olympic
Site] encourage healthy rivalry, stimulate
interchange of knowledge and ideas, strengthen
the brotherhood of nations, and in thus doing
so, help on the work of civilisation and promote
peace and prosperity throughout the world."
Prince of Wales, Opening Ceremony, 14 May 1908,
reported in *The Times*, 15 May 1908

*fig.*03
"London 2012 will be 'Everyone's Games',
everyone's 2012. This is the vision at the very
heart of our brand. It will define the venues
we build and the Games we hold and act as a
reminder of our promise to use the Olympic
spirit to inspire everyone and reach out to
young people around the world." Sebastian Coe,
Chairman, London Organising Committee of the
Olympic Games and Paralympic Games (LOCOG),
4 June 2007, www.london2012.com

*fig.*04
"The Olympics will bring the whole world to
London, a city where every nation has a resident
community whose influence has helped sculpt
our culture … It is a thrilling gift to the next
generation." Jude Kelly, Chair, Culture, Arts and
Education Committees 2012, *The Guardian*,
14 February 2005

The Seduction
of Capitalism, Crime
and the American
Way of Life

LAHARY PITTMAN

The genesis of this essay is a black and white documentary photography series on Manhattan's storied Lower East Side (LES), which was born out of being selected as the 2007-08 Artist-In-Residence for black and white darkroom photography at New York City's Henry Street Settlement, Abron's Art Center. To appreciate the correlation of the documentary series to the legacy of social reform, the historical importance of the Lower East Side and their relevance to recent American and world events, I offer this back-story:

In 1892, Lillian Wald, a 25-year-old nurse then enrolled in the Women's Medical College, volunteered to teach a class on home health care for immigrant women at the Louis Technical School on the Lower East Side. One day, she was approached by a young girl who kept repeating 'mommy', 'baby', 'blood'. Lillian gathered some sheets from her bed-making lesson and followed the child to her home, a cramped two-room tenement apartment. Inside, she found the child's mother who had recently given birth and was in need of health care. The doctor tending to her had left because she could not afford to pay him. This was Lillian's first experience with poverty; she called the episode her 'baptism by fire' and dedicated herself to bringing nursing care (and eventually education and access to the arts) to the immigrant poor on Manhattan's Lower East Side. Two years after this incident, she founded the Henry Street Settlement in order to provide nursing care and other aid to the poor and immigrants.[1]

Critical Cities Vol.3

The darkroom for the residency was provided by the nearby Educational Alliance Art School, part of the Educational Alliance, which has served downtown Manhattan since 1889. Originally a settlement house for East European Jews immigrating to New York City, the history of the Educational Alliance and the history of the Lower East Side are deeply intertwined. Like the Henry Street Settlement house, the Educational Alliance came to provide multiple strata of social and educational resources, as well as a prominent art school.

"The young immigrants' teenagers who took classes at the Alliance Art School grew up to be leading social realists and abstract painters of the 20th century."[2] Many of the most revered American artists of the century – Chaim Gross, Louise Nevelson, Mark Rothko, Raphael Soyer, Edward Hopper and Ben Shahn (depression era photographer for the Farm Security Administration) – either studied, taught or exhibited at the Educational Alliance Art School. In fact the entire geographic area of this part of downtown Manhattan is legendary for the depth of artists and world famous creatives such as Willem de Kooning, Bob Dylan, Edgar Allen Poe, Martin Scorsese, Jean Michel Basquiat and countless others.

With this litany of art stars, the bar is high for any downtown New York artist. My choice of subject for a new body of work for my residency was to document the important 2007-08 socio-cultural metamorphosis of the LES in correlation to national affairs (which included the surge toward the United States presidential election of an African American in 2008) and how the local/national metamorphosis reflected world events. I titled the series The Shifting Boundaries & Culture of Manhattan's Lower East Side. An LES critic's review of the exhibition of the series, at the Whitaker Gallery of the Educational Alliance, observed:

This exhibit is a contemporary photo essay on the changing Lower East Side. Pittman follows in the path of generations of documentary photographers who since the late 19th century have chronicled life on the Lower East Side. Jacob Riis documented the squalor of tenement life at the beginning of the turn of the century; Ben Shahn (an alumnus of the Educational Alliance) and others documented street life in the 1930s and 40s; Rebecca Lepkoff (another alumnus) documented the changes in the 1950s and 1960s. Shifting Boundaries catalogues the LES at yet another turning point. The Lower East Side, primarily made up of poor and working class residents, is rapidly seeing new luxury high-rise apartments and hotels being built on the site of former tenements. Expensive restaurants, hip bars, designer boutiques and art galleries are squeezing into ten foot wide storefronts that formerly housed family operated small businesses for decades.[3]

The range in time between Riis and Lepkoff, and from Lepkoff to myself, is equivalent. However an important divergence was assumed in Shifting Boundaries in contrast to my predecessors. Shifting Boundaries altered the historical application of street photography from a prior focus on people to a focus on urban art and the narrative found therein. The aim was to preserve yet re-dialogue urban art, street photography and their formal elements within the context of an innate American brand of socialist realism. This de-populated interpretation liberated vital elements to become a means of artistically and socially carbon-dating our society, while reconciling the future. The murals forewarn us, not only of events already in play, but of things to come.

The 1,000 negatives of Shifting Boundaries catalogue the LES at a turning point in which America is suffering what is being called the largest transfer of wealth in history. In addition to the temporal ambivalence of the black and white canvas, the visual style of Shifting Boundaries is characterised by aspherical prints, cave-drawing like murals, a sub-series of essays, signage interpreted as 'text messages', and antique toning – all serving to blur the boundaries of the 35mm documentary form with the fine art palette. An important secondary objective was to archive a record of endangered downtown murals, similar to the preservation efforts of cinematic film. According to New York City curators of urban art:

Photographs are an essential method of documenting graffiti since they are a permanent way to capture such a transient work of art.
Photography has prolifically prolonged the short-lived existence of graffiti pieces that were cleaned off, painted over and disbanded, while successfully becoming its own artistic form. In the absence of photographic images, graffiti would be all but a vague memory in the minds of New Yorkers. Photographs from the 1970s and 80s will provide the present day viewer with the opportunity to walk the streets of NYC painted inside out at the height of graffiti's explosion.[4]

In addition to having been a resident of the LES, I organised my street research by creating a grid of its historical boundaries, ranging from and inclusive of the Bowery, Greenwich Village, Alphabet City, Chinatown and all other relevant neighbourhoods. Then, as Denzel Washington's character told Angelina Jolie in *The Bone Collector*, I proceeded to "walk the grid".[5] Because Manhattan is a long sliver of an island (similar to the Yucatan peninsula), one full year was the right amount of time to thoroughly photograph, develop and process film, handmake museum-quality gelatin silver prints in the darkroom, as well as cross-catalogue negative scans and the technical data amassed.

Double Jeopardy

Three of the photographs from Shifting Boundaries illustrate the thematic drive of the project. The first, entitled *Double Jeopardy*,[6] represents a trend I became quite familiar with, where street art or assemblages would vary drastically between visits. They might be either completely removed by landlords or the municipality, or totally re-imaged by a different artist, tagged over, etc. For *Double Jeopardy* the setting was an alley gate that had been painted to represent a horizontally oriented American flag. Yet the real intrigue of the site was the second, vertically oriented, US flag flying above the gate. This second flag was extremely old, torn, ragged and soiled, and attached to a dirty clothesline running between the two buildings forming the alley. Because it was just tied onto a horizontal clothesline the flag could only fly vertically, and if there was no wind, it merely slumped un-graciously like a filthy, discarded dishrag.

On my first visit, the representational flag painted on the gate had nothing in the left uppermost rectangle where the stars are supposed to be. When I re-shot the location some months later, a street-writer had sprayed a scrawled facsimile for stars in the rectangle. I used two different lenses coupled to each other, with the second lens being aspherical, and lay in the gutter on my back directly under the gate, half on the sidewalk, half in the street, in order to get the angle of light diving down through the alley between the buildings, rendering the haphazard flag a translucent vertical veil.

The 'in-camera film effect', the sheer strangeness of the found assemblage, and the fact that the site was a real neighbourhood attraction all contribute to the image. The dirty striped and checkered cloth seems to symbolise a soiled and checkered history of the US government ranging from the Native American genocide to human rights abuses in Iraq.

This display of the flag was a pertinent observation – there is "a strict codified federal law (36 U.S.C. 173-178) passed by the 77th Congress in 1942 regarding the

Double Jeopardy, 2008

Hostile Takeover, 2007
OVER: *Liberation Goddess,* 2008

proper use and display of the American flag that states can impose penalties upon".[7]

The fact that the flags are desecrated, and don't fly or flow in the same direction, creates a contradiction that is at odds with the intended integrity of what the flag supposedly stands for, which, amplified by an overcast sky, made a foreboding atmosphere. The distortion of the image against the artificial nature of an aluminum gate-flag makes for an un-natural presentation of the 'stars and stripes', again giving pause to one's trust of representation. *Double Jeopardy* seemed an apt title – it looked and felt like a double-cross, engendering a sense of unease, distrust and suspicion. The literal definition of double jeopardy pertains to the legality of preventing a party from being prosecuted for the same crime twice. The conundrum, however, is that government crimes are routinely committed under the guise of national interests (i.e. the flag), and are not prosecuted even once. In October 2009, after President Obama was elected, "The National Lawyers Guild, seventeen human rights and civil rights organisations, and 45 prominent lawyers and civic leaders sent a letter to Attorney General Eric Holder … urging him to appoint a special independent prosecutor to investigate and prosecute Bush officials and lawyers".[8] Americans were as outraged as the international community over US government crimes, evidenced again in early 2010 when:

International arrest warrants were requested for George W. Bush, Richard (Dick) Cheney, Donald Rumsfeld, George Tenet, Condoleezza Rice and Alberto Gonzales at the International Criminal Court, The Hague, Netherlands by Professor of International Law Francis A. Boyle of the University of Illinois College of Law … for their criminal policy and practice of 'extraordinary rendition'. [However] the new Obama administration in the United States has made it perfectly clear by means of public statements by President Obama and his Attorney General Eric Holder that they are not going to open any criminal investigation of any of the Accused for these aforementioned Crimes against Humanity.[9]

Mounting efforts for justice persist:

George W. Bush had to call off a trip to Switzerland in February 2011 amid planned protests by human rights groups over the treatment of detainees at Guantánamo Bay and the threat of a warrant for his arrest … The visit would have been Bush's first to Europe since he admitted in his autobiography, Decision Points, in November (2010) that he had authorised the use of

waterboarding – simulated drowning – on detainees at Guantánamo … it is an
extraordinary development for a former US president to have his travel plans
curtailed in this way.[10]

Professor Boyle's criticism reflects legitimate and significant disenchantment
with broken campaign promises, including the choice *not* to close Guantánamo
Bay (as of this writing). Once again, any anticipation of a politician who appears
to be pure at heart seems doomed, as illustrated by that famous verse in the 1941
film classic: "Even a man who is pure at heart, and says his prayers at night, may
become a wolf when the wolfbane blooms and the autumn moon is bright."[11]
Except that instead of becoming the personification of evil themselves, the
undoing of many seemingly altruistic politicians is that of becoming inevitable
servants to the real bloodsuckers of modern-day capitalism and corporatism.

Liberation Goddess

The next print, *Liberation Goddess,*[12] is a visual documentation of what
appeared to be an interpretation and re-imagining of the Statue of Liberty
as an urban community icon. The subject of the mural is not identified by
the artist[13], yet the intention is clearly articulated in several ways. The figure
is female, represented in a heroic pose on top of a pedestal of either natural
or sculpted stone, like Lady Liberty, and draped in a cloth that curls around
and through her hips. There is no obfuscation of the fact that she is otherwise
naked. While the print was sepia/selenium toned in the darkroom it was still
discernible that she has the form and features of a woman of colour, attended
by flowing ribbons and flames (originally in rainbow colours) and adorned by
the dignity she accords the community through her nobility.

Unlike the original French-made sculpture in which both the heroine's
gaze and a torch are uplifted to a vision above, *Liberation Goddess* depicts a
divine, voluptuous woman with a straightforward gaze, and instead of a torch,
she is holding what can easily be perceived as 'the ghetto' itself. She cradles the
community defensively above her shoulders with both arms behind her head
like a shield against the buildings that are ravenously sought by corporate
developers aiming to gentrify the neighbourhood.

In fact, the very building this mural was painted on – an age-old
landmark drinking establishment known as the Mar's Bar – is under assault

by developers who had already purchased all the surrounding real estate in order to erect luxury high–rises and even forced the bar to remove graffiti from the front of the building (*Liberation Goddess* was new and situated on a side wall). Indeed, residents of communities across America have experienced an all out assault by banks and creditors to confiscate their homes via mortgage irregularities prompting the recent housing crisis. Alarmingly the middle class, and the lure of the 'American Dream', has been targeted for extinction:

> *Corporations are moving operations out of the US at breathtaking speed. Since the US government does not penalise them for doing so, there really is no incentive for them to stay ... American workers now must compete against a garment worker in China that makes approximately 86 cents an hour and a garment worker in Cambodia that makes approximately 22 cents an hour ... the average time needed to find a job has risen to a record 35.2 weeks ... Over 1.4 million Americans filed for personal bankruptcy in 2009, which represented a 32 percent increase over 2008 ... approximately 21 percent of all children in the United States are living below the poverty line in 2010 – the highest rate in 20 years.*[14]

Despite the middle-class housing crisis, post–9/11 corporate building construction in Manhattan ran rampant and unchecked while my photography residency was in progress. As reported by Associated Press writer Amy Westfeldt in a story titled 'NYC construction workers hold Mass for dead colleagues':

> *Thousands gathered at St. Patrick's Cathedral on Monday at a Mass organised by city construction workers to remember more than two dozen of their colleagues killed on the job in the past year. Workers, some who came straight from the job dressed in work boots and jeans, were joined by family members of some of the 26 union and non-union workers killed in the past year.*[15]

Events which occurred during my residency, and persist as of this writing, are a boisterous assertion that 'affluence supersedes community' and 'capitalism trumps patriotism'. My Shifting Boundaries series underlines the critical need to re-examine the counterpoint between a capitalist democracy and a socialist democracy.

Hostile Takeover

Hostile Takeover,[16] a bold black and white photograph, documents an acutely distressed, pasted poster trumpeting a dire warning of a New World Order within a circular rim of stars. Multiple tags by different writers are evident, including what seems to be the name 'Pablito' below the poster. However, due to small 'Obey' and 'Andre the giant' icons placed near the crested ends of the semi-circle scroll denoting the New World Order, it's more likely that attribution for the poster should go to Shepard Fairey. In my own consideration at the time, the phrase 'New World Order' alluded to the renegade alliance of certain governments with unscrupulous multinationals. However, the 2011 domino effect of Middle East dictators being ousted is now resulting in a *new* New World Order as young people wage 'Twitter and text take-backs' of their countries as remedies for decades-old repression by despots. Revealing insight into how and why dictators have been able to maintain strangleholds over their people can be discerned from an airing of the American public television programme *Newshour* wherein journalist Jim Lehrer interviewed the US Vice President Joe Biden:

JL: "The word, the word to describe the leadership of Mubarak and Egypt, and also in Tunisia before, was dictator. Should Mubarak be seen as a dictator?"

JB: "Look, Mubarak has been an ally of ours in a number of things and he's been very responsible on, relative to geopolitical interests in the region, Middle East peace efforts, the actions Egypt has taken relative to normalising the relationship with Israel. And I think that it would be, I would not refer to him as a dictator."[17]

Strategies to liberate cities from the infectious tide of predatory profiteering must operate in tandem with a resilient independent media. Vigilant fact checking and public condemnation of intentional data distortion and flawed media campaigns are imperatives for mobilising collective agitation. "As the historical lyrics of a song of the civil rights movement reminds us ... 'We Are The Ones We've Been Waiting For'."[18]

*All images gelatin silver prints, 40.64 x 50.8 cm © 2008 Lahary Pittman / Artists Rights Society (ARS), New York

1. Beatrice Siegel, *Lillian Wald of Henry Street* (New York: Macmillan, 1983) pp. 22-26.
2. Educational Alliance, Art School History, http://www.edalliance.org/index.php?submenu= ArtHistory&src=gendocs&ref=ArtHistory&category=Art%20School.
3. Educational Alliance Past Exhibits: Shifting Boundaries & Culture of Manhattan's Lower East Side, 7 January - 11 February 2009, photographs by Lahary Pittman, New York, <http:// www.edalliance.org/index.php?submenu=ArtGalleriesPast&src=gendocs&ref=PastExhibits &category=ArtsCulture#2009>.
4. Molly Sampson, Mario Ramos, Claudia Bumbac, 'History of Graffiti in NYC Reviewed in Exhibition at Benrimon Contemporary', 7 August 2010, http://www.artdaily.org/index. asp?int_sec=2&int_new=39270&b=History of Graffiti in NYC Reviewed in Exhibition at Benrimon Contemporary.
5. Phillip Noyce (dir.), *The Bone Collector* (Columbia Pictures/Universal Pictures, 1999).
6. Lahary Pittman, *Double Jeopardy*, 2008, gelatin silver print, 50.8 x 40.64 cm © 2008 Lahary Pittman / Artists Rights Society (ARS), New York.
7. 'The Flag Of The United States Of America', United States Code, http://www.usflag.org/ uscode36.html.
8. Marjorie Cohn, 'National Lawyers Guild and other human rights groups issue open letter to Eric Holder', 10 October 2009, http://www.atlanticfreepress.com/news/1/11963-national- lawyers-guild-and-other-human-rights-groups-issue-open-letter-to-eric-holder.html.
9. David Swan, 'ICC Complaint Filed Against Bush, Cheney, Rumsfeld, Tenet, Rice, Gonzales', 19 January 2010, http://www.democrats.com/node/21570.
10. Ewen MacAskill and Afua Hirsch, 'George Bush calls off trip to Switzerland', 6 February 2011, http://www.guardian.co.uk/law/2011/feb/06/george-bush-trip-to-switzerland.
11. George Waggner (dir.), *The Wolf Man* (Universal Pictures, 1941).
12. Lahary Pittman, *Liberation Goddess*, 2008, gelatin silver print, 40.64 x 50.8 cm © 2008 Lahary Pittman / Artists Rights Society (ARS), New York.
13. There was no apparent signature or identification of the artist on the mural.
14. Michael T. Snyder, '22 Statistics That Prove That The Middle Class Is Being Systematically Wiped Out Of Existence In America', 17 July 2010, http://inteldaily.com/2010/07/middle-class/.
15. Amy Westfield, 'NYC construction workers hold Mass for dead colleagues', 28 April 2008, http://www.usatoday.com/news/nation/2008-04-28-808973896_x.htm.
16. Lahary Pittman, *Hostile Takeover*, 2007, gelatin silver print, 50.8 x 40.64 cm © 2008 Lahary Pittman / Artists Rights Society (ARS), New York.
17. American Vice-President Joe Biden, Interview, *PBS Newshour*, 27 January 2011.
18. Harry C. Boyte, 'Civil rights history informs "We are the ones"', 25 February 2008, http:// www.startribune.com/templates/Print_This_Story?sid=15970347.

Unearthing the Other New Belgrade

From Unfinished Project Towards Critically Re-evaluated City

TIJANA STEVANOVIC

Whose space is the urban space of New Belgrade and what are the modes of knowledge production on the city? Space is generated not only by the building process but also through an active debate on how these building initiatives can be lived through. The modernist heritage of New Belgrade, as a primary built structure and something to be preserved, is not questioned here. Instead, the ideological modernist base of the city is considered in relation to its recent additions and in particular to the forms of participation in redoing it. This text seeks to create a dialogue, bring forward aspects of the architecture that are neglected in its conventional image, open up the critical public sphere and look into the potential spatial negotiation of power relations in New Belgrade today. It suggests moving away from discursive city identity narratives – modernist, transitional, post–socialist – and the often–implied negativity in critiquing such urban categories. This reassessment of local urban practices in New Belgrade is intended to show the universal potential of the city's unfinished past, rather than provide models for resisting the global homogenisation of urban settlements.

Property shifts

The starting point for looking into changes in New Belgrade's urban structure (and their reception) is the state crisis and economic and political turmoil during the 1990s. Due to the nature and recent date of these changes, they are largely undocumented and almost impossible to trace in legal archives, official architectural plans and urban planning documents, but their presence at the level of the citizen's everyday life cannot be denied.[1] Furthermore, these often-extralegal practices of the 1990s are now formalised and officially followed by state structures on a much larger scale and at a faster pace. In the face of these changes, and recognising the city's contested past and the uncertain plans for its future, it is important to investigate the scope of critical space available today.

New Belgrade is considered the fastest growing municipality[2] of Belgrade, Serbia. It has been recognised as such since after World War II, when the decision to create a modern capital for the new country, the Socialist Federal Republic (SFR) of Yugoslavia, was made. Located on the marshland between the left bank of the Sava River and the right bank of the Danube, opposite the centuries old nucleus of Belgrade, its site was the historical border of the Ottoman and Austro-Hungarian empires – a no-man's land – and, as a result, a state decision was required to establish a settlement there. New Belgrade is, therefore, a perfect example of a new city built on a *tabula rasa*, a space cleared of any impeding historical traumas, and a willed social product.

New Belgrade was conceptualised to bring the Yugoslav nations together around a common aim: building a city for the socialism to come,[3] for and by its people. However, unlike many other similar projects of socialist cities in history, New Belgrade has never been subjected to a unique development strategy of growth or a total top-down planning approach, even during its socialist period. The waves of actual political changes in the state have shaped its image differently, decade by decade, from the 1950s onwards.[4] In the late 1940s and early 50s, the initial competition as well as the first wave of building included the new state's governmental and administrative buildings in prominent positions on centrally planned axes, for example the Palace of Federation and Central Communist Committee building and the new railway station. The 1960s construction projects concentrated on providing housing for the rapidly growing city, and the decade of the 1970s was mostly characterised by the shift in planning circles towards self-managed urban communities and 'mega-blocks' of 2,000–3,000 inhabitants, envisioned as towns within the city. The 1980s saw the introduction of post-modern urban tendencies to break the big blocks into smaller units and bring back local centres of smaller scale.[5] Thus the politics of New Belgrade's urban development have often shifted, due partly, on the one hand, to giving citizens greater participation in decision–making, and on the other hand, to not consistently following one clear logic of planning for the six decades of its existence.

It is, however, the changes of the 1990s – the decade of war, the break–up of the old state and economic downturn in former Yugoslavia – that have been particularly drastic. Throughout the decade, changes in the city fabric were reflected in the dissolution of urban tissue through many individual (and, at the time, illegal) extensions, space partitioning and privatisation of the public realm, both metaphorically and literally. Once ideally imagined as a healthy and regulated capital, New Belgrade gradually became a marginal municipality, with illegal kiosks popping up on green lanes, flea markets and improvised petrol stations along the highway and main traffic arteries. Already existing social inequalities were exacerbated during the 1990s, resulting in the emergence on the territory of New Belgrade, and quite centrally positioned, of one of the biggest non–hygienic settlements in Europe, popularly called Cardboard City.[6] The uncertainty and absence of welfare services during the decade left citizens to act for themselves to secure their immediate daily needs. With the state's reluctance to either provide needed services or sanction illegal individual actions, the latter soon grew in such number that the black market started to dictate the city's overall image and its population's mobility. Paradoxically, as a result, government organs can be characterised as being out of the public realm, where we usually expect them to be situated.

The majority of these spatial imprints of political changes remain apparent today, but they have also been altered and have progressed in different directions.[7] They are more important as reflections of the transformation of social dialogue than as specific objects of architecture.

The official wave of social property privatisation throughout SFR Yugoslavia might, at first sight, seem to be the state's further withdrawal from governing the area. In the case of New Belgrade it happens to be extremely apparent in scale, since it has affected the entire, officially recognised, built structure of New Belgrade, which was originally conceptualised as social property, and would perhaps have been impossible to realise without this premise. New Belgrade does not have a history of private ownership, and was envisioned on precisely the opposite grounds – improvement of individual progress and the living environment by providing public facilities: vast green spaces in open blocks, communal centres free and accessible for everyone, good means of transportation and solid building design.

Licensing particularisation

The wave of Europe-wide political changes, together with the accelerating decline of Yugoslavia after Tito's death, motivated state officials to introduce changes in the property system in an effort to secure the financial situation of the state which was already shaken and in crisis. With the first steps in the privatisation of formerly social property[8] in New Belgrade during the late 1980s, in parallel with the slow break-up of Yugoslavia, it is interesting to compare the effects of the disbelief in the social system to the lost ideals in urban planning and the official restraint from any form of planned governance.

As a student, in the early 2000s, I used to live in my grandparents' apartment on the 7th floor of one of the residential buildings erected in central New Belgrade in 1961. One day the elevator did not work and, too tired to walk up seven floors, I decided to go to the next entrance (the estate had four entry points), take the lift there to the 8th floor and enter my wing through the rooftop door, which I remembered we used to do as children when we were playing. When I entered the Corbusier-style rooftop terrace, which was supposed to be the one, unique and unobstructed area for all four wings of the estate, I discovered that my childhood memories were quite different from the present reality. Someone had extended the communal room, which was originally used by some residents who had small apartments for drying their laundry, and now lived in that space. This extension had been done in such a way that it encompassed the public access to the building and the door I had planned to pass through. Years later someone knocked on my door, introduced herself as my neighbour and asked for my signature for the licence to legalise and make 'minor' and undefined changes (without an actual drawing of the base plan) to the extension I had discovered earlier. I refused, on the basis that it is public space that I need to have access to as a resident, still recalling how angry I was I had to walk those seven floors that night … I never discovered who let the person in there, if someone was renting out that part of the building to her and her family illegally, if some architect assisted them with the design, or if she received that licence. Yet that structure is still up there, existing and used. This is just one example of how the necessity to secure one's everyday life has pushed individuals to find flexible ways to extend the private into the public by simply reducing the latter.

With the limited sphere of public interaction and the absence of planning, the flexibility of the individual has become a more stable criterion for illustrating the city's affairs than any of its official urban concepts. Architecture as a discipline has lost its forward–looking role in the construction of progressive social ideas partly because of the state's withdrawal from housing production while the city's population was steadily growing. This sharp contrast is most apparent in the urban body of New Belgrade, compared to other parts of the city, because it is the space where the values of technology and modernist architecture as a discipline have been worshipped as socially progressive. The result has been most obvious in a decline in numbers in the state construction sector, but paradoxically, also in the explosion of informal building practices. Construction remains one of the most significant industries in Belgrade's economy today – someone provides the materials for those extensions and modifications, even if we exclude the professionals from making the design solutions for them – and New Belgrade is its biggest municipality with nearly 400,000 inhabitants.

On the level of urban decision–making, the partitioning of the public sphere and the balkanisation[9] of space has steadily led to the loss of a common ground on the level of planning. Nevertheless, the previously built, socialist city's infrastructure has not failed to provide a base and support for all the smaller and atomised changes. Indirectly, the solidity of its planning and design, although outdated, has triumphed in the present small additions to the already existing plot. In that sense, the new needs are reflected only as additions or alterations to already existing structure, and balkanisation has helped to both parcel the space and amalgamate the complex image of New Belgrade.

Dramatist and theorist, Borka Pavicevic[10] stresses that, due to the uncontrolled privatisation of the former social property and persistent simple reduction of what was once collective, basically the state itself has disappeared. She emphasises that 'retreat to a room' and anonymity have meant that the initiative and capacity to negotiate the common good have been in the hands of the residents themselves.[11] New Belgrade is paradigmatic ground for this claim, as it has been transformed almost entirely from social to private property, with ever–bigger reduction of public space, going in one direction. However, loss of control and a move away from top–down planning may be the hope for a more democratic use, but without neglecting the strategies of design.

A 'third way' transition?

What is usually understood by the term 'transition' in the cities of Eastern Europe can be easily subjugated by the political discourse and demand to access the EU, get closer to the developed west, by simply adopting its models as the only positive and progressive way, without any critical reflection on the global neoliberal non-democratic trend in the management of space. The notion of the 'transitional period' has held the central position in official narratives of state development in Serbia for the last two decades. During this period New Belgrade has witnessed the loss of its role both as a capital and as a leading example of social progress and hope. If we compare New Belgrade to other cities in the Yugoslav context, it is important to make a distinction on the basis of relevance to the state as a whole. Whereas, for example, following the break-up of the old state, Skopje or Prishtina are being rebuilt with a sense of national pride and being transformed from provincial towns into the capitals of the new states of Macedonia and Kosovo, New Belgrade has been reduced from a capital and an open, secular city to a marginal neighbourhood of Belgrade where shopping malls are deposited opposite fenced-off churches and churchyards. It has, in parallel, gone through the process of the institutional consecration of pre-modern ideas.

Today, there is still no consensus among authorities, investors and citizens, and no articulated official clear strategy for the development of the city, although New Belgrade still inevitably grows. Democratic changes and the aim of fast accession to the EU through 'transition' to a market economy have introduced another trend that ignores the widespread urban developments that happened throughout the previous decade and in the name of quick provision of needed services, such as office space and shopping malls.[12] The authorities today, much like the individual intrusions into 'unoccupied' public space, often easily decide to give the big investors great areas of land for little or no remuneration in exchange for the provision of shopping malls. Unwillingness to qualitatively define the changes that took place during the previous decade of state dissolution in the 1990s leads to the complete commercialisation of space. Commercialisation further constructs a base for the 'culturalisation'[13] of one hegemonic idea of the market and closes any space for critique, reducing it, thereby, to a simple oppositional practice as the most common means of political action.

Furthermore, New Belgrade citizens have capitalised on the privatisation of previous social property apartments during the time of the highest inflation in history.[14] Today, the market price of these apartments, which were obtained for very small sums, has risen more than 1,000 times in some cases. Even if not maintained for 50 years, these apartments' market value is the highest in Belgrade, in general, due to the good infrastructure and location. Paradoxically, selling off social property for inappropriate prices to private investors and the existing buildings' market prices benefit from each other.

Something is definitely going to happen here[15]

Boris Buden stresses that it is precisely by fragmentation and balkanisation of the cultural sphere that the unequivocal post-communist situation has been helped and produced.[16] The post-communist condition as a trope, formed on the basis of opposition to the previous regime, closes the circle of possible critical standpoints by simplification and diminution. Therefore, if we want to reassess the present depolitisation of space and New Belgrade's urban structure, it is important to look at the historical context of its roots: the particular changes that happened within the modernist city of New Belgrade and the attempts to neither align with east or west.

Contrary to the places of conflict and war in the region, in Belgrade during the 1990s another sort of a battle was fought – a battle for metaphorical territorial dominance through atomised, individual, city-fabric alterations. Could these illegal, individualised practices be acknowledged in official planning circles as a battle for difference? Can this be translated as a worthwhile idea, not design-wise, but in terms of a dissolved system of connections? On a larger scale, functions have deserted buildings or have been altered in a decade, but the existing structure and infrastructure have been capable of generating potentiality for new activities by being adaptable and reusable. In *International Competition for the New Belgrade Urban Structure Improvement*[17], Henri Lefebvre says that instead of solidity, the socialist city of New Belgrade has failed in providing a complete vision for the society to come. Yet, he adds, it is this unfinished form which is to be praised for its potential for innovation and new social exchange.[18]

Can these alterations, happening a decade after Lefebvre's statement, be seen as a critical cultural model belonging neither to planned de-politisation, nor to the explicitly expressed state politics? What are its potentials as an alternative to both? Tom Holert rightly notes: "Nobody can claim to be outside of design anymore."[19] What kind of space for critique of the modernist city is opened then, other than, on the one hand, a simple negation of the one-dimensional modernist ideology of progress or, on the other hand, a critique of the neoliberal commodification of space? What kind of authority presence is appropriate which would not repeat the mistakes of either of the two?

The present state of affairs reflects that in times of economic shortages and political changes a different system of spatial appropriation takes over from solid and permanent building production. Moreover, this type of spatial re-codification better addresses the impermanence of the contingent architectural discourse. It helps us see architecture as a means of connection, not reducing its role as a knowledge generator. The knowledge produced in such a way is not reducible to past uses or aesthetic commands, as Cedric Price suggested.[20] It is precisely by liberating New Belgrade's buildings from ultimately predetermined use that the new network and organic growth of interactions in the city can be established, as Lefebvre pointed out.[21] Citizens have inevitably participated in redesigning New Belgrade, over a long time period and in rather small steps, and it is only in accumulation that their actions can be seen as counter-hegemonic.

If we accept Irit Rogoff's hypothesis that learning can be traced in the series of turnings and that it is "we who are in movement, rather than it",[22] we can juxtapose this claim to the shifts and turns in New Belgrade's development, since there seems to be one constant in the development process from its earliest date: the continuation of discontinuity. From the modernist concept of a governmental capital, to the city of housing, and then to self-sustainable blocks, the urban pattern has never clearly demarcated a consistent approach. It is rather the lack of permanent solutions that characterises its neighbourhoods.[23] As the majority of New Belgrade citizens could inherit and privatise their apartments, there is a large number who have witnessed and participated, either passively or actively, in the 'turns' in the city's urban politics. Thus we are obliged to ask: What is the knowledge communicated through this large-scale transformative process? Is there a connective quality that can be learned and evaluated through an archive of this impermanence of ideas? What mode of archival action does this identification with systematic disruption of memory call for? As architect Ines Wiezman has elaborated:

The archive can reflect the very mechanisms of a society forming its discourse and possible field of action, but it can also function as an important laboratory for a critical cultural, or political discourse.[24]

In New Belgrade's alterations of urban fabric, we can trace only a fragmentary sort of collection which, due to its always-incomplete representation and reception, remains open and extendable in its use. But it is only by constant revision that the dialogue of social relations and environment can expand through time. The time interval occupying the unfinished can be understood as crucial for triggering the new reconnections for producing the critical knowledge. Holert reminds us that:

Attention to contingency and agency, to singularity and a 'place-based politics of subjectivation' can be enormously helpful in providing a framework for approaching cooperative cultural production in a different way – as a politics that boldly centres on the local and the particular without falling victim to a retrograde romanticism of the homogeneous community or the 'neighbourhood'.[25]

In their video *Something is definitely going to happen here*, duo Bik Van der Pol went to the site of the unfinished Museum of Revolution[26] in New Belgrade in order to question the role of the public in the creation of the urban landscape. They film the scene as it is, including passers-by and everything that comes into the picture, without acting, raising the question whether anything happened if there was no action produced other than recording what is on the site of the unfinished museum. By questioning whether the Museum of Revolution is possible as a concept, they aim to show that revolution cannot happen without the self-conscious production of knowledge. In a similar vein, Miessen and Obrist commit to "inquiring whether any accumulation and organisation of knowledge is productive – to the effect that it generates a narrative and/or history" and focusing "specifically on archives becoming productive due to their spatial framework".[27] Knowing that discontinuation, impermanence and lack of a steady vision have informed the city's development up to the present, it is the architects' task to rethink the possibilities for an active approach to archiving and learning from the social changes in the spatial framework of New Belgrade.

How can the architectural sphere address the city's 'transitional period' and its borderlines, if official relations to both the past and future of the city are still undefined? The recurring incapacity of conformist architectural strategy to define space usage can, as Cedric Price proposed, instead bring the critical stance towards "not–do".[28] As a constructive force, but different to building practice, architecture is, for Price, also comprised of the faculty of potentiality not to actualise an ideal. What can we learn from the experience of the reduction of the meaning and role of architecture in New Belgrade in the 1990s and 2000s? In accordance with Hannah Arendt's theoretical position of a refusal to take action as a political choice, what can this refusal to participate in building a public sphere mean for New Belgrade urbanity?

The city is, for both Lefebvre and Price, a contingent possibility rather than a determined structure. In Bik Van der Pol's video recording, all the passers–by contribute to that contingent category of 'becoming' a city. Here, in the absence of architecture, art as active discourse takes on the task of being a public space or the place for finding political meanings. Being visible means also being present, participating in forming a public space. However, what are the specific conditions of this participation? Architecture seems to have lost the power of deciding what is representable and which labour remains invisible in the cityscape. Thus, how is the spatial language of transformation translated into social changes and how can it be expressed in ways that will critically challenge prevailing concepts of architecture as profitable space?

In the absence of planning consensus, the use of structures remains flexible and on the periphery of rigid discipline. With the reduction of public space in New Belgrade, the atomised, individualised attempts to spatially appropriate the urban seem to be the only common denominator of citizens' power and inscription into the city. "Power not only acts on a subject but, in a transitive sense, enacts the subject into being."[29] Knowledge is the means for cultural revolution; citizens have the power to constantly reproduce new constellations of space and, therefore, new parameters of political participation. Thinking about New Belgrade, we are reminded that the city is a form that is ultimately socially produced. The boundaries of knowledge on space production and design lie in the architects' as well as the citizens' recognition of their right to Foucauldian micro–politics and self–transforming technologies as part of their 'right to the city'.

1. Many real estate developers profited from illegal construction projects, finding loopholes in the corrupted legal system for building structures on locations with unclear property histories. This was partly due to the state's appropriation of private property in the early communist era and its unresolved national strategy for denationalisation. Some benefited from this, others suffered, but everyone was aware of the fact that in a context of administrational void and institutional dissolution the most daring and those in need create ways of interacting with the city structure when architectural and urban planning circles have ceased to perform. Owing largely to the frequent political changes, and even changes in the country's borders (and therefore in the definition of what the state stands for) and with every new government, socialist planners failed to complete their own proclaimed goals. On the other hand – despite the absence of planning in the last two decades, the city emerges as 'the most desirable residential area'. See: Milica Topalovic, 'New Belgrade: The Modern City's Unstable Paradigms', in: *Unfinished Modernisations* (Zagreb: 2010) p. 15, http://www. unfinishedmodernisations.net/conference-unfinished-modernisations-outlinin-2.

2. 1953 census – 11,339; 1961 census – 33,347; 1971 census – 92,500; 1981 census – 173,541; 1991 census – 218,633; 2002 census – 217,773; 2006 estimation – 236,898; 2009 calculation – 388,354, accessible at: http://wapedia.mobi/en/Novi_Beograd.

3. The text of the youth work brigades' memorial plaque that commemorates the beginning of the construction of New Belgrade in 1948 says: "On that day the working people and youth of all the Yugoslav nations joined forces to erect the new Belgrade, to extend the beloved capital of the state of equal nations. To make the city bigger and better on this side of the Sava River, the city where the Communist Party of Yugoslavia headed by Comrade Tito started the uprising towards building yet another eternal symbol of the victorious liberation struggle of our people, led towards socialism by Marshal Tito, in the country built by the people themselves." (Author's translation).

4. After the split from the Eastern Block, Yugoslavia adopted a so-called 'third way' socialism, which followed neither the Soviet model completely nor the western example. It was this non-aligned position that enabled the introduction of, for example, social property, which is different from state property in other communist systems. Self-management was a later modification of governance, which was to improve the decentralisation of rights to individuals and greater participation of workers in governing the society.

5. See: Ljiljana Blagojevic, *Novi Beograd: Osporeni Modernizam* (Beograd: Zavod za udzbenike, 2007).

6. In Serbian, "Karton City" is named after its primary built material: cardboard (*karton*). It is mainly inhabited by Roma people, some of them refugees from the wars in the neighbouring territories of former Yugoslav republics, the majority unemployed and often living on social benefits. This community is the main recycling organisation in the city, since many of its residents collect cardboard and get remuneration for returning it for re-use in production processes.

7. The shopping mall in Block no. 70, where Chinese residents got permits for retail from Milosevic's government in the late 1990s, is still being used, but has an extension in the form of one more storage building on the neighbouring green plot; Roma slums that were demolished and relocated several times by the city authorities in 2009 still exist under the Gazela Bridge; the flea market has relocated from under the railway bridge to the nearby boulevard pavement; some kiosks have been removed, and some have been reinstalled following their demolition, etc.

8. It is important to discern again the notion of 'social property' in opposition to 'state property' in other socialist states. Social property is based on a concept of citizens' participation and ownership of the land and buildings, not the state's. Theoretically, governance in the Yugoslav self-managed system was brought closer to the individual citizen. The decision to privatise property with such a background would mean the burial

of the previous social contract.

9. "... balkanisation is not simply parcelisation, the creation of small entities at war with each other; it becomes synonymous with dehumanisation, deaesthetisation, destruction of civilisation." Maria Todorova, *Imagining the Balkans* (New York: Oxford University Press, 2009) p. 36. See also, Srdjan Jovanovic Weiss's research on balkanisation vis-à-vis democratisation process, http://roundtable.kein.org/node/792.

10. Borka Pavicevic, in: Albert Heta and Vala Osmani (eds), *The way between Belgrade and Prishtina* (Prishtina: Stacion Center, 2009) p. 83.

11. Borka Pavicevic, interview in *Pescanik*, 14/02/2011, http://www.pescanik.net.

12. Aerport City, Delta City and Usce shopping mall are all establishments built on land that previously belonged to the citizens, and which the state has given to private investors under special conditions for use, meaning almost for free. Former hotels Putnik and Yugoslavia have been sold to foreign private investors and the latter is being turned into a casino. Today it is private property where citizens have no or very limited access, mostly for commercial use.

13. Boris Buden, 'O kritici kao kontrakulturnom prevodjenju', in: *Prelom no.8/9* (Belgrade: Prelom Kolektiv, 2009) pp. 258–266.

14. The people living in the apartments at that moment had the right to purchase them, if they wanted to, and for very small sums.

15. Bik Van der Pol's video *Something is definitely going to happen here* was realised as part of an international project, entitled Differentiated Neighbourhoods, initiated by the Museum of Modern Art in Belgrade, curated by Zoran Eric. See http://www.artandresearch.org.uk/v3n2/vanderpol.php.

16. *ibid.*, Boris Buden (2009) p. 264.

17. Henri Lefebvre, Pierre Guilbaud and Serge Renaudie, 'International Competition for the New Belgrade Urban Structure Improvement' (1986), in: Sabine Bitter and Weber Helmut (eds), *Autogestion, or Henri Lefebvre in New Belgrade*, (Berlin: Sternberg Press, 2009) p. 1.

18. *ibid.*, Henri Lefebvre (2009) p. 6.

19. Tom Holert, 'Hidden Labour and the Delight of Otherness: Design and Post-Capitalist Politics', *e-flux journal*, 06/2010, http://www.e-flux.com/journal/view/152.

20. Cedric Price, *Re: CP*, Hans Ulrich Obrist (ed.) (Basel: Birkhäuser, 2003) p. 39.

21. *ibid.*, Henri Lefebvre (2009).

22. Irit Rogoff, 'Turning', *e-flux journal*, 11/2008, http://www.e-flux.com/journal/view/18.

23. The Palace of Federation was, for example, out of use during the wars with other republics of former Yugoslavia and due to the lack of representational bodies that it was supposed to house. Later its function was changed from representational to occasional usage, and only partial usage by Serbian governmental institutions today.

24. Ines Weizman, Kersten Geers and Moritz Küng, 'Archival Architects', *Displayer 03*, pp. 205–215, http://www.displayer-hfg.de/.

25. *ibid.*, Tom Holert (2010).

26. Designed by Vjenceslav Richter for the competition in 1961 but left in ruins since the foundations were laid.

27. Markus Miessen and Hans Ulrich Obrist, 'Archive As a Productive Space of Conflict', http://archive.hfg-karlsruhe.de/indexb.html.

28. *ibid.*, Cedric Price (2003) p. 67.

29. Judith Butler, *The Psychic Life of Power: Theories of Subjection* (Palo Alto: Stanford University Press, 1997) p. 16.

Zagreb's Empty Shop Windows and Transition *Flâneurs*

A True Story

BOJAN MUCKO

In research conducted in November 2009,[1] I examined the deterioration
and massive closures of small business offices in the city centre of Croatia's
capital. I mapped and photographed empty business premises, but also talked
with city officials. Eventually, both the emptiness behind numerous, dusty,
closed shop windows, and the distorted silhouettes of passers–by melted into
one and the same sign, signifying wider socio–political causes. There is a
socio–semiotic presumption in the background of my approach, but a purely
semiotic analysis would not be fruitful – I needed to hear voices, human
stories echoing in the emptiness behind the abandoned shop windows. So I
started to talk with craftspeople still surviving in Ilica Street, historically one
of the most important commercial streets in Zagreb. In the following text, the
craftspeople's and city officials' voices appear in italics, and even though my
narration is fictive, what I offer here is a true story.

A walk along Ilica Street, from Britanac Square to the tram loop,[2] gives the
wandering *flâneur* a somewhat grim experience of corridor emptiness. The
shiny shop windows at the beginning of Ilica, which simultaneously allow a
view of the classy shop interiors and reflect the busy silhouettes of numerous
passers–by, become rare after Mesnička Street and almost disappear after
Britanac Square. To be precise, the shop windows are there, but the optics have
changed; the reflection of the streets and the passers–by has become different.

If you happen to stop in front of the Iris shop at number 192, you'll have a hard time fixing your hair in front of the shop window. While you search for your silhouette in multiple layers of old dust, you might happen to notice a printed sign on the inside of the glazed door. The City Office for Economy is letting you know that the shop is temporarily closed from 22 July till 15 October. But if you study the date more carefully, you'll find that this three–month period was in 2002.

Soon you'll notice more signs such as "Thank you for your cooperation! We are closed until further notice", or "The store is closed", or "The City of Zagreb – For all information – City Office for Legal–Property Relations and the City's Assets; Department of Business Premises". Some of the handwritten shop–window messages, posted who–knows–when, are impossible to read due to faded ink. Sometimes, if you delve too deep into a shop window's void, it becomes unclear whether these goodbye messages relate to the empty shops behind them, or to the reflected street and people. If you get bored by the phenomenology, you might start quantifying Ilica's emptiness and find 50 closed shops in less than two kilometres.

Could the alarming number of empty retail spaces be a sign of some wider socio–political processes (and I'm not aiming at simplifications such as: "Ah, recession ...")? That question demands the transformation of the *flâneur* into a shop–window semiotician. Should you follow the references listed in the prevailing shop–window signs, you might head to the City Office for Legal–Property Relations and the City's Assets. There you will be fed a complex yet uniform story with the following key phrases: "nationalisation in the forties", "public ownership", "denationalisation in the nineties".

So, the living or business premises that were confiscated or nationalised during socialism used to fall into the public ownership category. Following the dissolution of Yugoslavia, the state of Croatia became the legal successor:

The property which was publicly owned and which was governed by former municipalities, that property, including the flats, the business premises and everything, according to the Act of the City of Zagreb and the Act of Local Self-Government and Administration, became the property of the City of Zagreb.[3]

But, during the late 1990s, an act was passed, which enabled the return of the confiscated property:

Following the passing of the Act on Compensation for Property Confiscated during the Communist Regime of Yugoslavia, between 1 January and 30 June 1997, the former owners had the right to submit requests for the return of the confiscated property. The act prescribed that the premises are to be returned in their material form and that any lease contracts cease to be valid with the day the decision becomes final and binding, but that the lessee has the right to use the space for a year under the current conditions. The flats were to be returned ... and the tenants had the right to buy the flats.

In short, residential and business premises that were leased by the municipality during the socialist period, were leased by the City of Zagreb during the 1990s. As for the business premises in Ilica, some of them, namely the craft workshops, have been leased to the same families since the 1930s despite the regime changes. These craft workshops sprang up in city premises during the Kingdom of Yugoslavia, and were leased by the city during the Independent State of Croatia in the first half of the 1940s. During socialism, they were treated as socially owned property and leased to the same occupants by the self–governing municipality. Then the dissolution of Yugoslavia and the constitution of the Republic of Croatia brought them back into the city's ownership to be leased, once again, to the same craftspeople.

Business premises that were privately owned before World War II, and which were confiscated from the owners (mostly Jewish) after the war, became socially owned during socialism (just like the city–owned premises). These were leased to craftspeople by the municipality, and then, from the dissolution of Yugoslavia until 1997, by the city. However, following the new legislation in 1997, former owners started to come forward. If they were able to prove that they were the legal successors of, for example, spaces that had been leased to craftspeople during the last 50 years, they could reclaim them. The new owners could, depending on their interest, make new lease contracts with the craftspeople or order them to leave within a year. That process emptied out many of Ilica's shops. For some reason, in most situations, the new owners were not interested in continuing the lease. For some (perhaps the same) reason, they were not interested in investing in the shops themselves either. So the shops remained empty, just like the shops whose legal status is still under debate (since it is not too wise to do business in a shop whose new owners could evict you at any time).

From the Ilica Street Reflections series,
November 2009, BOJAN MUCKO

Another reason for a shop to be empty could be that it was leased to a company which filed a bankruptcy claim. Such spaces, although they are owned by the city, are managed by a bankruptcy manager, who is allowed to use them at will, as long as the validity of their contract. So, if the manager is paying the city whatever the contract says they have to pay, they can keep the shop closed, sublet it, or do a number of things, until the bankruptcy process is completed.[4]

And that was the sketch of a cold, official synopsis about three 'subjects': (1) the city – the lessor, (2) the person – the lessee, and (3) the 'new' owner.

From this synopsis, it follows that the empty business premises and the dirty shop windows are a side effect of the relationship between those three subjects, determined by a greater historical socio–political context. Whether you like it or not, you're not able to change the context, so once again you assume the role of a *flâneur* and simple–mindedly start walking along Ilica. This time, your hair gets bad already at number 67 and your reflection once again falls onto a sign attached to the interior side of the glass. You get closer to the dense text and let your gaze rush through the title: "CONTRACT about business premise lease ..." It seems that the lessee, for some reason, decided to share the contents of their contract with accidental passers-by. You read on with interest. The contract is signed by the lessee – K.H., and the lessor – the City of Zagreb, represented by the mayor himself. You read through the contract signed in 2007 and discover that this space, 102.67 square metres in area, is part of a "building which is the object of compensation, according to the Act on Compensation for Property Confiscated during the Communist Regime of Yugoslavia" and that the lease contract is a "document of seizure". You then discover that "the rent is 89,639.91 kuna[5] (spelled out: eighty–nine thousand, six hundred and thirty–nine kuna)", and that "the 23,027.00 kuna deposit is included". However, you also find out that "in order to guarantee the regular payment of the rent ... the lessee gives two IOUs to the lessor: One to the amount of 1,000,000.00 kuna[6], the other one 100,000.00 kuna". In other words, the business premises are leased at £10,283.00 a month, but only provided that the lessee gives the city £134,031.92.

With your head spinning with all the zeros, you sit down in a nearby café to let the impressions settle down. In spite of your struggling with the legal terminology, you find it hard to resist the urge to attribute the six–zero context to the dingy transition politics. While the owner of the café serves you coffee, you engage in a conversation about the empty shops. Soon enough, you hear slightly muffled stories that can hardly fit into the city's official synopsis about the "three subjects".

The café's owner describes to you the (un)official process of lease–contract making, first with the former lessee, and then with the City of Zagreb. Once an empty shop was identified as suitable in size and location for a café, the proprietor searched for the owner of the property. Since the ownership of empty premises that are not owned by the city can only be deduced from neighbourhood gossip, the café's owner was lucky it was her own neighbourhood so she was acquainted with the previous lessee.

I shouldn't be telling you this, but in order to lease the place, I had to give her 5,000 euro in cash, for her to sign the contract. Only then would she terminate her contract [with the city]. Then I signed the contract." So, 5,000 euro to the Mrs who was out of business – the former lessee, *"and I paid the city her [the former lessee's] 20,000 euro debt"*, because the city assigns the former lessee's debt to the future one. *"For us small entrepreneurs, there is no debt cancellation. They won't evict the former owner, who should've been evicted when he hadn't paid two monthly rents. They didn't plug him out or lock his shop. Instead, the debt accumulated ... and then the city committee, for two long years, nine members of the committee never managed to meet, while I was paying the rent for two years* (before the café was opened).

So, first the bribe for the previous lessee, then paying his or her debt, then two years of paying the monthly rent to the city, and then, perhaps, they might be allowed to actually open the shop whose rent they had been paying for two years! While you're leaving the cafe, you lay your eyes on the tailor's shop and recall that the trousers you bought this morning, at the beginning of Ilica, are too wide, so you enter and greet the friendly tailor. While he is narrowing them, you start a topic he is acquainted with:

Some of them were returned to the owners[7] who raised the rents during the first month in order to kick the lessees out. Was it so because they couldn't stand the lessees who were in there? Was it pure, so to say, revenge? ... The other option was to be kicked out by the city, say I can't be two months late with the rent because I'd get kicked out right away. Now that's very interesting. All these shops, if you go and ask the city administration, have a 100,000.00 debt to them. That one up there, whatever it was, cosmetics, they had to pay, so it's told, 100,000.00 kuna of the previous owner's debt. It used to be a hardware store. Now you wonder, how can one be 100,000.00 in debt and be left alone in there for two or three years, while someone else can't? Very interesting! See, in 1997, and I think in 2002, I got a notice. I was on holiday [summertime at the Croatian seaside] *when the notice came, which said I had to remove the people and the things from the premises within seven days because I hadn't paid, I don't know, some rent. My old lady called ... and told me to come back right away* [to Zagreb] *because I was getting evicted. What the hell? So I came here, took care of everything* [he managed to prove that all the bills were paid and that the eviction had no legal grounds], *and they said: 'No, no, it was a mistake, a mistake.' But it was no mistake! I know it wasn't! And that's how it ended, but how can it be a mistake? They're not so stupid as to not know what they're doing, right? I think it was more like, 'We'd like to give the shop to one of our chaps, so we'll take care of this. Screw the little tailor'.*

How does one put together the stories by the café owner and the tailor? Her experience with the former lessee tells us about a city administration that tolerates the piling up of months of debt[8], and his experience tells us about rigorous surveillance by the lessors and attempts at eviction even when the rent has been duly paid. Of course, the stories can be brought together if we let go of the official "three subjects" myth, because the City of Zagreb is obviously the only subject, while the lessees are the objects of its high-handedness. The fact that the tailor was 'mistakenly' almost evicted from the space that his family had been leasing since 1936, was a sign of the covert interests of a certain subject within the city administration. The existence of covert interests can also be seen in the fact that the craftspeople who were trained in skills that were in short supply, such as tailors, were still not allowed to buy the premises, even though they had spent 70 odd years investing in them. So, even though the ownership of the shop is clean – it is a city-owned shop clear of any litigations – and despite the 20-year-old promise, it is a matter mentioned only within the election-campaign context:

Yes, no litigations, city-owned, and that fairytale about how we would buy

this and that. Those are stories for kids. I've been waiting 20 years for that to
happen. When will it? No way. That's a total make-believe. Four years ago, at
the Ban Jelačić Square, when we were signing new contracts, in 2005, we
paid the public notary 650.00 kuna for stamps because it was 'just about to
happen' … that we could buy. No way. My arse. They've been talking about
it since the independence. Our people have been pleading for everything and
these guys always say that no act was passed, no this, no that. It's all … they are
cheating all over the place.

You've managed to make the tailor miserable. A moment later you're back
in Ilica, in the second zone of the city, or as the local craftspeople say: "*in
the appendix*". Since you've managed to come all this way on foot, perhaps
you should seize the chance to visit the shoemaker who fixed your shoes last
week. It isn't convenient to go there by car ever since they installed sidewalk
poles and started charging for parking in the back alleys. And so you go to
the shoemaker's, where you find his mother, who is also his co-worker. You
recall that several years ago they had moved from one side of Ilica to the other,
and she explains that the first shop was returned to the owners during the
denationalisation. They didn't want to lease it to them anymore, so her son
started looking for another place. At first, he found a city-owned place in
Vodovodna Street.

Then he went to the local administration to ask whose place it was and if
he could lease it. They told him it was city-owned so he went to the city
government and who knows where else. Eventually, he lost about a year just
waiting. He even had the sign made. It's good that he didn't put it up. It was all
settled. We were going to get the place and we waited, and waited, and waited,
and finally they called him to tell him it wasn't city-owned at all. It was owned
by the state so the city couldn't lease it. The city had to settle with the state. It's
been like that ever since. They even told him they would let him know. It's been
seven or eight years and the place is still closed, which means that they haven't
settled the problem, right? The state and the city.

You step out of the shoemaker's workshop and stop to rethink for a second
in the empty street, with newly fixed shoes under your arm, narrowed
trousers in your bag, watching a nearby broken shop window distorting your

reflection. Finally, you have a new, somewhat Kafkaesque synopsis with two subjects and only one object: the state and the city versus the disempowered craftsperson. You try to walk on along Ilica, but you can't manage to enjoy its corridor emptiness anymore. The empty shop windows are suddenly imbued with meaning – they've acquired voices telling grim, burdened stories – and your reflection is all of a sudden a part of them. Who knows when you'll be returning here, "*in the appendix*" ... Transition *flâneurs* are, you think as you're leaving, having a hard time enjoying their walk.

*Thank you to Veljiko Linta for translation.

1. Research was conducted within the project Res Urbanae, under the NGO Association for Interdisciplinary and Intercultural Research (AIIR), http://www.uiii.org/.
2. The discussed part of Ilica Street is less than two kilometres long.
3. From the interview with the Deputy Head of the City Office for Legal–Property Relations and the City's Assets.
4. From an informal conversation with a former clerk of the City Office for Legal–Property Relations and the City's Assets.
5. Approximately £10,283.00.
6. Approximately £114,718.00.
7. This is about the property–return processes initiated after 1997, following the passing of the Act on Compensation for Property Confiscated during the Communist Regime of Yugoslavia.
8. Let us temporarily put aside the fact that those debts are transferred to future lessees.

ARCHIPELAGO

Introduction

DEEPA NAIK & TRENTON OLDFIELD

In late 2011 a new and revealing map was published. The map inadvertently exposed previously undocumented knowledge. Up until then it had been difficult to categorically list or chart all the financial districts pin-pricked across the planet. The large financial districts like London, New York, Hong Kong and Sydney were well known, however, the vast majority are relatively small in size and a significant percentage only built and occupied in the last decade.

Tellingly, it was the anti-capitalist and specifically anti-corporate banking protests beginning in late 2011 that finally revealed the geography of the early 21st-century's financial districts. This counter-cartography was unintentionally created by what is now commonly known as the 'Occupy Movement'. The protesters swarmed these spaces and set up campsites, which then became platforms for discussions and alternative sites of learning. Occupy's target was not a city's democratic institutions – parliament, public institutions, government departments or the like – but rather the centres of finance and business, those very specific conglomerations referred to as 'financial districts' or 'central business districts' (CBDs).

Occupy started on Wall Street in New York City on 17 September 2011, initiated and organised by the Vancouver-based organisation Adbusters.[1] The early protagonists claim to have been inspired by the revolutions underway in Tunisia and Egypt.[2] Before them, though not widely referenced, were the 'Red Shirts' in Thailand who occupied the main financial district and the airports in Bangkok in April 2010.

In London, one month after New York City, protesters attempted to occupy the privately owned[3] Paternoster Square, where the London Stock Exchange is located. The square was designed to be easily defended with just a handful of gateways, so it was no surprise that they were beaten out of the area within hours.[4] The protestors retreated, setting up a campsite adjacent to

Paternoster Square, in front of St Paul's Cathedral. This camp was eventually cleared by bailiffs, supported by City of London police, at midnight on 28 February 2012.[5]

In New York City an attempt at occupying Wall Street also resulted in a retreat by revolutionaries to the nearby privately owned Zuccotti Park. This site of protest was also brutally cleared by the police on 15 November 2011.[6]

Beyond the main centres, it is understood that over 950 other sites across 82 countries were temporarily occupied – some for hours, others for months. Most were forcefully cleared by the police, some fizzled out. It was a global phenomenon. And by-and-large it was site specific to 'spaces of finance'. Sites included the Stock Exchange in Taipei, the Reserve Bank of Australia in Sydney, Paradeplatz in Zurich and Bank of America in Pittsburg. Other 'occupations' of financial districts included the Wells Fargo and Bank of America in San Francisco and the European Central Bank (ECB) headquarters in Frankfurt.[7]

On 18 October 2011, three days after London's Occupy situated itself in Paternoster Square, the UK's *Guardian* newspaper published a map pin-pointing the Occupy protests across the planet.[8] Despite the sites of protest being predominantly located in the 'metaphorical west' – and it is vital that the financial districts not currently on the map, such as the many new districts in the 'global south' are added – it was the first disclosure of the global location and spread of financial districts.

By excluding the political borders, the map allows us to see a relationship between sites that was not made obvious before. They are 'islands', separated by distance but linked through intrinsic, perceived and technological connections. To use a scientific metaphor – very popular in most fields and increasingly so in 'urban studies' – to help unpack our argument, it is an archipelago. The largest natural archipelago in the world sits between the Indian and Pacific Oceans. It comprises over 17,500 islands and spans four time zones. Since 1945 it has been called the nation of Indonesia. Many of the islands are connected underneath the ocean – most as a result of their connection to the Sunda (Asia) and Sahul (Australia) continental plates. The crucial feature is that seemingly isolated islands far from each other are interdependent and connected by systems largely out of view and as a result of remarkable occurrences, such as volcanic eruptions, moving apart or clashing tectonic plates.

The financial districts, where astonishingly nothing happens but digital transactions and face-to-face meetings and which can exist on little more than a single road, like in Zagreb[9], are recognisable because of their predictable contemporary glass-and-tower architecture, conventional urban design, excellent transport connections, corporate food and clothing chain-shops and highly policed environment. Few places are as 'readable' as financial districts; it's hard not to know when you are in one. International airports, regularly offered up as 'non-places'[10], might even have a greater sense of place. The Vancouver international airport, for example, greets visitors in the arrival lounge with large screens depicting waterfalls, Stanley Park, whales, old growth forests and artwork by First Nations. Though arguably quite clichéd, there is no doubt the aim is to orient and immerse new arrivals into the specific atmosphere of local West Coast nature and history. The Hong Kong international airport is scattered with informational boards that chronicle the various histories of the city – local development, architecture, art, fashion, finance etc. In contrast, eating lunch in one of the underground malls in London's Canary Wharf would be hard to distinguish from a lunch break in one the underground malls in the CBD of Sydney, Singapore, Dubai, Chicago or Hong Kong. Even more uniform are the office spaces: endless rows of 'hot desks' adjacent to walls of over-priced, primary-colour abstract art – significantly reducing any need for an 'orientation' if moved to a different office and deleting any notion of 'culture shock' if relocated to another CBD. This predictability is apparently an important element of their attraction – 'similarity' is understood as efficiency and 'predictability' as exclusivity. As a result the concept and materiality of 'luxury' seems to have evened out across the world.

Desired, celebrated, ignored, distrusted or transformed into sites of protest and revolution – what can we learn about the most avant-garde spaces of modern capitalism? What do they mean for the future of how we might conceive of cities and our everyday lives? As the current crisis of capitalism can be traced through these 'financial service centres', the interrogation of these spaces, by a spectrum of disciplines and approaches, is ever more urgent.

The opening visual essay by Marisa Gonzalez documents a weekly occurrence in Hong Kong's financial district when well over one hundred thousand women 'invade' the site. A Deleuzian reading might suggest this to be a deterritorialising act where the women resist and create by de/re-coding the space. However, this would be another annoying nod to 'the dominant' while emboldening the capitalist sympathisers of those who wish to promote small acts of resistance among those of 'potentiality' and, consequently, no real threat. What happens every Sunday and bank holiday in Hong Kong is outside of these regularly offered ideas and should not be shoehorned into them.

Presenting the voices of the women alongside their photographs, artist Marisa Gonzalez instantaneously communicates a fundamental reality of early 21st-century global capitalism: inhumane exploitation of labour, in this case the everyday lives of migrant domestic workers. One aspect of the experience of Hong Kong's predominantly Philippine and Indonesian migrant domestic workforce is one day off per week and their entirely extraordinary use of the emptied financial district on that day.

The women explain how living in often extreme circumstances, which can include a combination of low pay, cramped working conditions, long hours, precarious rights and often racist employers, and the separation from family, particularly children, leads to acute feelings of alienation, depression and anxiety. The following quote is indicative of how many of the women interviewed feel about living as migrant workers: "We seem to be happy on our only day off ... but nobody knows the bitterness and loneliness inside us. It is a suffering we do not deserve even though we are poor."

It is not difficult to imagine the sense of relief on Saturday evening, knowing that tomorrow, for some of the day, there is chance to be with people in a similar situation, to meet with trade unionists, arrange the sending of parcels of clothes, food and sometimes gifts back to their families, to dance, to eat, to see friends, to be away and outside of work. It is mesmerising to imagine the female migrant workforce 'occupying', on a weekly basis, the streets of the City of London, Houston Texas or La Défense in Paris – across the archipelago. Such an event occurring every Sunday raises the proposition of not only a global union of migrant domestic workers but also a global action of migrant workers across the world 'occupying' their own downtown.

The next contribution is one woman's personal account of how she left her family in 1992 to work as a domestic helper in Hong Kong and of the struggles for decent working conditions. Vicky Casia-Cabantac was a teacher and, when she left her country, a teacher's salary was one-third of what she could earn as a domestic worker. In her brief but poignant paper, she explains how the first major alliance of Filipino migrant workers was established under the name the United Filipinos in Hong Kong to organise because "of our welfare, our situation as migrants which makes us victims of the policies of our own government in the Philippines". Together with other regionally based organisations, their first campaign was to stop Executive Order No. 856 in which migrant workers had to remit 50–70% of their total earnings to their government. This scheme, meant to generate income for the Philippines economy, would have had devastating effects for the many migrant workers and their families. Vicky, who is the deputy secretary general of the United Filipinos in Hong Kong, shares the crucial importance of having a space, "a territory", in which to meet with fellow workers one day a week to continue to campaign for their rights.

Women and the use of the public sphere are at the centre of the next essay by Demetris Taliotis and Evi Tselika. The financial district this time is the capital of Cyprus where the wealthiest and most influential financial institution – the banker and the marker of meaning – is the Cypriot Orthodox Church. Their essay 'The Sacred and the Naked: Undisciplined Research Mirroring Its Object' proposes a study not of the peripheral but central spaces and institutions. They pay particular attention to the absence of women in the church, the military and the public sphere, and problematise the role of Aphrodite as the patron goddess of the island, the goddess of divine prostitution and the main image communicated to the rest of the world via the government's tourism authority. We are asked to consider the ambiguities of the church as financial institution, property developer, marker of space as sacred and unexpected promoter of prostitution as cabaret.

Performance, despite protestations of efficiency, effectiveness and modernisation, remains a key element of life in the City of London. It is rare not to see men dressed in black tie on their way to an event organised by one of the numerous guilds, a Masonic lodge or an awards night organised by the Corporation of London. As many reading this will know, this ancient financial district is fixated on the maintenance and performance of rituals.[11]

The visual essay 'PINK: The Art of Being Confident' is a study of everyday performance, quite apart from formal and often secret rituals, one that was available for everyone to observe. In 2006 it was difficult not to notice a performance being undertaken by all manner of men working in the City of London. It shouldn't be overestimated. However, if you are interested in material culture, the performance of men wearing pink shirts along with brightly coloured pink ties is likely to be of interest.[12]

The impetus for taking the photographs was that this material culture seemed a metaphorical 'canary in the mine'. Perhaps absurd, perhaps unjustifiable (though bizarrely more foreseeing than most 'academics' and economists), to us, the pinks shirts and pink ties on these men sounded a warning, a loud and persistent alarm. A hyper-confident culture had taken over this financial district and it presaged an unknown imminent disaster. Perhaps even more worrying than in 2006, is their widespread return, after just a few years of absence. Is a greater disaster yet to unfold? Whatever the case, we doubt those photographed today would be smiling the way they did in 2006.

Following this, David Boulogne's series of photographs Make It A Good Experience – In The City and accompanying text offer a very personal experience with capitalism. An exploration of how and why, after years of avoidance, he finally succumbed to "taking credit" and an attempt "to understand a bit more about the agents of capitalism", the images are part therapy and part social study. Apart from a few London signatures, for example the double painted lines on the road, the images could be from any western financial district. The glass facades, deliberately positioned on the street, are not transparent but unexpectedly highly reflective. The search for idiosyncrasy among the suits proves fruitless. The black & white photographs create a sombre feeling that asks us to reflect on what looks to us like alienated though quite well-dressed workers.

Much has been written about the 'financial crisis' and the attraction of capitalism but David Boulogne's personal account has a unique edge because of his willingness to confess his relationship with capitalism: the flirting, the avoidance, the fling, the addiction and eventually the millstone punishment. His proposition is that we confront our own histories and make our confessions.

Financial districts are islands within their own nations, some more so than others. The City of London, for example, is independent from the rest of Britain. The British monarch must seek and be given approval to enter the City. Canary Wharf in East London is on private property and can only be entered through a few raised entrances while vehicle access is only via one garrisoned road. The financial district floats somewhere above the rest of London, attached by just a handful of escalators and a ramp.

Much less obvious are the mechanisms of enclosure and surveillance employed by the City of London. If you take your gaze off the clean streets and look up to the mature tree height a new canopy exists, one composed of multiple black cameras. No one can enter the City of London without being captured on camera; every street, tube station and road is monitored, every movement recorded, every car number plate captured, documented and filed. With just one or two adjustments to the road system and a few sentry boxes, the City of London can raise a boundary (the 'Ring of Steel') of which trespass has significant meaning.

The Ring of Steel relies not on traditional mechanisms of prevention but rather on the threat of retaliation, of brutal retaliation. The psychology that underpins the seeming success of the Ring of Steel is the fear of reprisal and humiliation. A protagonist would likely be successful at deploying the violence at their target but the threat of retaliation is understood as so great and the intelligence gathered so high that it has since kept the City of London 'terrorist free'. It wages a pre–emptive psychological war and in doing so, the City attempts yet again to lift itself up above the rest of London's citizens.

Among the many contributions to the TINAG festival's theme of Financial Districts was Henrietta Williams and George Gingell's 'Ring of Steel', a photographic exhibition and guided tour of the architecture of surveillance and defence in London's Square Mile. In this section, alongside Henrietta William's photographs is a conversation with the artist Jo Anne Butler, in which they detail the process and experience of setting out to first find, then map and photograph the Ring of Steel. We learn that the 21st–century uber digital border follows the same boundary markings and even uses some of the remaining ancient city walls.

The generally accepted argument is that London's Ring of Steel came about as a response to the bombing campaigns of the Irish Republican Army (IRA) that targeted financial, technological and communication companies involved in the perpetuation of a divided Ireland. London's Ring of Steel was based on Belfast's earlier version – a barbed wire and concrete block security installation built around Belfast's main shopping district – and, Henrietta Williams tells us, the main advisers for London's incarnation of the Ring of Steel were Belfast's police.

In its attempt to seclude and guard itself, the City has, Henrietta argues, completely reordered the flow of movement and the role of surveillance in our everyday lives. This becomes a powerful proposition when we learn that the over 100 entry points to the Square Mile have been reduced to just 19. The conversation also draws our attention to the role of everyday defensive architectures, such as the oversized flowerbeds outside Deutsche Bank. These flowerbeds are disguised defences used to protect the bank from possible vehicle-based attacks. Every piece of defensive architecture, every extra digital security check, every supernumerary security guard is an element in the strategy to separate the financial district from the everyday realities and people of the city it is in. In raising themselves up they expose what lies underneath, usually hidden and undisclosed. These financial islands and the companies within them have more in common and often more connections with other financial districts than with their own city.

Interrogating financial districts has in many ways been the sub-text to much of our work within and beyond This Is Not A Gateway. In the introduction to *Critical Cities Volume 2*[13] we argue that greater attention and study is needed on real and figurative 'centres'. We detail how the long-standing preoccupation with 'the fringe', with 'the edge', is a fixation of those who consciously or unconsciously don't wish to problematise and interrogate themselves, their own positions and their own privileges.[14] It is of course more comfortable to focus on 'the other' and 'the distant', which is somehow sexier ... edgier. We argue this is a phenomenon particularly endemic to academia and acute in urban and architectural studies.

It was inevitable financial districts would be the focus of the festival programme and several Myrdle Court Press books.[15] Being based in London and securing a festival venue overlooking the City, we chose to probe the forever intriguing Corporation of London and to expand the investigation and debate with contributions on financial districts from across the world. Our thesis was the materiality and social relations being performed in these spaces reflect capitalism's avant-garde; they might be the most percipient at revealing elements of what our lives are likely to be like in the future. We anticipated that spatial, psychological, sociological and design studies might contribute to understanding more of the current crisis of capitalism. At the time of the festival, the City of London's office occupation rate was at its lowest in decades,[16] so the festival also sought to re-propose what these spaces might be; could become.[17]

When we undertook the festival in 2010, interrogating financial districts was seen as an obscure endeavour. There were very few critical books on the subject and little available literature. This was transformed less than a year later when the courageous and revolutionary protesters started 'occupying' new and old financial districts right across the planet. Their focus on sites of finance (rather than government/democracy) has precipitated an unprecedented scale of investigation and attention that continues today. Some of the great analysis and insights that have been produced since 2010 include the novels *Capital* by John Lanchester and *Just Business* by Geraint Anderson, the academic studies *Psychoanalysis, Money and Economic Crisis* edited by David Bennett and *Towards a Socioanalysis of Money, Finance and Capitalism: Beneath the Surface of the Financial Industry* edited by Susan Long and Burkard Sievers, and the prolific banking blog 'Going native in the world of finance' by Joris Luyendijk.[18]

We note that, despite debilitating and punitive 'austerity' policies and most economies in double–dip recessions (depression!), few financial districts anywhere have not continued to expand and develop. The City of London, for example, has seen more tall buildings rise out of the ground since the financial crisis than in the previous boom decade. Regardless of how they are funded (mostly from Middle Eastern family dictatorships) they are managing to do something almost no one else is able to do – grow, and grow significantly – in a depression. More than ever, these spaces are floating above the rest of the city. Their materiality and social relations remain a focus for our work.

1. Adbusters, Occupy Campaign, http://www.adbusters.org/campaigns/occupywallstreet.
2. For more information see, http://occupywallst.org/about/.
3. Paternoster Square is owned by Mitsubishi Estate Co.
4. Entrance to the square was sealed off and a High Court injunction was granted against public access to the site. Paternoster Square is referred to as 'public space' in its plans, meaning the public has access to the site, however, as the area is not designated 'a public right of way' the owner can limit entry at any time.
5. The eviction from outside St Paul's Cathedral was contentious – while the majority within the church governorship aligned with the Corporation of London and wanted the protesters to be forcibly evicted, a handful supported Occupy and wished to negotiate for them to remain outside the premises. In October, when the decision to remove the protestors was made with the church's backing, Canon Chancellor Rev Giles Fraser resigned from his post in an act of protest. And later, following the backlash against the church's resolution to remove the anti–capitalist protesters, Rev Graeme Knowles, the Dean of St Paul's, subsequently resigned.
6. Zuccotti Park is owned by Brookfield Office Properties. Since the original eviction, there

have been several attempts to re–occupy the park; each met with evermore police violence.

7. For more information see, The Occupation Directory, a public listing of all known occupation sites built by and for the Occupy movement, http://directory.occupy.net/.

8. http://www.guardian.co.uk/news/datablog/interactive/2011/oct/18/occupy–protests–map–world.

9. The financial area in Zagreb is called 'Green Gold' and is situated in the lower city on Radnicka Street, at the junction with Vukovarska Street.

10. Marc Augé, *Non–Places: Introduction to an Anthropology of Supermodernity* (Verso: New York, 1995).

11. See for example, 'Events and Ceremonies' on the City of London website, http://www. cityoflondon.gov.uk/about–the–city/working–with–and–for–others/Pages/city–livery– companies.aspx; enthusiast historian on the East End and City, Barry Oneoff's website, http://barryoneoff.co.uk/html/ceremonies.html.

12. The photographic essay and short accompanying text is our first personal contribution to the *Critical Cities* books outside of editing and writing the introductory essays. Given that the topic for the festival was financial districts, we have broken our own rule and contributed directly to the festival programme and subsequently this book.

13. Deepa Naik and Trenton Oldfield, 'The Urban Industry and its Post–Critical Condition' in *Critical Cities: Ideas, Knowledge and Agitation from Emerging Urbanists Volume 2* (Myrdle Court Press: London, 2010) pp. 3–27.

14. The paper focused primarily on the professions entangled with the Urban Industry – architecture, academia, property development, design, urban regeneration, creative industries and visual cultures (along with the related foundations, festivals, media, PR and conferences).

15. For example, *Sign of the Times: An Alternative Reading of Collapse and Crisis in the City of London* (Myrdle Court Press: London, 2012).

16. For more information see, 'The City of London's Evidence Paper', which came out in September 2010, http://www.cityoflondon.gov.uk/services/environment–and–planning/ planning/planning–policy/local–development–framework/Documents/City%20of%20 London%20Office%20Evidence%20paper.pdf.

17. Other contributions to the festival programme included: 'Inside The City: An Anthropology of the Financial District' by Fiona Davies and Levent Kerimol, Partha Banerjee's 'Malice in Wonderland: A systemic and individual look at the psychology of the City and its workers [bankers etc] in the aftermath of the economic crisis' and Ignacio Costa's 'Mapping The Zone: Reflections on Global Capital' with large–scale photographs investigating the architectural configurations at Canary Wharf. The festival showed Marc Isaacs's documentary *Men of The City* nancial districts – one of the most potent being the university campus where over 50% of all courses are related to business and financial services.

18. John Lanchester, *Capital* (Faber and Faber: London, 2012); Geraint Anderson, *Just Business* (Headline: London, 2011); David Bennett (ed), *Psychoanalysis, Money and Economic Crisis* (Lawrence & Wishart: London, 2012); Susan Long and Burkard Sievers (eds), *Towards a Socioanalysis of Money, Finance and Capitalism: Beneath the Surface of the Financial Industry* (Routledge Press: Oxford, 2011); Joris Luyendijk, 'Going native in the world of finance' (14 September 2011 – present), http://www.guardian.co.uk/commentisfree/joris– luyendijk–banking–blog.

Female (Open) Space Invaders

MARISA GONZALEZ

On 1 May 2009, walking through the financial and commercial district of Hong Kong during my visit to the city, I was surprised at the unexpected sight of the public spaces invaded by a multitude of Filipino women. I learned that Hong Kong experiences this unusual transformation, generated by women workers, every Bank Holiday and every Sunday.

Hong Kong is one of the most developed areas in Asia, with a population of more than 7 million inhabitants, a large concentration of skyscrapers, and the highest density of population per square metre in the world. The city's financial and commercial centre houses the headquarters of big multinationals and major Asian banks, and the commercial malls and shopping streets of luxury brands that supply Asia's economic and social elites. It is a modern and cosmopolitan city: Asia's 'world city'. It imports not only a global flow of capital but also a global flow of people – the rich professionals from all over the world and the poorer migrant workers from Asia.

Among Hong Kong's migrant workforce are many of the more than 11 million Filipinos who work in foreign countries, i.e. more than 12% of the Philippines' population. Each year more than 1 million Filipinos leave their country looking for a job, and their government encourages and promotes this diaspora of its population because it is the country's principal inflow of foreign exchange. These emigrants, with their foreign currency remittances, are the main source of income for the Filipino economy. They remit more than 17 billion dollars each year and are considered 'national heroes' in the Philippines. This emigration includes a large number of women with high–level education and professional qualifications, who have to accept work in low–level jobs in foreign countries. They migrate to Hong Kong to work as 'domestic helpers' because the salaries they receive there are three times higher than a qualified worker's salary in the Philippines. However, in the Hong Kong context, their salary is lower than the 'minimal wage' of Chinese workers.

The migrant domestic workers in Hong Kong come mainly from the Philippines and from Indonesia[1]. Filipino women first began migrating to Hong Kong to do domestic work in the 1970s, and because of their ability to speak English, most of them worked for the British colonials and other foreigners and expatriates. In 1997, after 150 years as a British territory, Hong Kong became an Autonomous Territory of the People's Republic of China and, as the island's economy has developed, the education level of the locals has increased, as has the need for their children to speak English. The well-educated, English-speaking Filipino domestic workers continue to be in great demand. Some work for European families but the majority now work for Chinese families, and the recruitment of Filipino women as domestic workers has been institutionalised both in Hong Kong and in the Philippines. Almost all the women are recruited by agencies in Manila that exploit them by demanding very high commissions. They also demand good looks and even high school or college degrees, but they treat the women as servants even though, in most cases, they are more qualified than their employers. Today, more than 150,000 Filipino women work as 'domestic helpers' in Hong Kong.

Every Sunday, the executive professionals who own the city disappear. But the city does not remain a desert. Instead of emptiness or abandonment, the opposite appears. The city is taken over by thousands and thousands of women with suitcases and bags. In every street and square, there is a frenzy of activity. The lobby of Norman Foster's iconic HSBC Bank is invaded by crowds of women having picnics, playing cards or bingo, making clothes – a domestic appropriation of one of the most paradigmatic buildings of the 20th century.

A different sort of space, full of new life, is created and occupied by women, only women – Filipino domestic workers. A territory that was constructed with a specific urbanist purpose as the financial and commercial hub of this 'world city' is rebuilt, refocused and transformed into a small town. The women come together "in their town centre plaza, as a meeting point, as their own territory". Their traditions, habits and beliefs are the behavioural codes, implemented by them and accepted by the locals on Sundays. It is a unique use of the city, a pilgrimage in time and space that has the main streets of the financial district and its emblematic buildings, such as Foster's HSBC Bank, as its background.

On 1 May, a public holiday, I was able to contemplate this unusual vision and began a project to record the social and political activities of the Filipino domestic workers in the city space. Who were these women and what did they do?

By chance, in the main shopping area, I met Vicky Casia-Cabantac, a Filipino trade unionist. She was standing in the middle of the street that is closed to traffic every bank holiday, and campaigning for affiliation to the Gabriela network[2], which protects the rights of Filipino women. She told me that every Sunday, their one and only day off per week, this whole group of emigrant Filipino women, more than 150,000 of them, concentrate in the downtown centre to spend the day together, to socialise, relax and do personal errands. She explained that their population density generates the development of production systems like overseas deliveries, associations and unions, a parallel economy of exchange and transactions, and activities and organised logistics for the provision of their daily needs, resulting in a well-organised and autonomous social system.

The women occupy the same location every Sunday. They gather in groups according to their home regions and, in the footbridges at Exchange Square, they construct little cardboard-box *casitas* to define the extent of their territory and create each small group's enclosure of intimacy. They rest, sleep, eat, dance, read, in one word, 'live' on the streets despite the lack of privacy from passers-by.

The level of labour exploitation is extreme in most cases. Their working conditions are hard. All foreign domestic workers in Hong Kong are legally required to 'live in' at their employer's house, often in very close quarters or without their own space, without any privacy, without any room of their own. Many days they work more than 12 hours, and in the case of caring for the elderly or children, often 24 hours. When they have had problems of exploitation or abuse, they have not been able to initiate a legal procedure because 14 days after the termination of their contract they are expelled from the country and therefore cannot continue with their demand.

By law, domestic helpers have only two weeks of vacation every two years. This is their sole chance to visit their families. In Hong Kong there is no law on family reunification and no work permits for husbands, and these women can only connect with the lives of their relatives and their children in the Philippines through the telephone. In the interviews I conducted for the project, one woman said, "I am a single mother. I left my two children, my only treasures, to try luck abroad in Hong Kong. Here I get hard work, sacrifices, sadness, loneliness."

It is very difficult for the women to bear the isolation in which they live, separated not only from their family but also from each other every day of the week. For this reason Sunday is important to meet, communicate and reconnect. This day off it seems that they are happy because, in their groups, they can remember, remind each other and reproduce their identity, their strong roots and their culture. They sing together, play games, go to mass, do the transfer of their monthly salary and make boxes of clothes, food, gifts and toys to send to their families. In these luxury streets of Hong Kong, they celebrate their birthdays and the popular holidays of their fishing villages or small rural hometowns.

One of the women[3] explained: "On Sundays we feel happy in this foreign land. The parks and streets of the financial district of Hong Kong become Filipino territory, like the plazas of our little towns. The HSBC Bank is our cathedral and the cardboard *casitas* are our home. But we are homeless women."

These women change the meaning of the public space. Literally invading the downtown, redrawing the boundaries, delimiting their own territory, imposing their culture and creating new habits, they turn into nomads on their day off. They transform the ways of living, the content and signs of the space once a week. They transport their habits and traditions through leisure, rest, religion and culture, and they impose alternate codes on the space, building a new and unique human cartography. Their location is precise, constant. They turn the most cosmopolitan and commercial streets, and buildings designed by major architectural firms, into their own town plazas. The same space takes on different identities, depending on the day of the week. Thus, Hong Kong has two absolutely different cultures that are superimposed but do not co-exist at all.

In the testimonies I collected for the documentary, the women told me: "We seem to be happy in our only one day off a week, but nobody knows the bitterness and loneliness inside us. It is a suffering we do not deserve even though we are poor."

They are women who have sacrificed their personal life, leaving their home and their own society, to live alone in a hostile environment where they suffer racism and exploitation, in order to give their family and their children a better life. Yet migration can result in dysfunctional families. Later I travelled to the Philippines to visit their relatives, to see how they lived, how they felt the absence and the sacrifice of their mothers, wives or sisters.

As domestic workers, the women come to Hong Kong on temporary visas with a two-year renewable contract. Some repeatedly renew their contracts and spend their entire working life there, sending their salary to their family in the Philippines. Some of them are women with no land, who have been working in Hong Kong for 25 years, and now that their family financial responsibility is over they need to start saving for their own future.

In recent years their working conditions have been improving thanks to activism organised around several associations and trade unions for migrant workers. On the posters they carry in protest marches they display the word 'WISER', each letter standing for one of five demands: Workers' rights, Increased wages, Social services, Employment protection, and Rights of workers.

In March 2009, a newspaper article by columnist Chip Tsao calling the Philippines "a nation of servants" brought thousands of domestic helpers onto the streets in a strong protest against discrimination and contempt in their daily work.

In this developed society, in this era of globalisation, we have human working conditions close to slavery. And because it concerns women, women alone, and a community that is invisible for most of the week, the two governments involved are not looking for ways to improve the situation. However, the images and words[4] I recorded show the life of this community on their one day off, and they reveal that the women's family commitment, their responsibility, and their strength, creativity and energy can overcome their adverse situation, and that they have the capacity to eventually transform one of the most developed cities in the world.

All images from the series Filipinas in Hong Kong, 2010, MARISA GONZALEZ

1. Indonesian migrants are almost as numerous as the Filipino migrants in Hong Kong, but they are more exploited because they are less educated and generally have less knowledge of the English language.

2. The General Assembly Binding Women for Reforms, Integrity, Equality, Leadership, and Action (GABRIELA) is a network of Filipino grassroots organisations, institutions and programmes that address women's issues.

3. Testimony from Cecilia.

4. This project on the Filipino diaspora in Hong Kong premiered with an exhibition of 40 pictures, several videos and a 1-hour documentary film in the Evelyn Botella gallery in Madrid at the Photoespaña Festival in June–July 2010.

Casitas, Sundays, at the Exchange Square crosswalks, Hong Kong

Intimate grouping according to home region or affinity

I am Nora. I came from central Philippines, the island of Leite. I came to Hong Kong to work 27 years ago. The first contract was for two years and then I transferred to another family who I have been with for another 25 years. I have four children. All of them have finished university. I sacrificed my life here in Hong Kong because I wanted to send my children to go to the university. My children studied in Manila. I see them every two years, only holiday.

/

At work, only eating we can sit down. We work many days from 5.30 a.m. until 11 p.m., so we are tired the whole day. All day working. So, on Sunday we need to rest, be seated, all the day long.

I have stayed here in Hong Kong for 11 years already, yes that long. I came here for my son's future. I am earning much more money here than in the Philippines. I earn like 30,000 or 40,000 HK dollars a month(US$300). My employer now is British.

/

I finished my college in the University of San Agustin. I finished the first courses pre-dental, and shift to BS psychology, and then in Iloilo*. I worked as a secretary of one of the companies there. That's the time my sister wanted me to come here as domestic helper. My sister was working in Hong Kong already. She direct hired me because some of the employers wanted university degree.

* Iloilo is a city and a province of the Philippines located in the Western Visayas region.

/

Every month we go to the bank to send money to the Philippines to our families. Every Sunday we go to Mass, and after we do our shopping our most basic personal things that we can not do it during the week. After that we come back here to rest the whole afternoon. During the evening we are having dinner before we all go home. After dinner we separate each other and go back home about 8 o'clock in the evening.

Recruitment advert in the streets of Manila
OVER: Sunday, at the atrium of the HSBC Bank

Some agencies are hiring domestic helper to come over here to Hong Kong to work. Some agencies make salary deductions in the Philippines. They pay half of the placement fee. Another half is deducted from the salary by the time they arrive here. The agency makes a lot of money. After 3 or 4 months they finish their payment, then the agency asks the employer to terminate the contract, and then they hire another person again to make more money, to get another placement fee. Sometimes the girls borrow money from the bank. The collateral for the bank is the house and the lot of the parents, or their own piece of land that is their property. Or they borrow money from other people and the collateral is the piece of land. So the money they are paying to the agency is not enough yet to pay the placement fee.

/

To go to Hong Kong you have to be a high school graduate. Before you go to Hong Kong, the government has training centres, so you will be better skilled before you go to work, not only to Hong Kong but to other countries.

We fill the boxes and then we send them to the Filipinas, door to door. In two weeks they will receive them in the Philippines. We are here to send things to our loved ones in the Philippines. In this area, we generate a large packaging and logistics activity. We buy and fill the jumbo boxes to be transported in trunks to the port. Every Sunday thousands of boxes are sent by us to our country.

Packing boxes to send home

Window shopping

Religious activities

Campaigning

The United Filipinos in Hong Kong, the biggest alliance of the Filipinos in Hong Kong, was established since 1985 to protect the rights and welfare of our fellow Filipinos. We also campaigned for minimum wages' legislation, because once again the government excludes us from the minimum wages legislation.

/

I am outraged because the value of our salary is not enough anymore to sustain [our lives]. The reason why we come here is to be able to earn something to improve the economic conditions of our families. But the problem is, under this present condition … I am suffocated with all these financial difficulties. People are being punished twice. First, that you are forced into leaving your family behind. Second, is that while you work so hard, the amount of money that you get seems to be getting smaller and smaller, while you work harder and harder overseas.

*My sister had to go to work to Hong Kong. She sent all the money to
her children to pay their studies, food and clothing. Some other families, and
some of my sisters, they send the money to the husbands. But the
husband spends all the money gambling or with girls while the wife is working
hard in Hong Kong. The husband uses the money in not good habits.
If the husband and wife get separated, all the responsibility goes to the mother.
Specially if the husband has no work, all the responsibility goes to
the mother. This is why they have to go to work abroad as domestic helpers.*

/

*My name is Elmer. I am from the Philippines. I am married and have two
children, a boy and a girl. I am happily married. My mother
worked in Hong Kong as a domestic helper. She left me when I was nine years
old. She worked in Hong Kong for 25 years in two Chinese families.
She supported my education from the beginning to the end, until I graduated.
From Hong Kong she also sent me boxes with clothes, food; when I was
a child, a lot of toys. Only my mother brought me up. My father abandoned me
when I was two years old. This is part of Philippine life.*

Shoes are left outside the relaxing space

Relaxing together
OVER: On Sunday, the domestic helpers' day off, they meet in the
city centre at the HSBC Bank, among others

Creating place

Filipino Migrants in Hong Kong

VICKY CASIA-CABANTAC

The first wave of Filipino workers came to Hong Kong (HK) in the early 1970s and, at the time, Filipinos were the dominant population among migrant workers, reaching as many as 250,000. Domestic work is the main job for overseas Filipino workers (OFWs).

The United Filipinos in Hong Kong, the first major alliance of Filipino migrant workers, was established in 1985 as a result of our campaign to stop Executive Order No. 857, popularly known as Forced Remittance, which was instituted by the Marcos Administration in order to generate dollars for the Philippine economy. According to this decree, all OFWs were compelled to remit 50% to 70% of their total earnings. Other regionally based OFW organisations were also formed. The main reason we organise is because of our welfare, our situation as migrants which makes us victims of the policies of our own government in the Philippines. In 2004, with the passage in the Philippines of the Overseas Absentee Voting Law, Filipinos were given the opportunity to elect national government officials while living abroad. We then organised the Migrants Sectoral Party as our representative in the Philippine Congress. Unfortunately, although we garnered the most number of votes overseas, we did not reach the percentage of total votes to qualify our representative in congress.

In 2007, OFWs were represented in congress by the Gabriela Women's Party. We won two seats! Again, in the 10 May 2010 elections, we won two seats. All our hard work and campaigns paid off!

At the same time, here in Hong Kong, we also meet many problems with policies that really exploit us as migrants, and this is why we get together and work together to protect our rights and welfare. The Two-Week Rule, aka

New Conditions of Stay, is one of the discriminatory policies in Hong Kong since it requires a foreign domestic worker to leave Hong Kong 14 days after termination of contract, unless the reason for termination falls under the categories of: (1) death of employer, (2) redundancy or if the employer leaves the country, (3) financial reason or if the employer is unable to pay the helper's wages, and (4) violation of contract which requires evidence of proof to be submitted by the helper.

Downtown Hong Kong is a very small place and we tend to group by the regions we come from in the Filipinas. This is the landmark of our provinces and relatives. We designate a certain place to meet every Sunday, which is like our territory. We call it our territory, our meeting place, because it has become a habit to go there directly, to assemble whatever, discuss whatever, and then go to the parkways and all meet again in the afternoon. It is the close family ties that we bring here. Even if we are in the streets, or on the bridge, or in the park, we still bring our home values, and this all contributes to our unity as Filipinos.

In Hong Kong the majority of Filipino migrants, 90%, are women. There are a few men who work as drivers or gardeners, but most of us are women working as domestic helpers. That's why we have been labelled as a nation of servants; they call it the Filipino cultural group to our alliance.

We also work with other nations. Currently, Indonesians surpass the number of Filipinos in Hong Kong but they are more exploited because many of them do not receive the minimum allowable wage and they pay excessive recruitment fees through an agency that processes their contracts in Indonesia. We convene with other nations in a combined body, and this is the body – Filipinos are the biggest group there – that marches to influence the central government here in the central area. We campaign for minimum wages because, once again, the Hong Kong government excludes migrant workers from the legislation on minimum wages.

The Sacred and the Naked

Undisciplined Research Mirroring Its Object

PWC (PUBLIC WORKS CHORA)'S DEMETRIS TALIOTIS *&*
EVI TSELIKA IN CONVERSATION

The following text is a compulsive and compulsory research splinter concerning Cypriot public space, who claims it and who inhabits it, and the intense visual stamping that occurs on the territory and on the bodies of inhabitants. Through a methodology of exchange of findings and comparing seemingly absurd facts that prescribe the local, PWC probes into the concepts of urban space, ownership and accessibility, the contemporary art market and the idea of social engagement in Cyprus's highly fragmented spaces.

Fictional and factional figures acquired are utilised to examine the role and function of the Cypriot Orthodox Church, which is the richest financial institution on the island.[1] A main character in this analysis is the activities of the autocephalous Church of Cyprus, a defining player in the production of public art, cultural identity and state wealth. Another is the metaphorical use of the tourist icon of Aphrodite, which the Cypriot state has adopted to promote itself as the island of love. This is ironic in the context of high levels of illegal prostitution and sex slavery that are found within urban and rural settings,[2] and further highlights the disparity in the representation of the sexes in both religious and high–level state management.

By actively quantifying unquantifiable notions that

are highly predominant both in the specific place and in its representation abroad, one more element brought into focus is the direct interplay between economy, market and cultural patterns and production. Through comparisons and direct use of quantifying graphs to speak in terms of visual ventures, social phenomena, ownership and the idiosyncrasies that characterise the Cypriot locale, we aim to present the work of PWC in an innovative manner that plays with notions of the financial urban centre. This is not manifested as an analysis of the visual graphs but rather the graphs act as stepping stones for a discussion on increasingly prominent matters of critical glocal concern.

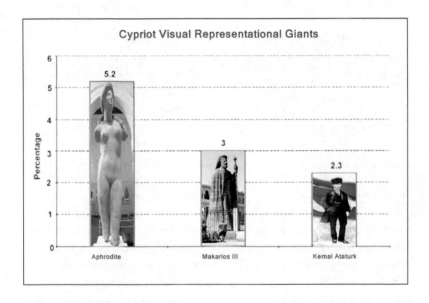

Cypriot Visual Representational Giants

Aphrodite – the patron goddess of the island, who seems to have been a reinterpretation of the Eastern Mediterranean goddess Astarte. The worship of Aphrodite, which spanned a period of thousands of years on the island, was manifested in the form of divine prostitution.

Archbishop Makarios III – the first president of the island, from 1960 up until his death in 1977. He was also the head of the Greek Orthodox Church.

Kemal Ataturk – the first president of Turkey and the person credited as the creator of the modern Turkish state. In North Cyprus his influence is highly present in the construction of the secular character of the social reality of Turkish Cypriots.

These three representational giants for the locale can be seen in busts and sculptures, images on walls, on key rings and t-shirts. All three speak of the notions of Greekness, Turkishness and Cypriotness: creating direct links and metaphors for the insistence on identity politics that define the island and maintain it in its position as a still not formed coherent state.

DT: When talking about Cyprus I always remember these lines from Seferis:

And this island: who knows it? I've lived my life hearing names I've never heard before ...[3]

The onomasiology of public space could not have evaded Cyprus. That definition of land ownership via the proprietorship of names, later developed by the British empire into the land registry, has shaped the modern use and history of Cyprus as an island. Nonetheless, the Cypriot onomasiology of public space has remained minimal and liminal. Geographically restricted.

From *Κύπρις Αφροδίτη* (Cyprus Aphrodite) to Kibris, the naming, the ownership of space has firmly remained within the remit of *blessed (μακάρια/ makaria*[4]) sanctification. Between altar, church bell and minaret. Driving through Cyprus – who walks anyway? – one can see how the privatised space has been shaped by this relationship of land and sacredness. Domestic, commercial and state architecture roars with farcical attempts to mimic in order to partake in this patrimony.

This fixation with ownership, with the 'House' – only equalled by the Cypriot fixation with that Berlinesque division of the island, exemplified in Nicosia – has left a visible gap in any discussion of the public space in Nicosia as a public's space. Moreover, whereas the big guys – Makarios and Kemal – are everywhere to be seen and in a sense privatise, once more, any public space by providing it with either of their distinct community identities (community not communal), Aphrodite is either in the museum or on cabaret and strip club signs, or on coconut-scented beach towels, and as the logo of other controversial 'delights'.

ET: As one lies on a beach towel adorned with Aphrodite's curvy figure one cannot help but wonder how come there are no

Makarios-decorated towels to be found? I guess it would be too sacrilegious for naked tourist bodies to lie on the Ethnarch's face. The use of the image of the patron goddess of Cyprus in juxtaposition with the dominant male figures of Makarios III, who represents the Cypriot Orthodox church (an entity devoid of women), and Kemal Ataturk, who can be taken to represent the secular Turkish Army (another entity defined by female absence), is highlighted in the above graph and can be interpreted through the concepts of ethnicity, sex, gender and male/female balances and equilibriums.

An important element, and one that is largely understudied in the case of Cypriot discourse, is how the ethnic lines can also be interpreted as lines of gender. Far removed from times when woman worship described the island context, the local landscape is now quite largely embedded with the masculine stamping of ethno-nationalism. According to gender peace analysts, the bi-polar political system on the island is an expression of the male dominating power structure. The gender lines and inequality remain highly prevalent. Due to the focus on the 'ethnic' problem, many social issues go unresolved. Cyprus, with its repeated representation as a young maiden who needs protection and its ardent relations with the two ethnic communities in the respective motherlands, depicts a set of gender relations that refer back to the structures of nationalist ideology that was passionately preached by both Makarios III and Kemal Ataturk. As Cynthia Cockburn indicates, "patriarchy and ethno-nationalism are partners in theory, sexism and racism are partners in practice".[5]

DT: Talking of sexism, I also wonder how many nudes the Church of Cyprus art collection has? How many depictions of Aphrodite, Venus, whatever? It was the first public art collection on the island,[6] initiated by Archbishop Makarios himself in 1963,[7] and is still the only one accessible online – part of it at least. Amongst Lefteris Economou's painting *Great Female Marches 1989–1991* and portraits of the Greek royal family, do they have Aphroditesque nudes?

ET: The nude Cypriot female body is an absent notion.

The 'desirable nude body' is something reserved for the large numbers of foreign women who work in the gentlemen's nightclubs. What we used to be faced with instead was the use of the Cypriot female body as a means for political propaganda, which further maintained the myth of the maiden Cyprus that needs protection. The recurrent images of Greek Cypriot women becoming a wall of remembrance through the demonstrations up until the late 1990s, especially at the Ledra Palace checkpoint in Nicosia, and asking for the recovery of their missing persons,[8] has now become a thing of the past, as the missing are being exhumed and people being put to rest. Cypriot women in Cyprus are minimally represented in the army, absent from the church's managerial ranks. Whereas foreign women in Cyprus are mostly treated as sex objects in the many strip clubs found in Nicosia, as well as being sexually harassed across the island.[9] The large mono–cultural dominance within the two ethnically divided parts has resulted in patterns of racism that are now causing increasing problems as the migration levels are constantly rising and there is minimal assistance from the state for the integration of these migrants and their children into Cypriot society.[10] Cyprus at the present moment demonstrates a social scape that has come to be inscribed by multiculturalism. However, there is a persistent lack of state policy towards the smooth integration of its most recent inhabitants.[11]

DT: As the current President Christofias said during his locally infamous speech at the Brookings Institution in Washington in late 2010, Cyprus is one big geographical victim of rape, an Aphrodite deflowered: "So as you know, Cyprus is a very, very beautiful island. A whole island. But unfortunately, let me say it's been raped and we have to restore the visions of Cyprus. The island of Cyprus is famous as the island of love. It is the island of Aphrodite, as you know."

Cyprus, the rape victim in Christofias speech, is the Cyprus of the coup of 15 July 1974, the Greek junta coup, and of the subsequent Turkish invasion/ peace operation on 20 July 1974. But other macho penis formations have been present for quite some time, before and after July 1974, forcing themselves through and on the island as land. Geologically, Cyprus is characterised by arid valleys and eroding beaches. All of its urban centres can be either found by the sea or in the singular case of Nicosia across a plain. Architecturally, minarets and Greek Orthodox churches, Venetian walls and gothic cathedrals, tropical modernist[12] blocks of flats and, most recently, nondescript hotel resorts (designed it seems especially to incorporate bulbous breasts and big, fat penises), all diametrically oppose the vernacular architecture of Cyprus with its low–ceiling, mud–brick buildings.

ET: The worship of Aphrodite in ancient Cyprus revolved around the notion of 'sacred prostitution'. This flourished on the island during the classical period (475–325 BC). It is said that young girls would serve as priestesses in the temple of the goddess and wander the land offering themselves in the name of their goddess. It is also reported that all women would have to do this once in their life in honour of Aphrodite. They would sit in the outside public space with their hand extended waiting for a man to put in a coin, which would then lead to sexual intercourse and an offering. Another myth has it that as Paphos was the main centre for the worship of Aphrodite many would come there from other places and even before their boats docked at the harbour the women of the island would be taken onto the ships and offer themselves in honour of the goddess.[13] Today, a far cry from the worship of the goddess, the sex workers on the

Gentlemen's Clubs and Cypriot Cabarets
50%

Cypriot Orthodox Churches under construction
50%

island are predominantly from other countries mainly in Eastern Europe's ex-Soviet bloc, Asia, Latin America and the Near East. Prostitution is still to this day predominantly female and the Greek name for a sex worker or prostitute is *ierodouli*, a 'slave of the sacred'.

ET: It could be claimed that the Cypriot art historical legacy has long revolved around the church's murals, icons and paintings. As the richest institution on the island, the church owns huge amounts of artistic religious relics,[14] which form part of its financial portfolio. Cyprus is also known as the 'island of the saints', a notion that is not surprising if one sees the number of churches that are to be found on its small territory. It is a number that is constantly increasing as church construction has been occurring at an unprecedented rate. With a new cathedral that will surpass 22 metres in height being planned in the old centre of Nicosia, the play of power seems to still constitute a firm reality in the landscape.

In the Nicosia suburb of Aglantzia, in one street that is three kilometres long there are three churches – one per kilometre.

The spiritual significance of this architectural symbolism is all but forgotten as they sprout in the landscape like mushrooms after the rain, and one cannot help but wonder what their function is in an increasingly secular island?[15]

DT: The secular is, though, another sacred notion. Another church-manifested notion. Archbishop Makarios was also the first president of the Republic and stayed there for 17 years. Of course there were democratic elections, but the percentage of Makarios approval was steadily in the high 90s, even after his death in 1977. Therefore the notion of the secular Cypriot state passes through the church of Cyprus. It was the archbishop's palace that was most heavily bombed during the coup, and it was there that they tried to assassinate Makarios in March 1971 – Makarios the president.

In a sense, the secular state is but the prostitute of the church, as the state is still highly co-dependent on the church in a variety of ways. A mode of transition from uber-Byzantinism to contemporary Middle Eastern and Eastern Mediterranean politics. Authoritarian, leader-cantered and violent. The numerous churches stand, spread out, not as reminders of the sacred but as indirect reminders of the state itself.

ET: And speaking of *secular prostitutes*, the focus shifts again to the contemporary sex industry of Cyprus. The island has become a major transit point for prostitutes in the Eastern Mediterranean and the EU authorities accuse the Cypriot state of being highly tolerant of illegal prostitution as it bears witness to the exploitation of countless young women from all over the world. Women are brought over for supposed jobs as waitresses or domestic workers and are then forced into the sex trade, either by their employer or through lack of other forms of work. Many are not allowed to move freely and are housed in groups in apartment blocks and managed strictly by their pimps. The cabaret venues that are plentiful in the city become much more prominent at night and if one walks in the main square of the old town in the early hours of the morning, the girls that work in the sex industry are all eating after the night's work. It is one of the few times that they seem to make a strong presence in the public space. Sex trafficking occurs within a multitude of venues used by Cyprus's commercial sex industry, including cabarets, bars, pubs and massage parlours, often disguised as private apartments and located throughout both urban and rural settings.

DT: Since 2009, to legally get a job in the cabarets – and by extension in the massage parlours – you need to have at least a ballet school diploma. This came about after the claims of cabaret owners – whose businesses are often housed in church-owned property – that what the cabarets offer and promote is art. Again, via names, playing with the word 'artiste' (αρτίστα του καπαρέ, a cabaret artist), they made a most impressive conjectural leap. This wasn't prostitution, and if it was it was in the name of art. As with any conjecture, this too allowed for a multiplicity of proposals, from a multitude of sources, as to what a cabaret is and how it is supposed to work – not the best business practice when you are trying to control a secretive and tightly knit organisation like sex trafficking, and in conjunction with some high-profile Viagra-related deaths albeit urban legend ones

(Mr Kamougiaros, one of the most famous cabaret owners and 'artiste' agents in Cyprus, apparently died after consuming one blue pill too many), the cabaret industry started experiencing a decline. The outcome of this decline was that the South East Asian immigrant community, who up to that point had been meeting in the few public gardens and even fewer social support centres on their days off, rented out these former cabarets and turned them into 'ethnic' clubs.

ET: Cyprus's fragmented public space, sphere and realm all seem to highlight the male/ female interplay as it is witnessed

vis–à–vis the economic structures of the local. Two very prominent money–makers are compared and contrasted here: the Orthodox Church and the Cypriot sex industry. One claims to be the producer of culture, the other of artistic performance. What both industries unquestionably produce is huge amounts of yearly profit. Profit that is sedulously concealed, in both cases, from the opinion of the Cypriot public. There appears to be very little willingness to accept criticality in this heavily indoctrinated and nepotism– defined social landscape.

DT: Regardless of all the talk of Cyprus having an orderly, if violated, public space – both partly

The Cypriot Merman, July 2009, EVANTHIA TSELIKA

due to its position as an ex–colony in the Eastern Mediterranean – it is very difficult to talk about this space in a concrete way, to academically research it. It is a haphazard social phenomenon, an unresearchable, scattered and unclassifiable conglomeration. The role of the church is, of course, a primary factor – historically, socially, politically – but if one wants to further any research into Cypriot public space the only way is by embracing this space's absurdity, its eroding porosity and its jumping jacks flashing in every other empty lot, churchyard and pavement. Yes, the public space of Cyprus mirrors international trends; yes, it is layered, but it is also boiling, overflowing, hidden and found in bibliographies and data one cannot even start imagining! Can such a 'thing' qualify as a topic for an academic discipline of research? Does such research even need to be disciplined?

1. "The total economic wealth of the Cyprus Church, which includes the revenue of all its episcopacies and Monasteries amounts to 847.707.976 Euros. The total income in 2008 amounted to 46.012.584 Euros, while total expenditure to 46.167.043 Euros. The Church of Cyprus's income include 970.000 Euros from liturgical income (such as petty cash donations from church goers, candles etc), approximately 10 million Euros from the state towards the priests' salaries, 17 million Euros from investments and rents, roughly 1.3 million Euros from other activities and 1.5 million Euros from stocks." Fiscal audit of the Church of Cyprus, 2008, p. 24.
2. See H. Kiatipis, N. Ioannou and I.Nicolaou (eds), *The Trade of Girls* (Nicosia: Ekseliksi Publishers, 2004).
3. George Seferis, 'Helen', *Log Book III* (1955).
4. This is a conjectural, textual reference to his beatitude Archbishop Makarios III, aka Archbishop The Blessed III.
5. Cynthia Cockburn, *The Line: Women, Partition and the Gender Order in Cyprus* (London and New York: ZED Books, 2004) p. 198.
6. For more information on the politics and contents of this collection, see http://www.makariosfoundation.org.cy/.
7. 1963, three years after the independence of Cyprus as a republic, was also the year when ethnic bi–communal troubles amongst Greek and Turkish Cypriots became violent, the focus of which was the December events on the west of the island.
8. One of the human tragedies and urban myths of the 1974 Turkish invasion/peace operation is the number of male persons who were never accounted for. These were assumed to be alive and captured by the Turkish army, numbering to approximately 1,619. This number is under constant renegotiation after the recent finds of mass graves on both sides of the island but particularly in the military graveyard of Nicosia. On 28 April 2011 the number of still unaccounted for 'missing persons' is believed to be around 500.
9. See, for example, the experience of Alice Wang, a Chinese American Fulbright scholar

living in Limassol, Cyprus, http://www.cyprus-mail.com/opinions/aphrodite-s-home-cruel-place/20110313.

10. For an analysis of migration in the south part of Nicosia, see the 2008 report *Migrant Cities Research, Nicosia South* by Olga Demetriou. This can be accessed at http://www.prio.no/Cyprus/Publications/.

11. Cyprus geographically can be found at the crossroads of three continents and it is the easternmost entry point into the European Union. In 2010 and 2011 there have occurred various instances of clashes in Cyprus amongst Cypriot locals and migrants of varying nationalities (mostly from South East Asia, Africa and the Middle East), both adults and teenagers within educational establishments. A fact that characterises the treatment of migrants even at the hands of the police is an illegal Pakistani immigrant's choice to jump out of the window, something that proved fatal, rather than face the policemen (http://www.inews.gr/135/kypros-pakistanos-protimise-to-thanato-apo-ti-syllipsi.htm).

12. Tropical Architecture is not a style but rather an approach to architecture that asks for design to be conceived in response to the needs and opportunities of a specific region – although it is not inherently opposed to global potentials. A tropical modernist architecture is defined by its location. An excellent example of this is the work of Brazilian architect Oscar Niemeyer. See Alexander Tzonis, Liane Lefaivre and Bruno Stagno (eds), *Tropical Architecture: Critical Regionalism in the Age of Globalization* (London: Wiley Academic, 2001).

13. See Nickie Roberts, *Whores in History: Prostitution in Western Society* (London: Harper Collins, 1992).

14. The Archbishop's palace houses three museums within its Nicosia foundation; see http://www.makariosfoundation.org.cy/. Kykkos Monastery is the richest one on the island, both in term of monetary income and artefact ownership; see http://www.kykkos-museum.cy.net/index2.html.

15. Orthodox Church (87.9% of the Greek Cypriot population) attendance remains quite high throughout generations with 37.9% of frequent churchgoers. However this is lower than the 46.2% of the previous generation, as well as being much more for social reasons rather than spiritual. For figures and further analysis see *Survey on Political and National Perceptions*, http://docs.google.com/viewer?a=v&q=cache:DatLjd2BX3cJ:www.prio.no/misc/Download.a spx%3Ffile%3D%252Fcscw%252Frd%252FReplication%2BData%252Ffile49645_survey_com bined.doc+church+atendance+cyprus&hl=en&gl=uk&pid=bl&srcid=ADGEEShXgiiCmLp StqoWf9lUoxbQIg5_lvGymTwKZHh6JV-0YTA3wk1j4JseMgHxZ7CAchTubkYiW6cjbJ6_Qx EpZxsYsSXOVhZ6dwAPwGQdkdetoLSkOBYq-mFnh_S28AHpqONtVv98&sig=AHIEtbSP qXBO7C9GrFApLH_21zUrGlzzeQ.

PINK

The Art of Being Confident

NANNA NIELSEN & TRENTON OLDFIELD

If you had any interest in the people who worked in or around the financial services industries in the previous decade, it was difficult not to notice the concentration and number of men wearing pink shirts and pink ties. In an attempt to better understand a little of the shrouded mechanisms of the City of London and the confidence of the men who choose to wear pink to work, we set out to create a photographic archive of this time and phenomenon.

Exactly why and when men started wearing pink coloured shirts to work in the financial districts of cities remains ambiguous. Pink is a colour often associated with Barbie dresses, pre–pubescent girls' bedrooms or even 'pink movies' – femininity. According to our research, in the past men were most often seen to wear pink shirts or jackets when they were hunting. Perhaps unsurprisingly the narrative of pink shirts is now intertwined with a global corporate retail clothing chain store established in the 1980s called PINK, which suggests it is named after a supposedly well–known 18th–century tailor, Thomas Pink, who may have made pink hunting jackets.

The summer of 2006, the period in which we took the photographs, was exceptional in many ways. If you look back over news archives, you will see much of it was taken up with celebrity gossip and launches of new technologies such as mobile devices, online social networking platforms and the world's largest jumbo jets. There were reports of occasional, though not catastrophic, natural disasters alongside detailed reports of ongoing economic growth of nations and across the globe. Britain, despite funding at least two significant wars abroad, was experiencing its longest period of economic growth on record. The financial services industries and the City of London, where these men we photographed worked, in spite of being onerously understudied, were generally agreed to be the 'goose that laid the golden egg' and somehow therefore remote and mythical.

Western Europe had a general air of confidence and bullishness about itself, and the financial districts were the geographies where confidence was so high that you could – if you walked or cycled through them as we did – touch it, smell it and see it. Were the pink shirts a symbol of the much written about, highly educated, responsible, sensitive, metro–sexual though confident banker or a symbolic 'canary in the mine', a sign that 'the City' was over confident and therefore collapse was imminent? Was 'the City' no longer vulnerable to a self–preserving public school old boys' network, and instead now in the safe hands of a new type of individual, one who made decisions in a modern businesslike manner, emotionless and as a result of sophisticated scientific analysis? We wondered if the 'the City', despite being awash with scientific graphs and business models, was still dependent on the emotion of confidence.

All images from the series Pink: The Art of Being Confident, 2006, NANNA NIELSEN & TRENTON OLDFIELD

I Confess

DAVID BOULOGNE

I confess I regularly dream the impossible and I find it good for my creativity. Life is precious and my aim is to feel connected to the world. I wish people could care a bit more and think of the future by learning from the past. I left my country for something I thought would suit me more. I found something I am disappointed with. This made me realise who I am and that such a perfect place doesn't exist. I confess I am a dreamer and I wish for better days. My dreams are not of gold or silver but of human exchange, respect and care. Someone said 'we are what we eat', and I could suggest 'we are what we dream of'. The Americans could be British too, but in the end it is simply a dream. And to wake up is always terrifying.

First impressions

I came to London from Paris in the late 1990s as word had it that the creative industries were booming in the era of New Labour. Being a freelance photographer has never been well recognised in France, so I was in search of better prospects over the pond. Starting from scratch, I did various jobs and, as time went by, I began to understand the new British spending culture.

The continental approach back then was more conservative and access to capital was long and laborious. In order to start a small enterprise in Europe you need to pay upfront for many legislations that make your existence already difficult. You then have to pay many taxes on salaries and you are heavily taxed on your yearly profits. The whole procedure is very heavy. In both public and private sectors the system is strongly built on education and somehow on classes, even if the distinctions are not as obvious as in Britain. That division is translated into the working environment where vacancies are not filled based on meritocracy but where diplomas and networks are vital. Overall the working reality is subject to a very strong hierarchy of rulers and followers.

The followers will never be offered better positions and the rulers (cadres) will always sit on their little cloud. And if you wish to create your own business, most people point at you as if you intend to betray them and join the other side. In the end, as a person who tries to engage novelty and create jobs, you find yourself very disillusioned. The French mentality and its reality teach you to abandon your dreams and to become subject to the state by demanding its assistance. This is the reason why people tend to show not much dedication to their work. This is why there has been a lot of unemployment for the last 20 years. And finally, this is the reason why so many people like me left.

In London, life seemed much lighter to endure. Many people had several credit cards and loans to live with. A year after I arrived I found a position as a wedding photographer. The job was interesting, versatile and fulfilling. I started up an agency with the owner but I didn't want to be involved in ownership and shares. My interest lay in learning skills, as much as a photographer as a salesperson and agent. The agency took off very quickly. Our assignments took us all around the world, to the most luxurious locations. I could practice my love for reportage photography and evolve in truly amazing and unaffordable places. This was a kind of dreamland, which I appreciated all the more remembering my background. Most of our clients were couples who were happy to use their credit card to pay their suppliers to secure a memorable and luxurious event. They would also be in the process of buying a house, about to enjoy a lush and gorgeous honeymoon, and be simultaneously planning a baby. All these things require a lot of money, but for most of them it seemed pointless to question what tomorrow would be like. Their wealth was considered deserved and long lasting.

A move to credit

I couldn't get my head around people's behaviour towards capital and investment. People had many preconceived ideas of fame and wealth associated with my trade. I also realised that if I wanted to move forward and stand a chance of keeping some sort of credibility I had to consider credit. London was not made to serve a careful approach like mine but to generate money. There was no chance I could improve my business by standing firm on my values, i.e. to save and spend according to what you really earn. It was obvious not only that credit was needed but also that it was the usual way to proceed. I therefore applied for credit and obtained it without any effort. I guess it was considered normal, despite my very low income and being a single freelancer.

Suddenly work slowed down and as I was about to hit my limit I contacted the credit company. I needed an extension. They could see my recent history and they predicted things would not get any better in the near future. Therefore they refused my request. My clients were late with payments, bills piled up, I was stuck. Those times were hard and edgy. I was living by the day. I couldn't repay my credit, and the interest I had to pay to the credit company was building up, adding to my problems. I didn't see any way out. I also felt very let down by the credit company – so welcoming at first and so distant the next day. I really felt disgusted and strangled. Shortly after that work picked up. There was a ray of hope and a tiny improvement in my bank statement. I received then a surprise phone call from them. They were offering me a loan of £80,000 … *no comment!*

This experience taught me how fragile we are, and how the banks and the likes play with you as if you were a puppet. This is a harsh and sad reality. It shows that the weak and vulnerable are the best customers for a credit company.

I was strongly determined to clear off that debt. Fortunately, work became more regular and customers started to pay on time. When I eventually paid it back in full 18 months later, I felt like the richest man in the world. The massive burden had finally disappeared and the future felt full of promise once more. After that episode I decided I would never buy any property in the capital where the prices, encouraged by the burning economy, would never match my resources. I started to make my own decisions about how to run my business. I was fed up with people who were full of praise and recommendations but who actually didn't have anything to prove those recommendations would work. I realised that most people, especially in the metropolis, fantasise and follow a general trend without careful thinking. In fact, rational and dedicated people are very rare.

Creative bounce

I wanted to understand a bit more about the agents of capitalism and I decided to start a photographic project about the City of London.[1] I asked a successful trader and amateur art buyer to invest in my project and he accepted. I was free to capture the subject with my own eyes and words.

After a few months it became clear that the world I was photographing was pernicious and secretive. The transparent and/or reflective skyscrapers were hiding greed at full flow. My intention was not to document the district from within the towers but to photograph its agents in the street, on common and public ground, on their daily stroll. I wanted to discover some kind of idiosyncrasy that identified and linked those people. I eventually realised that there was none to be found. They simply looked like everybody.

This triggered a new direction in my reflections on the capitalist concept. The boom experienced in the late 1990s was widely generated by the belief we construct in 'better prospects', and how much we are prepared to pay the price for its realisation. Lies, speculation, hypothesis and fear are all abstract concepts that fuel ultra-capitalism. Whereas capitalism is based on competition of real goods and real assets, ultra-capitalism makes gambling as banal as going to your local for a cappuccino. And those economies driving the so-called modern world are profiting from exploitation of poorer countries around the globe. No wonder then that some parts of the world are tired and react with violence.

Following 9/11 some people in Britain vigorously criticised the Arab world. Being French, I occasionally had to take criticism for the non-involvement of my country in the Iraq war, and show my support for that choice. But let's not forget that at the same time France was selling record quantities of weapons to fuel the war. The London bombings in 2005 perhaps made some people in Britain suddenly realise that maybe they, and their lifestyles, did have something to do with the anger coming from the Middle East. Distorted mass media coverage and propaganda play a big role and they are not the monopoly of dictatorships. They are closely connected to ultra-capitalism and operate continuously everywhere.

Addictive system

The capitalist system has spread widely despite the different regimes and religions. We have left behind us all sorts of religious and/or political dogmas that don't seem to work. The elite realised that one way to gain control was through popularity by feeding the masses' belief that we can all live the 'American Dream'. The trouble we are facing in recent decades is that governments have lost their power of decision and handed it over indirectly to the conglomerates. By allowing mega–powers to exploit the system and rapidly increase their assets we can only become more disillusioned and frightened. The capitalist system, by definition, is not designed towards fairness, but the ultra–capitalists want even more and are stretching the system to the extremes, so it divides and snaps badly. All we can see is that greed has become widespread at every level, in every class and situation. In the west, we express ourselves in the manner the system allows, whether we like it or not, because we depend, day–to–day, on that very system.

The more we are given, the more we spend. The more we have, the more we lose ourselves and expect the impossible. This pretence is exponential and the deciders can manipulate that behaviour as much as they want. They have real power and believe they are untouchable. As power and fortune are indefinitely combined they achieve that ultimate goal of being demigods. By encouraging ultra–capitalism we produce greed, lies, fear and isolation. The common idea that this sort of 'successful' economy is good for everyone is the biggest lie ever promoted because it relies on people's fantasies. The real money always goes to a small margin at the top.

A prosperous and harmonious society can only work through education and care. We could envisage a new system that would enforce some strict regulations and methods for sharing openly and fairly, and benefiting participants as much as communities in need. This vision can only work if the government has a strong role in the economy. We cannot continue letting the conglomerates decide for the nations. The current situation is immoral and highly dangerous.

Moral responsibility

Faith has faded and we have turned towards something more material, satisfying and realistic. But, in invoking capitalism to the full, we have abandoned our moral responsibilities. Capitalism has succeeded in splitting up communities. We have traded acts of sharing and compassion for disguised arrogance. Greed is simply tempting and legal.

When a predominant idea takes over we need to install a counter balance, and this can only be found in politics or reason. Our governments and politicians are meant to be an assembly of wise members elected to set rules in a just order for the nation and to fulfil their role as ambassadors for better and fair societies. And of course, that doesn't happen, because success in the economy is tied with electoral success and therefore power. So once again, power and self-interest prevails. As the corporations will not stop gambling and profiting, it is our responsibility to force our governments to re-institute their dominant position in decision-making. The very essence of capitalism is designed to fail anytime. We do not have to follow its rollercoaster plan that only profits a very small number of people. Most people do not realise that they have a voice and opinions to express, and that by remaining silent they hand themselves over to the existing system.

Confession of a consumer

We are all bound to the financial crisis and I hope the most recent one will trigger some doubts about our system. Capitalism charms because it gives you what you feel you need. It doesn't make you think or act responsibly. But there is no point in attempting to break the system by installing a new one just as radical. All extremisms are destined to fail. A wiser, more responsible and profound way requires a pause. We must engage with the idea that government must take action to stop the privileging of the private sector. The government must work for the people. Elected politicians have to stop the habit of doing dodgy business with conglomerates for personal benefit. We have to start thinking long term, stop being complacent, and derail the lethal gambling ideology.

But the first thing we must do is stop blaming others. We all have to share our responsibility in the highs and lows of fragile capitalism. Based on a moral principle, the banking system in which we participate is responsible for the huge sums of money it makes, the troubles that result and for the stability of our nations. We have a voice, we have some power, and we have a duty to our families and communities. If we do not like or trust the system we must say it and work together to change it. There will always be clever, selfish people who exploit a certain system to profit and maximise personal benefit so we need to speak up for reforms to impose stricter and fairer rules.

Certainly our standard of living, or at least our material wealth, has increased, but we pay a high price for it. And part of that high price, commonly known as credit, and the interest we pay on it, is yet more benefit for the elite. By idealising and imagining that we need more, we make their fortunes grow and our fortunes diminish. So the system is not as good as we expected. By implementing more futile dreams, which the elite encourage through the media, we have become hooked consumers that feed a minority. We are the ones to blame for praising such a foolish myth.

We need to grow up, become aware of the system we are feeding, act reasonably and feel responsible. By revolt or disconnection, we must present our real aspirations to the various institutions and those we elect into positions of authority. And first, if we want to move forward, we must take that initial, vital step of recognising and confessing our present complicity in the system. We have to face, question and take responsibility for our reality and our actions. The governments must take action and show their authority. The conglomerates must lower their targets and redefine their goals.

We need to understand that the human legacy and the planet are at stake. Our first reasonable act for a better world could be a confession.

1. This essay is an extension of the photographic installation presented at TINAG Festival 2010, which combined a slideshow of Boulogne's work Make It A Good Experience – In The City with an invitation to visitors to write their 'confessions' about their relationship to the City of London and pin them on the adjacent wall.

All images from the series Make It A Good Experience – In The City,
2002, DAVID BOULOGNE

London's Ring of Steel Uncovered

HENRIETTA WILLIAMS *&* JO ANNE BUTLER
IN CONVERSATION

Entering the Panopticon: London's Ring of Steel[1] is a project comprising a series of photographs, an interactive map and a series of walking tours created by photographer Henrietta Williams and map maker George Gingell. It was exhibited in the 2010 TINAG festival.[2]

JB: There is a rich body of work by artists who interrogate notions of borders. How did your interest in photographing walls and fences develop?

HW: Binary opposites and tension points within cities and landscapes have always fascinated me. A number of years ago, living in Ireland, I became interested in the continuing issues of division in Belfast and began to use photography to explore landscapes around interface areas.[3] Often I photographed quite banal scenes that had a very recent history that was being covered up somehow. In a way, this has become the basis of all my work since. I have continued to use photography as a way of exploring the complexity of landscape and memory. I am particularly drawn to 'urban amenities' that are often used as a form of disguise. I can't think of anything more interesting than becoming an expert in reading the urban landscape, that's my ambition. It enriches your everyday experience of the city you live in.

JB: And how did this lead to the work on London's Ring of Steel?

HW: I became intrigued by the notion of this invisible border that I had heard about that surrounded the City of London. This followed on from some of my earlier Belfast-based work ... in fact the idea for the development of the Ring of Steel itself actually came from Belfast. The term 'Ring of Steel' was commonly used to describe a security installation built in the 1970s around the central shopping area of Belfast. It was made of concrete blocks and barbed wire, and then later a series of high metal gates, quite literally a ring of steel. Following the IRA bombing in Bishopsgate in 1993, the City of London police worked closely with the Royal Ulster Constabluary to design the 'Ring' in London. So not only the threat but also the proposed solution was coming from Northern Ireland. The London Ring of Steel was purposefully much less visible, and, as I was living in London, I wanted to know where this hidden border was. I started working with a map maker, George Gingell. We spent days walking the boundary of the City, trying to work out exactly where the Ring of Steel began and where it ended.

JB: It's interesting that in an age when everything in the city, even a plant pot in a public space, has to get planning permission, usually after public consultations, you had to search for this 'construction' in public space.

HW: When we began researching we realised that there wasn't any map of the cordon in public circulation. So the Ring of Steel began to take on this sort of mythological status in my head. With the Freedom of Information Act we are all led to believe that these sorts of things are in the public domain. Yet everything was so vague, we couldn't find any proper map to work from. George and I wanted to play detective and pin it down. Then we became fascinated by the idea that the Ring of Steel almost exactly followed the historic system of defence, the Roman–built London Wall. The project was really very collaborative. I did the photography, George made the map, we walked it together. We each brought different skills to the project. But the ideas came from both of us. We both wanted to make the invisible, visible. And one of our main reasons for making the 3D map was to make the Ring of Steel visually accessible to the public.

Remnants of London Wall at 1 London Wall, 2011
All images from Ring of Steel, 2010–2011, HENRIETTA WILLIAMS

JB: Initially London's Ring of Steel was a temporary malleable system of bollards – what Coaffee calls the "Ring of Plastic"[4] – but this then evolved into a more permanent and, as you say, *invisible* system. Was it hard to find the Ring and what does it actually look like?

HW: Once you know what you are looking for, it actually becomes quite easy to trace. The Ring of Steel consists of a series of sentry boxes, bollards and vehicle-recognition cameras. Street patterns have been re-drawn with one-way systems, flower planting and trees blocking roads. Also, alongside all of this, the City of London police worked with local businesses and landowners to install private CCTVs. As I understand it, the Ring of Steel in Belfast was a very visible gated structure, a bit like the city's interface walls. In London, on the other hand, the authorities became concerned about the system being too visible. It was felt that if it was overtly visible then effectively the IRA would have 'won' and succeeded in turning a sizeable chunk of central London into a kind of battleground. There is a really interesting issue here about the socially acceptable aesthetics

of defence. The initial ring, the 'Ring of Plastic' was constructed from temporary road blocks but people felt the blocks had negative associations with war zones. So, gradually, they were replaced with a new permanent system designed to blend into the urban landscape. Before working on this project I regularly walked through and around the bollards and sentry boxes without realising what I was looking at. And many people doing our walking tour had a similar reaction. Of course, those from academic and planning backgrounds had prior knowledge. But for most people, you walk through urban environments all the time and you don't notice these things. I suppose, once you know what to look for, it is visible, but until then, it is a kind of secret.

JB: Imagining that feeling, realising that you are being watched, monitored, recorded, that there is this surveillance system all around – I wonder if people have become indifferent to CCTV cameras tracking their movements? You say there are close to four million CCTV cameras in Britain?[5]

HW: It's very difficult to actually

pin down the number, but it's believed there are around four million CCTV cameras in the UK. So yes, I think people have become pretty indifferent to CCTV in London now. It seems to have become an accepted part of city life.

JB: And how then does the Ring of Steel differ from those other more general areas of surveillance and CCTV?

HW: Well, fundamentally, the Ring of Steel was created specifically for vehicles. It's a complete system of organisation that changes the movement and flow of vehicles through the City. The idea was to reorganise access, so that relatively few policemen could be used to cover the entire area of the Square Mile. Now there are only 19 entry points. So there are only 19 cameras to be checked, and only 19 sentry boxes that need to be manned to monitor all the entry points to London's financial district.

JB: So, two-thirds of all the streets entering the City of London have been closed?[6]

HW: Exactly. Prior to this, there would have been roughly 100 entry points – a huge police operation to man – now, there are only 19 entry points. Also, new financial buildings tend to be built within the cordon, rather than outside, so there is now a much more defined border between the financial area and the rest of the city. Walking along the perimeter, mapping the Ring of Steel, the shift from skyscrapers to low rise has really become quite marked. The 3D map provides a very clear sense of the high-rise buildings that make up the City being encircled by the Ring of Steel.

JB: In your text accompanying this work you write that "we now live in a society in which we are unwittingly ordered and controlled, where security and safety are paramount".[7] But cities, since their origin, have always been defensive mechanisms. Stephen Graham[8] notes that the City of London is built on the ruin of the fortified capital of Roman control. And there is a memory in the landscape of the separation that persists – this is clear in the way the Ring of Steel runs alongside the ancient city wall. Later on, the Tower of London was built in a highly strategic position on the river and in relation to the sea. So London has long been a location that was defended – a site of defensive control. All this makes me wonder why we would be surprised that "security and safety are paramount"?

HW: Well, one would assume that we have moved forwards since the Middle Ages. And when people study urban planning today they emphasise contemporary urban concerns such as 'lingering through the city', 'engaging with the city', 'activating public space' ... rather than notions of protection. Perhaps it's because the solid Roman line of defence has now become an invisible wall of surveillance that is permeable. So maybe this is the surprise. Instead of bricks and mortar, protection is a line of thin bollards, artfully placed, and CCTV cameras.

JB: But, going back to your text, are people "*unwittingly* ordered and controlled"? Or are authority, control and security what people want and expect from cities? In certain cities, the sense of authority is palpable.

HW: Well, people like the idea of being protected, so, in the abstract, the City of London's Ring of Steel might seem attractive. But if people understand how it actually affects how they operate through the City – this is very different. People begin to think: 'I'm not really allowed to hang around on this street', or 'this street has now been sold as a defence measure to a private security company and is watched over by a private security guard who can tell me what to do'. When we did the walking tour of the Ring of Steel as part of the TINAG exhibition, there was an incident on one particular street, which is a *private* street but still a *public byway*.[9] When we arrived the security guard immediately wanted us gone, but we were a group of 30 people, which was helpful. We then engaged the security guard in a discussion about how it was our civil right to walk through this public byway. The Ring of Steel raises questions about contemporary notions of public and private.

JB: In his essay 'Imperial Bedroom'[10], about the American 'obsession' with privacy and the public reaction to the Clinton/Lewinsky scandal, Jonathan Franzen writes: "If privacy depends on the expectation of invisibility then the expectation of visibility is what defines public space ... how sweet the promenade, everyone needs a promenade sometimes, a place to go when you want to announce to the world that you have a new suit." There is an extent to which, when you are in a public place, you expect, and maybe even want, to be visible. And particularly with the rise of social networking sites such as Facebook, we are willingly self–publishing details of our 'private' lives online all the time. Critics might ask why we would feel that surveillance systems in public places are an invasion of our privacy.

HW: I guess this is because surveillance is about remote policing. An extreme example of its power and dangers is the helicopter attack video released by Wikileaks in 2010. In the video you see that the American soldiers, using surveilliance cameras, believe that a Reuters cameraman on the ground is a terrorist holding a gun so they shoot him and all the people with him. Or think of the killing of Charles de Menezes in London. The police, looking at grainy CCTV images, thought that he was a terrorist. He ran when men holding guns chased him. He

didn't stop because he presumably thought the men were criminals and were going to shoot him. And it turned out that they were the police, in plain clothes, and they did shoot him. That's one way in which surveillance becomes really frightening. So it's not just about being visible – that's kind of ok. The problem arises when people consider that remote visibility is a perfect tool and make decisions that are totally removed from the situation on the ground. At its best, CCTV can record events that help prevent crime and trace criminals, but at its worst, ordinary civilians get shot dead by the police or soldiers who believe them to be terrorists. I think that's a very big gap.

JB: Franzen[11] also writes "genuine public space is a space where every citizen is welcome to be present". On first reading this seems obvious. But maybe not?

HW: It *seems* obvious but these ideas about public space are definitely being corroded. The public realm is being dismantled. Writing about the privatisation of public spaces in the UK[12], Anna Minton describes an area in Manchester in which there is a

Sentry box and CCTV camera for number plate recognition,
New Fetter Lane, 2010

large private shopping mall, and surrounding it there are streets, outdoor streets, but which are in fact privately owned by the shopping mall. The kids in this area have the highest rate of ASBOs[13] in the UK. This seems to be more than a coincidence. Really, prior to the Ring of Steel, we didn't have this sort of surveillance society. It can be seen as the beginning of the surveillance society in the UK, and because it was deemed to be so sucessful it was then exported across the rest of the city, and the country. I think this makes the Ring of Steel very significant. Today London has more CCTV cameras than New York. So my own interest in the Ring of Steel is not simply the system itself, but what it led to, in terms of helping to create a society where constant surveillance is the norm.

JB: It also led to the creation of a sequence of these banal, anonymous spaces, specifically designed to discourage people from lingering. Hertzberger, Whyte and Gehl[14] write about ways we can design the built environment to actively encourage social interaction, whereas in the City of London they are actively setting out to do the opposite. There are strategies used to prevent people from loitering, for example in McDonalds they seem to deliberately use uncomfortable seats and stark bright lights because they don't want you to linger. Is it a similar approach?

HW: It is a little different. The City of London is an affluent and commercial environment. Spaces tend to look very clean and crisp. There are plants and water features. Benches are marble rather than plastic. But, most importantly, there isn't anything social in the spaces – no coffee shops, no sandwich bars, no street vendors. And if you don't put a café on your privately owned street people will walk through; they can't get a coffee and sit down in a pool of sunlight. These areas are also closely watched. If you do anything 'wrong' you will be moved on. So I suppose it's a combination of not offering any services, or any reason to stay, and a not too overt, but still very present, private security force.

JB: Teenagers are often accused of 'loitering' when they are just 'hanging out', relaxing, something that is really important for people to do. The current 'policing' of the City seems to treat urban inhabitants like itinerant teenagers. What is it that is going on in the City that makes 'hanging out' so dangerous? And what happens to societies in which the impulse to 'hang out' is restricted?

HW: Well, the only people who are welcome in the City are those engaging with it as a capitalist environment. Much of the City has been either privatised or made into Business Improvement Districts (BIDs)[15] controlled by property developers and business owners, so the urban environment becomes solely about generating money. Consumers are welcome, but others are excluded, the city becomes sanitised as certain people become airbrushed out of certain areas. This denies the possibility of having spaces where different types of people mix. The city becomes compartmentalised rather than being an amazing urban melting pot – the joys of urban life are the unimagined possibilities of exactly these potential interactions. Any location in which just one sort of person is invited to linger is a bad idea. And of course there is also the feeling that high levels

of security actually contribute to people's sense of fear. Anna Minton writes that there is "mounting evidence that far from promoting the feelings of reassurance and safety promised in the developers' brochures, it is the blatantly security–conscious environments themselves which are responsible for growing levels of fear".[16]

JB: There are certainly parallels here with the 'regeneration' of interface zones in Belfast, which you have also documented. In particular the use of plants and water features to create this anonymous security cordon reminds me of the former battlegrounds of the interface which have now become generic business parks, car parks and hotels. In both cases the anonymous and generic is used to neutralise these territorialised spaces.

HW: Yes, there are similarities – spaces being softened, yet remaining heavily policed and with access being controlled and limited. I think that we are so accustomed to seeing images of battlegrounds that urban planners have become very careful to avoid using that language in civilian environments. So, for example, there is reinforced steel and concrete in front of Deutsche Bank on London Wall but it appears in the shape of planting boxes, and there is an increased protection zone between the road and the building but it takes the form of a 'generous' pavement. Also, on one of our walking tours we had a member of the Camden planning authority who told me about a bench they were designing that was a defence against joy riding. I'm fascinated by this idea of banal objects having a secret role.

JB: The word 'secret' crops up again and again. You liken the Ring of Steel to Bentham's Panopticon although that is a single central tower of surveillance rather than a cordon of 'secret' surveillance. Of course, *feeling* constantly watched, whether the tower is occupied or not, is what you might call the 'success' of the Panopticon system.

HW: It was Foucault's reading of the Panopticon as a kind of metaphor that I was thinking of. And the operation of Bentham's Panopticon is, in many ways, similar to how CCTV functions within contemporary society. Just

like the prisoner, we don't know when we are being watched, but we modify our behaviour accordingly. It's less direct and more codified, but it's the same thing. It is also worth noting that whereas Bentham's design was for a prison, CCTV is used to trace and track the movements of *everyone* within view in public spaces.

JB: So maybe one of the functions of the Ring of Steel today is the *semblance* or *image* of order and control rather than the actuality? Kieran Long, for instance, mentions this[17], and that post 9/11, this type of defence strategy focused on car-borne terrorism is slightly defunct. The international terror alert in 2010 was sparked by devices transported in UPS packages, for example. Often it seems that things like airport security with their 3D body scanners really just point to the impossibility of the task of defence in the modern era.

HW: In many ways controlling cars does seem defunct, but on the other hand, Mayor Bloomberg is looking into installing a similar system in Manhattan. It seems that preventing someone from driving a van packed with explosives into a key area remains a fairly useful defence strategy. In fact the system of surveillance has actually been extended much further west than we think since the introduction of the congestion charge cameras.

JB: The walking tour, with the precedent and legacy of the Situationist *derive*[18] through to more contemporary urban walkers including Iain Sinclair and Will Self, is an interesting format. Why did you decide to use it for this particular project?

HW: From the outset, the mapping process, finding the Ring of Steel, was all about walking. George gathered some maps from the internet and we started walking, trying to piece it together. We walked it for four days, figuring out how it worked and photographing every element of it as we went along. The act of walking was what made the project interesting to me, and one of the great things about doing the walking tours was that we could engage with loads of members of the general public – a broad mix of people not just the art and architecture crowd. It's interesting to hear from a taxi driver what they think. They are hugely

knowledgeable about the city streets and can talk about the Ring of Steel from the point of view of driving restrictions and regulations. The need to build up a broader picture like this is really critical.

JB: It is also interesting the way in which the walking tour has resonances with tourism and marketing campaigns to package and sell cities. The historic city walls are considered suitable fodder for the tourist but CCTV and bollards are not. There is something subversive about using the format of the walking tour to show people the 'history' of now – the politics of security in the contemporary urban environment.

HW: Actually, someone could set up a commercial walking tour to see the Ring of Steel. We've had so many people wanting to come on the tour and, interestingly, they were not tourists but mostly people who live and work in London, open to new ways of reading the urban landscape and wanting to gain deeper understanding of what has happened and is happening in the City. The walking tour format gives a real sense of the border line at the edge of the City of London and contemporary power politics

Roman remains of the London Wall lie in the basement
of Merrill Lynch, King Edward Street, 2010

Private CCTV camera within the Ring of Steel,
Spital Square, 2010

and links this to the historical politics of the Roman/Medieval wall which consistently intersects with the contemporary Ring.

JB: Of course, there is a rich resonance here between the traditions of cartography and power. Stephen Graham writes that: "One can readily forget that many of the world's cities originate, at least in part, as military constructions. The history of the imagination, construction and inhabitation of urban places cannot be told without considering the central role of such places as the critical sites of militarised power and control."[19] The very same thing might be said of mapping.

HW: Yes I agree. Historically people have always made maps as tools for conquering swathes of land. When I worked in Belfast I became interested in what was excluded from maps. Interface walls, for example, are not included on any ordnance survey maps. Obviously they are marked on military maps, but because they are technically classed as temporary structures they are excluded from maps in the public domain. So in a way, with the Ring of Steel map, we're questioning that idea of what is 'suitable' to include or exclude on a map for the general public.

JB: What do you think is the key issue in hand for the public?

HW: The idea of 'fortress urbanism'[20] really needs to be addressed by a much wider group than just urban planners. The way our cities operate should be of concern to everyone living within them. The Ring of Steel has led to the normalisation of fortress urbanism, privatised space and CCTVs in London today. The City of London has become a model where techniques are adapted from conflict zones and modified for civilian use. As Anna Minton clearly details, this is now feeding out across the rest of the country.[21] Stephen Graham warns against viewing the spaces and infrastructures of city life as "passive backdrops to the propagation of violence or the construction of security". He believes that "the way cities and urban spaces are produced and restructured ... actually help[s] constitute these strategies and fantasies".[22] Ultimately, we need to think more about the effect that these kinds of places are having on our society.

1. The Ring of Steel is a network of counter–terrorist installations that was installed from 1993 onwards to protect the City of London. Created in the aftermath of the IRA bombing of Bishopsgate, the so–called 'Ring' aims to prevent and track terrorist activity targeting the City of London.

2. See the full project and the 3D map online at: www.henriettawilliams.com.

3. An interface is a Northern Irish term defined as: "the boundary between Catholic (Nationalist) and Protestant (Unionist) areas, especially where two highly segregated areas are situated close to each other, are known as interface areas. In many such areas of Belfast the interface is marked by a physical barrier known as a 'peaceline'." See http://cain.ulst.ac.uk.

4. Jon Coaffee, *Terrorism, Risk and the Global City* (Farnham: Ashgate, 2009).

5. Stephen Graham, *Cities Under Siege: The New Military Urbanism* (London: Verso Books, 2010).

6. *ibid.*, Coaffee (2009).

7. www.henriettawilliams.com.

8. *ibid.*, Graham (2010).

9. The area around Snowden Street is a perfect example of the privatisation of public streets described by Anna Minton: "As the twenty–first century corporate estates take over large parts of the city, the last decade has seen a huge shift in landownership, away from the streets, public places and buildings in public ownership and towards the creation of new private estates, primarily given over to shopping and office complexes, which, while not actually gated, feel very much like separate enclaves." Anna Minton, *Ground Control* (London: Penguin Books, 2009).

10. Jonathan Franzen, *Imperial Bedroom: How to Be Alone* (London: Fourth Estate, 2002).

11. *ibid.*, Franzen (2002).

12. *ibid.*, Minton (2009).

13. An Anti–Social Behaviour Order or ASBO is a civil order made against a person who has been shown, on the balance of evidence, to have engaged in anti–social behaviour. See http://en.wikipedia.org.

14. See writings by Herman Hertzberger, William Whyte and Jan Gehl.

15. "BIDs are a way of running the city which is based on the type of management models taught at business school ... [it] is geared towards creating the optimum trading environment." *ibid.*, Minton (2009).

16. *ibid.*, Minton (2009).

17. Kieran Long, 'So can the secret Ring of Steel save the City from terrorism?', *Evening Standard*, 15 October 2010.

18. "One of the basic situationist practices is the *dérive* [literally: 'drifting'], a technique of rapid passage through varied ambiances. *Dérives* involve playful–constructive behavior and awareness of psychogeographical effects, and are thus quite different from the classic notions of journey or stroll." Guy Debord, 'Theory of the Dérive', *Internationale Situationiste*, No. 2, December 1958.

19. *ibid.*, Graham (2010).

20. *ibid.*, Minton (2009).

21. *ibid.*, Minton (2009).

22. *ibid.*, Graham (2010).

AGENCY

4

Introduction

DEEPA NAIK & TRENTON OLDFIELD

Even if you tried to pretend it wasn't the case, an undeniably very large percentage of the history of the human world is the history of slavery and the subsequent attempts to break free, to escape tyranny in its many guises. In being 'free' the endeavour is to gain (or regain) and then strive to maintain control and 'agency' over one's own life.[1] How much traction does one have 'over' one's own life, from everyday actions to self-defining how one wishes to live? What are the contexts or conditions in which we live that help to determine our lives?

Despite slavery being illegal in all but a few countries, there are, today, greater numbers of people enslaved than at the height of the trans–Atlantic slave trade. The percentage of people enslaved is lower, though the overall number is higher.[2] And almost equally pernicious is the fact that today, despite claims of advanced 'civilisation', vast populations of people are indentured workers in cities: domestic workers, ship builders, labourers, drivers, nannies, factory workers and general labourers. In addition, many are now indentured by debt and as a result tens of millions have little to no agency over their lives for the foreseeable future. Furthermore, it is often the practice that debt, if not cleared, is inherited, forcing a debtor's children into servitude and labour.

Since the 'financial catastrophe' diagnosed in late 2008, unemployment in the UK has increased by one third; youth unemployment has doubled with the number of 16–24 year olds without a job in the UK rising to 1.04 million.[3] At the same time, for those who do have jobs, wages have been significantly decreased, by 3.5%, failing to keep pace with inflation.[4] And a recent government policy now forces the unemployed to work for their unemployment benefits through 'placements' with large companies including supermarkets.[5] Prisoners in the UK are now working for £3 a day for multinational companies.[6] In Greece, the situation is worse with wages reduced by 45% and unemployment tripling from 400,000 to 1.2 million people.[7] Americans have experienced an 8.5% increase in unemployment and, depending on the sector, a reduction of between 3% and 20% in their wages.[8] There is tremendous downward pressure on wages and salaries. Without decent wages and with compulsory labour programmes, people, particularly young people, have significantly less agency than many of their parents experienced. People are worried that the parliament–authorised 'austerity measures' could mean a return to workhouses and grinding insistent poverty. There is palpable concern that people are once again losing control over their everyday lives; their real or perceived sense of agency is decreasing.

The pursuit of agency (happiness?) and the problematisation of citizenship was one of the driving motivations for establishing This Is Not A Gateway. We refer to this impetus in our introduction 'Emergent Agitation: Knowledge as Urban Politics' in *Critical Cities: Volume 1*,[9] where we argue that: "Clear and un-romanticised understandings of the dynamics of power are more pertinent than ever as people increasingly assert their right to agency in their lives."[10] It was foreseeable that the always–present imperative to be able to determine one's own future was only going to increase in urgency and vigour.

There was also an awareness that something remarkable was happening across the planet. While cities were increasingly becoming home for more people, evidence showed there were fewer opportunities for critical discussions, debates and exhibitions.[11] Moreover, there is a serious decline in respect for and faith in the parliamentary systems, political parties and supporting 'democratic institutions'. A serious and pronounced democratic deficit exists, one that will likely be the defining issue of the 21st century. This democratic deficit is intrinsic to the proposition of the Four Horsemen of the Apocalypse, who, according to Slavoj Zizek, currently represent the worldwide ecological crisis, imbalances within the economic system, the biogenetic revolution, and exploding social divisions and ruptures.[12]

The five essays in this chapter provide us with direct experience of specific events where individuals and groups have either resisted attempts at reducing their agency or set out to forge new possibilities for greater control over their lives. Quite by chance all five contributions are set in London. It is a city of polar realities.

On May Day 2010, four separate protests, representing the Four Horsemen of the Apocalypse, converged on Parliament Square in Westminster, London. They held a people's assembly that evolved into what is now known as the 'Democracy Village'. The village existed for many months though eventually, like many other sites of protest, it was brutally cleared by private security guards, with the police looking on. For close to two years afterwards Parliament Square was surrounded by 8-foot fences – Westminster Council and the Greater London Authority feared the activists would return.

One of the protagonists was Siraj Izhar and his essay 'Democracy Village: The Nomos and Topos of the Post-Political' is a brilliant treatise on his experience of village life, what it means to camp, and how mainstream contemporary politics is the suspension of democracy and introduction of a risk management strategy in its stead. He reflects on the 'extralegal' forms of political agency and what it means to confront a corrupt institution in its own garden. The essay reproduces several communications directly related to the Democracy Village. These include a conversation between two recently returned British soldiers, the proceedings of the court case in which the Mayor of London evoked legal proceedings to remove the people's assembly, an insight into the fracture between the camp and long-term protesters Brian Haw and Barbara Tucker, and the interaction between Stuart Holmes and Justice Griffiths Williams. It's raw, honest, provocative.

The following paper 'Resistance, then What? Reflections of the Spirit of '68 Group' brings together individual statements and a conversation between members of a reading group that formed as a result of a workshop at the TINAG festival.[13] The premise of the text is that there is deficit of agency and an urgent need for resistance to the self-generating momentum of the social and political elites' increasing inequality. Their questions, motivated by the failures of the Spring of '68, set out to rip apart the political methodologies employed in recent political protests and movements in Western Europe.

The first part is comprised of individual contributions on a specific issue. Judith Ryser, who was on the Paris barricades, explores whether the conditions for revolution exist at present and wonders if more incremental and experimental initiatives that can be shared and tested in anticipation of revolutionary times, might be more realistic. Romeo DelaCruz draws on his personal experience of revolutionary Philippines and asks why the protesting UK students were so surprised when a politician said one thing before an election and did another thing after the election. He suggests a "solidaric general protest" initiative is needed, rather than individual protests that focus on specific issues and by definition leave others out. Christina Garrido effectively demolishes the happily held consensus that the 1992 Barcelona Olympics was 'a good thing'. Furthermore we learn how the post–Olympic resistance, which was largely performance and *in situ*, was either laughed at or appropriated by the big museums and art institutions. She argues the '68 protests established a long inheritance of failed revolutionary methodologies that undoubtedly ought to be left behind. Richard Carter contrasts the context of '68 with the 'theatre of spectacle' on our screens today and wonders if the protests in North Africa, on the UK's streets and elsewhere are "instinctual responses of the intimidated ... or the authentic corollary of radical free thought".

The papers in this chapter are important provocations to an urgent and much needed discussion around the role of protest, the methodologies employed and their lack of success in producing social justice let alone revolutionary transformations. More provocation is needed, particularly where ideas on revolutionary methodologies remain romanticised despite and possibly because of their continual transformative failure.

The focus of David Rosenberg's essay is a pivotal confrontation that took place in East London in October of 1936. This was an act of defence rather than revolutionary action. However, it was one of the few defeats of fascism before the horrors of World War II. 'East End Battleground: Defending Multicultural Spaces and Lives' is an insight into and a reminder of how other people's agendas can quickly engulf an area, a group of people, or both, and sometimes quite unexpectedly. Control over one's own life is often dependent on seemingly unrelated shifts and turns elsewhere.

The essay takes us onto the streets of the largely Jewish neighbourhood around Brick Lane in the mid 1930s on the day it was surrounded by four columns of 'black shirts', the 'uniformed' members of the British Union of Fascists led by Sir Oswald Mosley. David Rosenberg details what we now know as the Battle of Cable Street. In doing so we learn a great deal about Oswald Mosley, who seems to have been a sordid political opportunist of unrelenting self-belief; a member of most political parties until irresolvable disagreements, and seducer of both the landed wealthy and the cotton workers, miners and unemployed.

Realising it might be difficult to penetrate East London, the four columns were marshalled within the City of London, with the support of many hundreds of specifically drafted-in police. On their first attempt to enter via Whitechapel High Street the fascists were stopped by thousands of people creating a human wall strengthened with abandoned trams and vehicles. Mosley's 'black shirts' retreated to the sanctuary of the City of London, regrouped, and then tried to enter the East End along the very straight though narrow Cable Street. Despite significant police support for the fascists they were defeated in a brutal battle. Police arrested 84 people – 79 were anti-fascists, and a good number of them were sent to jail. In the Battle of Cable Street many thousands of people put their bodies on the line in order to successfully defend the spaces for self-determining multicultural lives in East London. Organised political party-based fascism did not recover in Britain. Just 75 years old, this is a story of such importance it might well have been told in the opening ceremony of the 2012 London Olympics.

Notably, David Rosenberg connects contemporary questions around 'broken Britain', the so-called failure of multiculturalism and David Cameron's cultural policies, to the political propaganda that unfailing prevails during difficult economic periods. Despite its much-touted promise of individualism and independence, hyper-capitalism – in its pursuit of efficiency, effectiveness, monopoly and shareholder dividends – systematically deletes spaces for non-conformists and independent-minded people. Small independent businesses that address local needs, usually run by local people (often a family) in small shops, are a source of great confusion to corporate capitalists. The independent cornershop, made famous and romanticised across the world because Margaret Thatcher's father owned one, is very difficult to find in Britain today. Temporary street markets and vendors are generally tolerated as picturesque, 'ethnic' and easily moveable. It is this constellation that provides the backdrop to Ruth Allen and Mital Patel's contribution, 'We Write the Story of Our Town: A Folk Tale of 21st-Century Tottenham'. It is a razor sharp confrontational exposé of the methodologies, including storytelling and future archiving, employed by the Wards Corner Community Coalition in order to 'wrong-foot' a paternalistic, belittling and disingenuous local authority and property developer.

Wards Corner is what planners today call a 'mixed-use community'. Along with 'high-density urban living' it is currently the ultimate (rhetorical) aim of every planner, developer and government.[14] The large Wards Corner building includes over 60 independent shops, many homes and an indoor food and produce market. A property developer wishes to bulldoze everything and replace the existing mixed-use neighbourhood with over 200 market-price apartments and a number of large floor plan shops along the street.

Located in Tottenham, not far from where London's police shot and killed an unarmed young man, Mark Duggan, while he was sitting in the backseat of a taxi, Wards Corner is also not far from where the 2011 London 'insurrections' first ignited. It is in the London Borough of Haringey, a council that has fashioned itself, as the authors so brilliantly summarise, as "downtrodden, neglected and helpless" and pleads for the "dynamism, energy and creativity" of the private sector to help solve its seemingly endless conundrums. The authors also succinctly explain the psychological erosion of agency that occurs in these conditions:

"One of the reasons the corporations are successful in selling us consumerist dreams (including the dream of corporate regeneration) is because they develop and then offer to cure our internalised negative views of ourselves and our communities. We are 'not good enough', 'not affluent enough'. Tottenham has been relentlessly fed this sort of view of itself for too long, by the press, by politicians, by officers of the council. It is demoralising and inhibits actions. We become vulnerable to almost colonial intrusion from outside forces as our confidence and our ability to tell our own story is diminished."

This scenario is so familiar and regular it's hard to imagine why it wouldn't simply go ahead. The paper shows, however, that despite ongoing attempts at alienation the coalition was able to bring together a broad collection of local people, with sometimes quite different interests, and then set about meticulously turning the disregard for their capabilities and humanity back on the council and developer, exposing their disrespect and contempt, and in the process increasing the community's agency and group cohesion. The developers, the borough and the 'regeneration' teams have been wrong–footed by the Wards Corner community taking the lead, creating a community plan and pre–empting shifts in tactics.

Contemporary tactics for revolutionary change is a subject seldom discussed and, it seems, of little interest to today's activists. At least, here in Western Europe, there appears to be a nostalgia or some kind of blindness that makes it difficult for people to move beyond the methods of the mid to late 1800s. Perhaps it has something to do with the new and impressive abundance of dissenting materials that appeared at that time thanks to the availability the printing press and the invention of photography? More recent revolutionary struggles, like those to end colonial imperialism in the mid 1950s, might be at least as useful? That said, it is difficult to find one organisation that states a revolutionary aim as explicitly as William Morris's declaration for the Socialist League in 1885:

> *"Fellow citizens, we come before you as a body advocating the principles of revolutionary international socialism; that is, we seek a change in the basis of society – a change which would destroy the distinctions of classes and nationalities."*

Hassan Mahamdallie's paper 'William Morris – The Practical Utopian' examines one of the great fighters for increased personal agency. Author of a recently published book[15] and lively and provocative session on Morris at the festival[16], Hassan tackles head on the assumption that William Morris was "a utopian who sought refuge from industrialism in a world of medieval fantasy". Morris was born into significant wealth, educated at the University of Oxford and "designed expensive wallpaper" but, as Hassan Mahamdallie carefully shows, it is precisely these contradictory features that are useful in comprehending elements of this tumultuous period. It was a time when there was a great number of individual 'upper and middle class traitors'. They included Marx and Engels, among many others. Rather than maintain and perpetuate the status quo, these individuals, in different and often contradictory ways, set about increasing the agency and independence of others.

Morris is well known for his decorative arts and little known for his revolutionary socialism and powerful novels. We learn he was an internationalist when at the time imperialism was the dominant ideology. He was ardently anti-war and, as a result, denigrated by much of the establishment. And he was committed to improving workers' living conditions and particularly concerned with the forced movement of people from the countryside to cities:

> *"It is profit which draws men into enormous unmanageable aggregations called towns, for instance; profit which crowds them up when they are there into quarters without gardens or open spaces; profit which won't take the most ordinary precautions against wrapping a whole district in a cloud of sulphurous smoke; which turns beautiful rivers into filthy sewers, which condemns all but the rich to live in houses idiotically cramped and confined at the best, and at the worst in houses for whose wretchedness there is no name."[17]*

Morris's writings offer many ideas and practices that are highly relevant for conditions today. The people's revolutions in Tunisia and Egypt and the recent insurrections in the cities of England, Greece and Spain have been exhilarating moments of possibility and agency. Everywhere around the world there is the presence, often on the streets, of people insisting on having greater agency over their lives, be it the students in Quebec, the indigenous peoples of Peru or the miners of South Africa. To re–use a phrase from journalist Paul Mason: "it's kicking off everywhere."[18] It is, as we all know, also a time of considerable oppression, with 'austerity' and 'financial crisis' being used to significantly reduce wages, limit welfare and criminalise dissent and revolution. How can cities ensure democracy and prosperity for their citizens? What mechanisms and methods might we employ, as tens of millions more people live on less and less surface area, to enable people to increase their independence and ability to determine their own lives?

1. John Shand (ed.), *Central Issues of Philosophy* (Blackwell Publishing: West Sussex, 2009).
2. Kevin Bales, Zoe Trodd and Alex Kent Williamson, *Modern Slavery: The Secret World of 27 Million People* (Portobello Books: London, 2009).
3. House of Commons Library, Economic Indicators Research Paper, 01 May 2012.
4. James Ball, 'UK incomes fall 3.5% in real terms, ONS study reveals', *The Guardian*, 23 November 2011.
5. Shiv Malik, 'Million jobless may face six months unpaid work or have benefits stopped', *The Guardian*, 29 July 2012.
6. Shiv Malik, 'Prisoners paid £3 a day to work at call centre that has fired other staff', *The Guardian*, 8 August 2012.
7. David Gow, 'Greeks face further wage cuts as price of latest bailout', *The Guardian*, 21 February 2012.
8. Sudeep Reddy, 'Downturn's Ugly Trademark: Steep, Lasting Drop in Wages', *Wall Street Journal*, 11 January 2011.
9. Deepa Naik and Trenton Oldfield (eds), *Critical Cities: Ideas, Knowledge and Agitation Volume 1* (Myrdle Court Press: London, 2009) pp. 14–21.
10. *ibid.*, Naik and Oldfield (2009) p. 16.
11. Since 2007 we have been collecting data on urban forums, including price, professional fields and communities represented, gender and ethnicity of speakers. We call this research 'Keys to the City'.
12. Slavoj Zizek, *Living In The End Times* (Verso: London, 2011).
13. The workshop initiated by Judith Ryser was called '1968 to Now: Can we ever progress?' and was held on 24 October 2010 at Hanbury Hall, London.
14. For more about this prevailing urban development strategy see the section 'Erase, Stretch,

Relinquish'.

15. Hassan Mahamdallie, *Crossing the River of Fire: The Socialism of William Morris* (Redwords: London, 2008).

16. Hassan Mahamdallie hosted a session called 'William Morris – Street revolutionary and urban visionary' on 23 October 2010 at Hanbury Hall, London.

17. A.L. Morton, *Political Writings of William Morris* (Lawrence & Wishart: London, 1979) p. 153.

18. Paul Mason, *Why It's Kicking Off Everywhere: The New Global Revolutions* (Verso: London, 2012).

Democracy Village

The Nomos and Topos of the Post-Political

SIRAJ IZHAR

I

Squaddy 1: It's tit for tat. It's no disrespect to what our guys do, they do the same thing, it's tit for tat. We're proud of what we do and they're proud of what they do ... you knowwhatImean, it's never gonna work, our boys do what they do best and they do exactly the same, it's just one of em things, it's tit for tat and it always will be.
Squaddy 2: Long as our government remembers to protect our troops, yeah.
Squaddy 1: Government do! Right, I'm not going to be a fucking asshole here ... I went to I–rak in 2006, right, with bare minimal equipment. I go to Afghanistan September, I can see the massive difference in kit, weaponry to fight the Taliban.
Squaddy 2: Everyone should have it.
Squaddy 1: Everyone does get it.
Squaddy 2: They don't.
Squaddy 1: People in this country can't see what we get, where have you been?
Squaddy 2: Kandahar, mate.
Squaddy 1: Kandahar. Tell you what, I will walk away before I punch you out now.
Squaddy 2: You ain't talking right.
Squaddy 1: Yeah, I will walk away before I punch you out.
Squaddy 2: Yeah right, fuck off then.

Peter Sloterdijk[1] wrote the fable about an inflatable parliament, an air–conditioned tent, that could be parachuted onto invaded cultures and countries like Afghanistan: instant democracy and its infrastructures delivered from up above. Military adventurism always returns home in some perverse form and here it's the human face of the blowback, servicemen abandoned by the state engaged in drink–fuelled catfights with nothing else to do. We are in Parliament Square, Westminster. Big Ben hovers above, a giant moon glowing on a campsite of some 40 tents. Unlike Sloterdijk's fable, the tents here have emerged from below as it were, popping up as pathological mushrooms from the cracks within society and its legal frameworks, evading the endlessly devolved myriad of market–led new laws, patched up for several years by anti–terrorism laws and new policing measures like SOCPA (Serious Organised Crime and Police Act 2005), ASBOs (Anti–Social Behaviour Orders) and so forth.

Established within all the narratives of meltdown, the Democracy Village press release of May Day 2010 stated that the Four Horsemen of the Apocalypse would converge on Parliament Square, from different corners of the city, to convene a People's Assembly with the decree: "The War in Afghanistan is at an end, Parliament Square is now occupied to ensure implementation of this legislation by the people."

Lacking any infrastructure or amenities, without sanitation facilities, the camp has to sustain itself day and night through 'skip–diving' for discarded waste food and furtively accessing local hospitals, hostels and bars for toilets.

Since Guantanamo, the camp in its various forms has been the subject of renewed focus in contemporary political discourse, most recently theorised by Agamben to define the relationship between state and citizen, between sovereign power and human subject. For Agamben, the camp is not an anomaly, a historical aberration, but in fact the "hidden matrix" of our political system, its *nomos*, its power materialised in multiple forms.[2] The significance of the camp is, thus, not so much as a physical entity but as a symbolic one. The camp is the site that figurates and fixes the border between the subject and the state, between us as bare life, bare human existence without political representation, and us as citizens within a political constitution. The camp as such is the all–pervasive defining space of the political.

For contemporary activism, the camp becomes performative as the site to re–engage the dynamics of the relationship between the state and the subject citizen, the testing space for possible political constellations and forms of political agency. The camp already has a rich lineage in activism, as in Greenham Common during the 70s Cold War era, but in 2010 activism operates in a markedly changed environment. Now there is no Cold War but an unending War on Terror, internalised within law and order, extending the reach of the state into the privacy of everyday life. This is supposedly the 'post–political'.

The post–political refers to the way the state today has relinquished much of its control to private interests, what Jacques Rancière describes as the "suspension of politics, the reduction of state to mere police agent servicing the (consensually established) needs of market forces".[3] Thus political governance today operates primarily through processes of risk management; in other words, governance no longer seeks political solutions to political problems, but instead attempts to break down the political into management control exercises, often through the creation of new laws and bylaws that regulate citizens' behaviour and reduce potential disorder. The administration of society is no longer contained by institutions with identifiable boundaries, such certainties as schools and parliament, but mediated through new technologies. The borders of institutions progressively dissolve with the advent of what Deleuze described as the "societies of control" in which digital communications and technologies produce the organisational space and with it a new topology of power.[4] With the society of control, power is dispersed and pervasive, there is no longer an inside or outside. The matrix of the new *topos* is total control and total transparency.

In the post–political, transparency becomes the source of distributed anxiety, which is the base matter of the society of control. If the camp is the hidden matrix of the *nomos*, transparency constitutes the matrix of the *topos* of the society of control.

II

Mayor of London versus Democracy Village
Royal Courts of Justice at the Strand

The Mayor and the GLA (Greater London Authority) seek injunctions against the Democracy Village camp in order to repossess Parliament Square. Simon Grinter, Head of Squares Management for the GLA, takes the witness stand, answering questions from his counsel QC Ashley Underwood for the Mayor of London. He bemoans the loss of his capacity to exercise his duties, unable to make the square available to officially sanctioned demonstrations and to tourists. He is distressed by the damage to the turf, and describes the welcoming desk set up by Democracy Village as a control desk for monitoring who comes onto the square. One can palpably sense the pain of separation of a man from his duties for the care and control of Parliament Square. He is the honest broker caught in-between in this conflict. But the cross-examination from Democracy Village defendants begins.

Friend', who has no home, asks, "Would the GLA consider an application from someone who has no money to pay for the public liability insurance to get your permission to protest? Someone who has no address? Where do I fit in your form? Would you ever approve?"

"Extremely unlikely," confesses Grinter.

Friend continues, referring to the scale of human damage and ecological destruction being wrought on the planet by government policy, in particular its military adventures abroad and the ongoing killing of civilians: "Would you say it is possible to commit a lesser crime to prevent a greater crime?" Simon Grinter is baffled.

Friend tries to help, maintaining that his presence in Parliament Square is necessary to bring the government to account: "If you were asked in a death camp to take your family to the gas chambers, would you do it?"

The judge intercedes on the Grinter's behalf, declaring these matters not relevant to the court.

But such questions continue with fellow Democracy Village defendant Professor Chris Knight. "Do you think the democracy protesters in China applied for public liability insurance for Tiananmen Square?" he asks with reference to the Mayor's bylaw requirements.

Again the judge steps in. "Don't answer that question," he tells Simon Grinter, and addressing Professor Knight, "He speaks for policy, not the reasons behind it. He is an employee." Then, just to remind everyone how the judicial process works, the judge adds an advisory note for the court speaking very slowly: "Parliament makes laws. Judges interpret them."

Democracy Village as a living village was set up to confront the other 'parliament' across the road, to confront institutional power with village life. The proximity of confrontation, through the occupation of Parliament Square, is essential – it forces an intimate correspondence between space and power through the sharing of the same *topos*. The activism as an intervention is to force this intimacy on the state, to conjoin through the camp the *topos* and the *nomos* of the political. The *topos* is the spatial dimension inscribed into the structure of the state, of sovereignty; the *nomos* is the socially normalised ordering of experience, of what is taken for granted, as self evident, the law internalised within culture.

The apparatus of state will seek to both deny the conjunction and reinstate its distance, but post–political sovereignty is a double–edged entity. Its *modus operandi* is damage limitation which safeguards vested executive interests through compartmentalisation and devolution. In the case of Parliament Square, the title to the grass is held by Her Majesty the Queen, the pavement is vested in the Westminster City Council. The management of the square is the duty of the Mayor of London's office, the GLA, who manage their responsibilities through the Trafalgar Square and Parliament Square bylaws 2002. These bylaws regulate the conduct of the public and run to some nine pages with an exhaustive list of conditions that all citizens must abide by: to *not*, without prior consent from the mayor, make a speech; to *not* exhibit any notice; to *not* engage in any political activity; to *not* erect a tent ... and so forth. With these bylaws, the mayor now seeks an injunction through the courts against Democracy Village to prevent the villagers from camping in the square. The bylaws, as a classic illustration of the model of political governance, provide a bounded legal space, an encapsulation, which renders all arguments outside their specific terms out of jurisdiction to any activity in Parliament Square.

For Democracy Village, engaging the legal process in the form of such 'juridico–discursive' model of power is a diversion. But it is nonetheless a necessary diversion for it is productive of the space and the time to embed the village as reality, to experiment in the making of *its* social imaginary in the public domain. But the law courts are not the site of activism or political agency *per se*. Rather the camp is the real site, the camp embodies a rejection of the state's way of being, and asserts a countervailing *nomos* of a completely different way of being. But how to formulate this way of being: through resistance, through the alternative, through rejection? What are the ways of constituting this? Whilst resistance and rejection are easier to envisage, the alternative imaginary is a more complex construct.

However, new political imaginaries cannot come into being through theory – they require a primary *jump* into reality, a jump that involves a lived theatre of engagement and intervention.

In this sense, the camp with its transitional nature functions as a social device of a political imaginary in the form of a transitional *phenomenon*, which enables

Legal bundles from the Mayor of London's lawyers, Eversheds,
delivered to democracy villagers by anonymous couriers in time
for breakfast reading, 2010, SIRAJ IZHAR

a bridge onto a yet unarticulated space beyond the present. This space then draws in the narratives, illusion and disillusion, as intermediate areas of experiencing to which inner reality and external reality both contribute in making it real.

In his essay on 'Transitional Objects and Transitional Phenomena', psychoanalyst Donald Winnicott sketches out the mother–infant relationship and the role of a transitional object in the development of the next phases of relationship.[5] In one of his diagrams, Winnicott illustrates the space between the mother and the infant as mediated by illusion as "the infant can not know at first what is to be created". The illusion is an external reality that corresponds to the infant's own capacity to create. Later the illusion is replaced by a transitional object which creates a neutral area of possible experience, one that is not structured by normative codes of reality acceptance; this creates a direct continuity between one phase and another which comes into being. So it is with the relationship between the state or sovereignty and the subject citizen or bare life in the creation of new social imaginaries.

Articulation of space in–between the relational entities – the mother and infant, the state and new forms of subject–hood – is a primary undertaking which requires the invention and intervention of material means: the transitional objects and phenomena. If these do not exist, they have to be invented and find a place and space in reality before they can be a channel for what is currently beyond the present state of experience. Otherwise the potential remains in the sphere of illusion.

It is through creative political agency that such production of new forms of the transitional for bridging the space of the political materialises. This takes place, becomes concrete, through situations which, in themselves, form the loci of becoming, combining the aesthetic and the political.

III

It's late evening, mid summer. Within the tent, one can hear a voice periodically: "Stop the murder!" Then again: "Stop the murder!" On leaving the tent, one can see it's Dan from the village holding up a placard and walking anti–clockwise round Parliament Square whilst traffic flows round him clockwise. The Parliament Square Heritage wardens with their Chubb uniforms, emblematic of the extent of the privatisation of our culture, meekly watch from the north end. But it is only a matter of time before a policeman crosses

over from the House of Commons and threatens to pull Dan over for breach of the peace. Villagers come to his rescue. Then out of nowhere, another voice, this time over a megaphone, booms out. It's Barbara Tucker, emerging out from her station where she and Brian Haw have faced down the House of Commons for 10 years. They feel trespassed upon, their own campaign undermined by Democracy Village and dragged into court by the GLA.
"You have absolute disregard for our feelings."
"You don't have any feelings for how fucked the world is."
"You don't have any feelings for us, dragging us into your corrupt proceedings ..."
Brian Haw follows behind with his crutches, holding up his video camera. The policeman is disorientated but continues, "Once more and I will arrest you." There is confusion. Who is speaking to whom? But it's common knowledge that Brian Haw and Barbara Tucker are authorised to use the megaphone though it's usually turned on the parliamentarians across the road; for them this is a diversion. The policeman returns to Dan: "I am working for a living, forget the uniform, as a civil person I want you to keep quiet. I know about you, your protest."
"We pay your wages, it's not about you, us, it's about the bigger things in life."
"Good little lambs, completely indifferent to others, coming up with fairy stories."
Barbara Tucker intrudes once more on the megaphone, and retreats. It's over to the policeman. "I will give you one last warning. Keep quiet or I will arrest you," he says, pulling out the radio to summon support.
"I will kiss the ground as you want me to," Dan pleads. Then, "My brother," he says, addressing the policeman, "See the little stubs, I was born in Brazil, the CIA distributed crack to support the military." Dan pulls out his stub of an arm. The policeman softens. A conversation ensues. The policeman gives his name: Edmund. Dan carries on letting Edmund the policeman know that Glaxo were using untested drugs in Brazil and that had aggravated his condition considerably. "So why can't you sue Glaxo?" Edmund asks.

The realpolitics of life in the camp was that of a village initiated by activists but progressively populated by the homeless and those living on the margins of life – the junkie, the alcoholic ... Democracy Village, as an open autonomous space, brought all sections of life onto Parliament Square and provided a haven. While this raised questions not only about the value of political agency of those living on the margins within political campaigns, at the same time it created opportunities for activists to articulate the philosophy of governance of the village, the *nomos* of the square, *its* laws of exemption, *its* structures of inclusion and exclusion.

Deployment of the camp as a transitional object enables a bridge onto a new phase of the political through the making of an intermediary space of experience. If this space is deterritorialised by new agents, how does it withstand the forces of fragmentation and thereafter enable a meaningful evolution into the new imaginary rather than collapsing into regression and fragmentation?

In this sense, the inter–relationship with lives lived on the margins of social, political, cultural, economic and geographical borders is instrumental to the making of the camp. Through the inclusion of what may be called 'performative marginality', the day–to–day fault lines emerge within the life of the camp and out of these the multiple identities of life and politics, their coagulation. What is otherwise rendered useless or invisible by the state *nomos*, by the managerial processes of the post–political where the excluded "is prevented from politicising his predicament of exclusion",[6] becomes a working part of the framework of the village and the building of its autonomous politics as democracy.

This is the camp in its second phase as praxis, beyond the initial jump, the intervention, the occupation and the making of the transitional. As praxis, the *process* of democracy begins with the embryonic unit, with the single person's agency, and then, on engagement with another, enters what R.D. Laing in *Politics of Experience* called "the field of inter–experience". Through the building blocks of the field of inter–experience, we comprehend why political process often results in the alienation of experience.

R.D. Laing articulates the basic understanding in the field of inter–experience as this: "Your experience of me is invisible to me. My experience of you is invisible to you." Equally, "The other person's behaviour is an experience of mine; my behaviour is an experience of the other."[7] Thus, while the political is rooted in experience, in terms of experience we are invisible to each other; thus so much of human behaviour is in the form of unilateral or bilateral attempts to eliminate experience. In its socialised form, politics is often the negation of experience, political reality the alienation of experience.

The praxis progressively evolves into a new phase, beyond its confrontation with the state to an exploration of practice itself, which can contain the democratic possibilities for a different model of politics – the how–to institute the social theatres for a politics of integration of experience. Political agency or activism that defines itself by resistance or protest against identifiable hegemonic entities, like corporations or military, is easier to articulate and valorise as a sort of foreground; agency that involves the making of ontological realities at the level of experience requires a greater complexity of social forms, involving dimensions that are often hidden and remain in the background.

IV

Democracy Village defendant Stuart Holmes, in response to why he is in Parliament Square, presents evidence on the effect of depleted uranium on Iraqi babies. He has photographs, documents, but after a few minutes the judge cuts him short, "It's simply not relevant." To the bylaws.
Holmes protests, holding up photos of a deformed baby, "Your Honour, are we getting a fair trial?"
"It's not a free for all," Justice Griffiths Williams replies.
Holmes then asks, "Are you ex–military?"
The judge is taken aback. He goes quiet for a few moments. The QCs and lawyers look on.
"Territorial Army 1967," he declares.

Another improvised question comes on the afternoon of 22 June from Louis James Stainee, who has infiltrated the courtroom possibly under the ruse of a being a Mackenzie friend (a lay person who may attend court to assist a defendant).
"Are you under oath?" he asks the startled judge.
"I am not a witness, I am not required to take the oath."
"Then you might be an imposter? Will you take the oath?"
"Under what law?"
"Under Common Law."
The judge asks Louis James Stainee to leave the court. The 'Mackenzie friend' stands his ground. The judge then declares it is impossible to continue till Stainee is removed.
"All stand."
The judge retires from the court. The entire legal machinery has juddered to a standstill.

Louis James Stainee is ecstatic.
"Man overboard! Man overboard!"
The ranks of legal professionals, barristers and solicitors look on in incredulous silence.
Finally two muscular court attendants arrive. The courtroom ergonomics are pretty tight and Louis is holding firm. Verbal exchanges get progressively nastier by the minute.
"Get out of my way."
"Shut your mouth."
The court attendants make a grab; Louis bangs his head.
Someone calls out, "Assault! Help!"
Another, "Call the ambulance please."
But Louis is dragged out. The court is sombre. In half an hour the judge returns in a dark mood. The public gallery he insists must be vacated henceforth and so it is. There is a brief return to the tedium of due process the following day.
Barristers ask, "Please refer to page 110 of the legal bundle ..." and so forth, followed by the shuffling of pages, the quiet passing of memos ...

With the post–political, the institution of the political is marked by what Kierkegaard would describe as "blocked ontology", "ontology at a standstill".[8] If political ontology is blocked by an endlessly circular due process of the post–political, containing all dialogue within its terms, what stratagems, what devices, what means do we use to get beyond it? Interventions are actions that are invariably temporal. Courtroom dramas, however eventful, always conclude with the predictable.

Transcending contingency, temporality may start with the transitional object to establish a grasp of the unknown and progressively figurate, in the field of inter–experience, to lead to new types of practice, but it has to culminate with an integration of the aesthetics of politics and the politics of aesthetics – a *sensus communis*, a common sensibility, to carry forward.

The aesthetics in activism is often perceived as the absence of form and structure, but only because it evolves through fundamentally different processes of mediation with life to that of normative bourgeois objectification. It is through the aesthetics that multiple disconnected narratives can find a common framework, a commonality, and can intersect progressively to become an epic form. In this process of making, through which often unconnected subjects – the homeless, the intellectual, the professional – may come and go, they interweave to create form for the common sensibility.

With Democracy Village, this critically lay in the conjunction of the two words, 'democracy' and 'village'; a form of adumbrated parataxis, the placing together of two unrelated concepts, each with its utopian trajectory: democracy as the *nomos* in its utopian form, the village as *topos* in its utopian form.

Adorno has referred to parataxis as "the agency of form",[9] form being the vehicle for new potentialities by which the particular contents find their expression. In this process, in the dynamics between form as *statis*, as image, and form as fluidity, as narrative, form becomes itself a content, and form's own self–emancipation. At Parliament Square, the subject of the form and the content is democracy as embodiment of the political, and its sensible realisation the aesthetics of the village. Depending on the perspective of different subject positions, everyone can imagine the idealised form of such a parataxis, both as image and as narrative. In the course of time, as the narrative unfolds with the unexpected and the inevitable – and given the realities of life within a traffic island – a projected idealisation as utopia turns into a space of regenerative crisis, a crisis heterotopia, and then, with further time, undeniably stagnates into de–generative dystopia – the cycle of utopia enacted and inverted. These are the natural stages of any sustained social inter-vention, but each of these stages opens up a different dimension of the *nomos* to allow the emergence of alternative realities to find shape within *social form*.

1. Peter Sloterdijk, G–I–O Global Instant Objects, http://www.g–i–o.com/pp1.htm.
2. Giorgio Agamben, *Homo Sacer* (Torino: Einaudi, 1995).
3. Jacques Rancière, *The Politics of Aesthetics: The Distribution of the Sensible* (London and New York: Continuum, 2004).
4. Gilles Deleuze, 'Postscript on the Societies of Control', *October*, 59, Winter 1992, pp. 3–7.
5. Donald Winnicott, *Playing and Reality* (London: Tavistock Publications, 1971).
6. *ibid.*, Jacques Rancière (2004).
7. R.D. Laing, *The Politics of Experience and The Bird of Paradise* (Harmondsworth: Penguin, 1967).
8. Theodor W. Adorno, 'Kierkegaard: Construction of the Aesthetic', in Brian O'Connor (ed.), *The Adorno Reader* (Oxford: Blackwell, 2000) quoted in Steven Helming, 'Constellation and Critique: Adorno's Constellation, Benjamin's Dialectical Image', http://pmc.iath.virginia. edu/text–only/issue.903/14.1helmling.txt.
9. Theodor W. Adorno, 'Parataxis: On Hölderlin's Late Poetry', *Notes to Literature*, Vol. 2 (New York: Columbia University Press, 1992).

Resistance,
then What?

Reflections of the Spirit of '68 Group[1]

RICHARD CARTER, ROMEO DELACRUZ, CRISTINA GARRIDO, ANA POVOAS,
JUDITH RYSER & MARTIN SLAVIN

Starting points

JR: '68 and now – Why do current protesters against authoritarian governance refer so often to '68, considering that it did not achieve the desired result?[2] As a student manifesting against established values I was on the barricades, which were followed by workers' demands for better conditions, but '68 spawned even more authoritarian governments. Some argue that the material conditions were not pre-revolutionary,[3] but are they now? Is a neoliberal austerity period sufficient to provoke more than frustration or rebellion? How can those who share dissatisfaction initiate a mass movement that would have political effects?

Although the baby–boom generation achieved some societal goals, such as free higher education for all, these achievements are now being eroded. Is there sufficient idealism to rescue egalitarian goals, or is the legacy of individualism too overwhelming, underpinned by the idea of the Big Society and personal resilience? The most challenging question is that even if protests achieve results, could they be turned into positive energy capable of mobilising lasting support? How could they contribute to consensus on a more democratic, more open society that would improve social and spatial justice, attributes which are at the centre of academic debate?[4] Considering the generalised implosion of left politics in Europe, there is little opportunity to unite progressive voices. It may be in the gift of the social sector to invent alternative social commitment, civic innovation, institutional structures. Even if current resistance spawned an alternative model of society, how could it be implemented in space and place? What actions could change the trend towards increasing social, economic and spatial polarisation? Perhaps incremental initiatives would be a more realistic means to redress the worst excesses of top–down spatial interventions, attenuate ensuing gentrification processes, share experimental knowledge widely, and thereby strengthen participatory democracy.

RD: London student demonstrations: A right to the city? – The 'Demolition 10.11.10' marked a new dawn for British politics but showed the contradictions of the student movement. Marching with 50,000 protesters, I asked myself if it was the students' manifestation of their 'right to the city'.[5] While venting anger on the Liberal Democrats' breaking of their election pledge was a logical response to an act of betrayal, it clearly showed the naivety and lack of political maturity amongst students and their leaders. Having an onerous contract of pledges with politicians, without any penalty for non–compliance, the National Union of Students (NUS) neglected the usual experience that politicians say one thing before the election and do another when in power. By arguing that tuition fee increase and abolition of maintenance allowance were threats to social mobility, without an alternative proposal and a critical examination of the system that produces social inequalities in Britain, the students failed to advance the need for political, social, economic and cultural transformation. "Any contemporary struggle to envision a reconstruction of the social process has to confront the problem of how to overthrow the structures (both physical and institutional) that the free market has itself produced."[6]

The Millbank Tower siege by radical students and anarchists polarised the student movement. Their direct action and occupation caught media attention and rattled the politicians, but it caused division amongst student ranks and isolation from the public. Breaking political apathy and radicalising the students, the series of demonstrations, walk–outs, sit–ins and occupations that evolved thereafter are a significant step towards "democratic experimentalism"[7] that balances practical progress and individual emancipation. However, to inhabit the city and to sustain resistance, the students should work for a shared goal and organise a "solidaric general protest"[8] with other sectors, groups and communities affected by the coalition government's policies.

CG: Barcelona 1992 and the mediatic resistance – When Barcelona was announced in 1986 as host city for the 1992 Olympics, I remember the excitement everyone around me felt about being selected for such an international event. What we could not know was that the Olympics were to be the beginning of the end of what was once a small grey town, without status, but still full of life. The council began immediately to regenerate the urban landscape, and this became a model for other cities – internationally acclaimed as the 'Barcelona Model'[9] – but was slowly realised as a disaster for locals. It created a monumentalisation of the city in order to project itself internationally, rather than an attempt to satisfy local culture and its necessities.[10]

Before and during the 1992 Olympics, there was almost no resistance. It was later, when locals realised Barcelona was becoming an unpleasant place to live in and how it had been turned into a stage, a "city of the spectacle",[11] that resistance began to formulate. The intellectual and creative classes of the city self–organised. New collectives such as Las Agencias and Ariadna Pi, among others, arose and started creating actions around town. Most of these activists operated *in situ*, and although that was a major part of their strength, the real power was in their appropriation and *detournement* of official media language and codes to alternative ideas.

Though this symbolic resistance was appropriate and necessary for the moment, this one effort proved not effective enough. Most of these actions were absorbed and aestheticised by big museums like Museu d'Art Contemporani de Barcelona

(MACBA),[12] and others were simply dismissed as a joke, due to their spirit of festivity and celebration. Hence there is a need to rethink the modes of operation we have been using – most of them the legacies of '68 and other resistance movements of the 20th century – to create new types of action, which are not merely symbolic, but which are actually effective in order to achieve the change we would like to see.

JR: Impact of London 2012 Olympic Games on locality –
Mega–projects such as the Olympic Games are in a league of their own due to their sheer scale and compulsory timeframe. Of supra–national importance, they are masterminded by remote players who have different agendas from the host cities, despite them being crucial partners. For London, hosting the games means confirming its 'world city' status, besides generating profitable development for its regeneration industry and financial sector. Securitisation, a brainchild of the liberalised financial system, has transformed the rules of engagement of such mega–projects by converting real estate into a footloose commodity, tradable on international stock markets, and effectively dislocating the built environment from its use value.

No wonder, mega–projects have become the Mecca of the development industry, yielding extraordinary profits, benefiting from public subsidies, externalising risks, and being 'too big to go under'. Mediating initial disruption in a selected location and assisted by immovable tight deadlines, regeneration consortia constitute powerful institutional instruments, combining land ownership, regulatory powers, public purse, development know–how and marketing. Their crucible is the legacy promise, but in London's East End the Olympics have simply accelerated regeneration already planned as a private sector–led undertaking with public sector input of land and infrastructure.

A crucial part of the regeneration process is the narrative devised to appease the local population and convince it of legacy benefits.[13] In reality, most of the local residents, businesses, allotment users and others were displaced, and few may be relocated on the site.[14] The local community stands little chance of obtaining access to land, let alone owning and developing sites within the legacy programme.

In more general terms, mega–projects cannot confirm or refute whether urban change implies destruction, invasion, segregation or polarisation, and whether there exists a path dependency between creative colonisation of abandoned sites and gentrification.

AP: Critical experience with resistance and compliance: Undefended beliefs – My participation in the Spirit of '68 discussions has been rooted in personal ambivalence. While discussing alternatives to the neoliberal production of our times, I was simultaneously working for an architects' practice co–responsible for the masterplans of the 2012 London Olympics and its legacy, the resistance to which is mentioned here. This ambiguity enabled me to sense what motivates the members of groups that are often regarded as radically opposed to such mainstream interventions. I observed the same intellectual rigour, dedication of enormous amounts of personal time and eagerness among them to challenge the top–down directives through any breach or opportunity. Such empirical

observations resume a common feeling of entrapment. This shared feeling is the basis for the evolution from tactics of opposition to tactics of collaboration, an abandonment of puritanism that recalls Sennett's claims in *The Uses of Disorder*.[15] Since individuals' revision of values and conduct seem necessary to sustain deep societal change, this can be provoked through exposure to plurality, awareness raising and reciprocal learning. Relationships between people construct a dialogue towards the necessary level of abstraction that can unite different agendas in the exploration of what needs doing. Local and national scales are transcended through the alliance[16] of these groups that are capable of pressing governments' governance towards citizens' sense of reasonableness.

The '68 revolution of values didn't extend to the majority, or so the election of de Gaulle makes us believe, but there seems to have been a moment of suspension, when people were willing to revise their values.[17] Raising awareness on how the lives we lead sustain or weaken the order of things that we criticise can slowly promote value revision. Diverse experiences, skills, assets, ideas, actions can be articulated pragmatically to challenge the mediation of capital power. Do such groups, which seek an independent civil condition, need to be plural, cosmopolitan? Can they be linked into wider alliances (where academia has a role to play)? It may be a way of working with the strength of critical thinking while preserving the subjectivity of the parts.

Resistance and disobedience remain a public demonstration whenever formal politics deviate from the socially acceptable. As Rawls has put it: "given the often predatory aims of state power ... a general willingness to resist the state's claims is all the more necessary."[18]

RC: Outlook: Provocation –

Forty–three years later, we can view the black–and–white rage of '68 and be struck by both the parallels with, and the remoteness from, our contemporary "theatre of spectacle".[19] The Paris barricades retain their potent allure, but new dramatic images are being reflected on our screens. The mass student demonstrations of late 2010 have seen the rod of the people thrust through the royal window, and the flame of democratic rebellion has ignited

the Arab world. The ignored and the marginalised are taking to the streets in physical manifestations of outrage. To what extent are these mass actions the simple instinctual response of the intimidated? Or the authentic corollary of radical free thought? If the spirit of '68 is characterised by its failure to deliver real and lasting change,[20] do we have the right to expect anything more this time around? It is still possible to see ours as an age of "totalitarian democracy" where "everyone will allow the right to speak, but none will allow it to be taken".[21] The twittering blogosphere seems symptomatic of our fatally apolitical passivity, which has permitted the erosion of real–life community and fostered a culture of consumerism. We are mindful of the inefficacy of the 2003 mass demonstrations against the Iraq war in London, the "biggest in British history",[22] ignored by the UK government. In our present era of economic freefall, it is the middle–class liberal consumer, not his working–class forbear, who remains subjugated by the status quo. For Debordian anarchists, it is merely the image of a radically free social connectivity, which is sold to us by big business, the commodity fetishism or the invasive marketisation of personal subjectivity via 'http personalisation'. This 'social interactivity' can seem a hopelessly sanitised counterfeit of the unstructured *derive* freely conducted by night through the sleazier working–class districts and bars of the unadulterated 20th–century city by the Situationiste Internationale and their associates.[23]

Questions arising

What is the symbolic resonance of '68 with contemporary action?

RD: The idea that the students can ignite political change is a romantic interpretation of the '68 movement and a myth that is being nurtured by those in the student movement, as appeared on the placards of the 'Demolition 10.11.10' demonstrations. A more realistic mass movement is the 'people power' phenomenon, which is multi–sectoral, inclusive and participatory. It toppled dictatorships in the Philippines in 1986 and in Tunisia and Egypt recently.

CG: I personally think resistance in the so–called 'developed countries' is always very safe. We go out and demonstrate for a few hours. But then we go back home to sit comfortably in front of our computer with a cup of tea and we go back to work the next day because it's Monday. Not many people are willing to risk their jobs or their wealthy situation. Big revolutions are only effective when people are willing to take risks. A clear example of that has been the recent revolution in Egypt. We should think about that when we talk about effective resistance as well. What risks are we willing to take? What are we ready to lose, or to win? In western countries we flirt with the idea continuously, but we might not be actually ready to create a real change.

How does mass media alter the spectacular event?

RC: I am intrigued by the narcissism of the student protesters filming themselves on their mobile phones, and the apparent choreography of the smashed window event at Millbank. The lack of ideology seems manifest in their single issue politics and the one–liner style of their banners (Tory Cu*ts). Have they really considered the wider effects on society of the public sector cuts and formulated a proper alternative manifesto? For me, the image that was equivalent of '68 was that provocative pole shoved through Camilla and Charles's limousine window by a passing anarchist who couldn't quite believe his luck!

AP: I share that concern, and perhaps we can compare this fully gadget–equipped youth parade to the revolutionary style of beards and inflamed speeches fed by the left stars of the 60s. Jenny Diski's account[24] of the practised confusion between liberation and libertarianism seems to point in the direction that counter–youth–culture can be a blockage of youth efforts towards change beyond rebellion.

JR: In *Fight Back*,[25] there are many articles that discuss the use of contemporary media and social network sites. What I find interesting is how they enable diffuse co–operation, online and offline combined, very flexible and responsive, as an alternative to a centralised, hierarchical, leadership–led model of operation.

RD: The use of new media technology democratised access and control of information and facilitated multiple realities. The use of text messaging, internet, video and social networks challenges the role of traditional and mainstream media. It allows the demonstrators to document 'the moment', to share their experiences with others and to counter the establishment's interpretations. The demonstrators' use of video cameras in the G20 demonstration challenged the official declarations, and the use of social network media strained the resources of the Metropolitan Police. Text messaging facilitated the popular uprising and ousting of the president in the Philippines in 2001. Similarly, mobile phones were used to contest the establishment's position in Iran and to document the chaos in Egypt, Tunisia and Libya.

AP: I think there is also a psychological component to it, which I imagine to be the sense of security in the face of the risk accepted when taking to the streets, in particular to overthrow lifelong presidents and dictators as we are watching in the Arab world. I wonder if new technologies are not allowing the expansion of a neighbouring pattern that often rules encounters in the intimate scales of friendship and kinship – "If you are doing it, I will do it also!" – to critical political events of national scale. We can also ask if a parallel psychological effect of trust is not playing a crucial part in the succession of uprisings in Tunisia, Egypt, Libya, etc., through the communication of confidence that change is possible, informally circulated through those same technologies and despite the repressive blackouts.

What will be the legacy of resistance?

JR: For me the biggest hurdle is the transition from a reactive stance (protest against something we can all agree) to a positive anticipatory position to work towards an alternative system of governance, an alternative economic model, for running higher education or whatever. How to turn this means into an end when protest has succeeded? How to agree on a goal and elaborate how to implement it, with whom? With what timetable? With what legitimacy?

RD: Resistance creates new institutions. Once the resistance becomes successful, these institutions are legitimised and the implementation of change is transferred to them, leaving behind the people in the process. This is the start of a new problem as institutions alone are not capable of changing society. People should be an integral part of the whole process. The institutionalisation of participatory democracy is not a guarantee as its mechanics can be still subject to those who have power and control resources.

CG: In one of our group conversations, Martin said that after his research on the Olympics, he arrived at the realisation that almost no effective resistance can be done once decisions are made. He suggested that, to be effective, resistance needs to be done before, or at the time of, the decision–making. That might be a very good tip for future Olympics and other mega–events.

JR: Choosing an ideal time to act makes sense. However, in the case of the 2012 Olympics, for the people who were displaced and those who are still around, there is no next ideal time. They will have to devise new modes of resistance or, better still, anticipatory initiatives so that they can respond to any opportunity that presents itself from now on. The legacy game is still in limbo and may present new openings.

AP: Post–games development is not going to happen overnight and development plots may be fenced off for up to 40 years. In fact, the Olympic Delivery Authority (ODA) commissioned a "Transformation masterplan" to deal with the period immediately after the games.

The idea of allowing interim uses throughout the site seemed a logical way to deal with the interest of the visiting experience and security issues. However, it was never developed as the ODA insisted on a landscaped strategy, perhaps concerned over future legal rights of use. But collaboration between the official teams of masterplanners, activists and communities could have pressed for the reasonable claim to use empty land. Being back with a foot in there would have created much more scope to influence the future of the place.

CG: Making politics can be a new form of resistance. Aida Sánchez de Serdio argues that in every little group there are always institutional and bureaucratic processes that need to be done.[26]

I consider that nowadays activism should get involved in political and bureaucratic processes in order to achieve more. I am not suggesting that little actions are not useful. Any kind of resistance (symbolic or not, micro or macro, passive or active … and at any time) is in my opinion always necessary. However, seeing how resistance has been created and used until now, I am of the opinion that we should find ways in which this resistance leads to effectiveness. That is, that resistance is the means to an end, rather than an end in itself.

Has free thought been sold with the marketisation of democracy?

RC: Having just seen Duncan Campbell's film *Bernadette* (2006) documenting Devlin's activism against the British occupation in 60s Northern Ireland, you cannot fail to be struck by her saintly charisma and competence at 21 years of age – though she was ultimately martyred by the media. I think this type of militant, but compassionate, real–world idealism is something shared by the '68–ers (that I know) and lacking in later generations who have become atomised by the effects of individualism. Too often we 'younger generations' are afraid to speak our minds, but all too keen to reflect ourselves in illusory, self-congratulatory mirrors like YouTube, Facebook, pointless online petitions and the rest; we seem very superficial by comparison.

JR: You may have a point, but are all youngsters that narcissistic or shy? I think you are very hard on yourselves. Again in *Fight Back*,[27] there are interesting accounts of effective dialogue during sit-ins at various universities.

AP: Richard, this makes me think of one of your narratives when you described the desolation of understanding that the sublime rock songs of your teenage times were in fact consumables producing the same emotions in a whole generation. Martin probably would say that you were a victim of marketisation and contributed to the perpetuation of the consumerist-based system. Yet that didn't prevent you from developing your critical thinking. So, to me, the question is whether products and behaviours of apparent lightness are compatible with the development of the

capacity for critical participation in civil society. Provocatively, whether those citizens would be willing to waive those products, should the complex links between economic survival and the geography of world problems entangled in their production become accessible knowledge? Is it a form of resistance to produce research that seeks to clarify those relationships and make them clear to the general public?

RC: I was thinking of "seriality",[28] Sartre's conception that those who control the media are capable of simulating unique subjective experience and mass marketing it to a population unaware of each other's existence – as in Bentham's Panopticon. I suppose, in this sense, the internet has been effective at disrupting distribution and control by a single source, as did rock music in the past.

RD: In his idea of democratic experimentalism, Unger[29] recognises the conflict between personal need and the demands of democracy. But he argues that this can be mediated by intense political engagement and persistent popular political action. I guess this was the experience of the students who were radicalised by their experiences during their action. While you may say that their use of the media is narcissistic, the students used it to advance their political agenda. Their frustrations with the politicians and the Met police intensified their participation in, and call for more, demonstrations.

Opposition or subversion?

RC: I'm for subversion: head–on opposition will inevitably result in disappointment. It is through creative listening to the needs and desires of others that we can understand our own position better and engage in synthetic dialogue with the opposition. The danger lies in failing to reassess one's own stated aims dynamically. While I cannot really believe in the capitalist 'bogeyman' – call me *'un bourgeois'* – the corrosive effects of ill–considered and short–termist profiteering are real and present.

JR: I agree with that, although purists may condemn us. The Bromley–by–Bow Centre is an example of a group demonstrating by doing, succeeding where everybody thought they would fail or give up, and finally invited

into the mainstream. The danger is to slide gradually into someone else's outlook and to comply with their agenda. Therefore it is important to have an internal organisation that remains self–critical and innovative.

AP: Indeed, the Bromley–by–Bow Centre is engaged with the Olympics through the Water City initiative. What worries me is the less apparent relations of the pros and cons of playing with the devil. Andrew Mawson,[30] founder of the centre, refers in his book to the social gains devised in a business with Tesco. While, in Mawson's perspective, the collaboration with Tesco offered an opportunity for the integration of a group of Bengali women in the neighbourhood, I have difficulties with Tesco's destruction of much of the British built environment and its exploitation of the bottom of the capitalist production chain.[31]

CG: Traditionally, power and resistance have been understood as a bipolar relationship. Lately, the words 'participation' and 'co–operation' have been discussed in relation to this. I think these are key words for further steps of resistance and change. These methodologies have proved themselves to work in different arenas, such as the internet, academic research or activist action. They tend to erode power relations considerably. Also, teamwork and negotiations have proved to be much more effective in terms of achieving goals.

RD: Opposition challenges the system, overthrows the structures and creates an alternative in the quickest possible time. Subversion does not guarantee a change of structure, takes too long to do and may in fact strengthen the structure. The risk of being co–opted by the system is very high.

Can dissent work in coalition?

JR: Take the student protests in London. The law of increasing fees has been voted. Can students collaborate with universities to make the best of a bad world? How does this relate to David Willetts'[32] offensive to produce a student charter – ignoring that many 'contracts' between universities and students who have accepted a place there already exist – notwithstanding the fact that such a top–down centralised initiative from a government minister flies in the face of localism and a self–determining Big Society?

RD: Collaborating with university officials is a palliative approach and does not address the politico–economic and socio–cultural issues surrounding British higher education. The idea of participatory governance is good, but it will mean an overhauling of the highly hierarchical structures of British universities in particular and society in general.

RC: We have discussed before the problem of complexity arising from negotiating between different and competing interest groups. For every successful campaign reflecting the true diversity of values within the group, there are probably at least as many 'good intentions' that are distorted by the domineering attitude of a minority, resulting in the apathy of the majority. Ours is just a little experiment in self–determination dynamics. My experience of bureaucratic 'community consultation' has often been less than inspiring. It is usually characterised by the privileged 'decision–makers', excluding the poorly educated, the overworked and the 'otherwise busy', and orchestrated to suit the timetable and the foregone conclusions of the administrators. I think this is where sociological theory can probably improve the decision–making process. For me, it is not as simple as 'bottom–up' governance. A self–organised and structured hierarchy is necessary for action to be effective. There must first of all be a will to listen, and second, a will to act.

Where next?

Those of us liberals who attempt to work within the system, to mitigate the excesses of unbridled marketisation of public space, free education and to defend the rights of equal access for all, face continual compromise by the conformist exploitation of our instinctive goodwill, the private sector's insistence on quantifiable 'deliverables' where 'value' is invariably judged in a single numerical dimension, and 'efficiencies' measured only in momentary profit.

Conversely, situation–based activities of artists have developed 'ecological' praxis of mutual interdependence between environment, socius and psyche,[33] and community–led independent organisations such as Growing Communities[34] seek to supplant the hegemony of supply and distribution. It is in these small–scale, pragmatic, community–based initiatives that we see the resurgent development of 'social milieux', organised around positive economic exchange of ideas and commodities where genuine profits are made in nurturing physical, psychological and social environments through active participation in change.

It remains to be seen whether the Big Society is just a cynical ruse by the UK coalition to save money while masquerading as 'social enterprise'. Meanwhile, apolitical community groups, charities, activists and the voluntary sector are being visibly renewed by a sense of shared purpose and common interest. Whether in the 'No to Academies' campaign[35] opposing the intrusion of corporate business interests into the state education system, or the web–based multi–issue lobbyists group called '38 degrees',[36] ordinary people are finding a collective voice across the political and class divides in the establishment of networks of subjective exchange across both physical and artificial space.

1. Spirit of '68 is a self-selected cosmopolitan group formed to examine why the events of '68 did not result in a less authoritarian society. It is exploring resistance against autocratic governance and ways to transform resistance into participatory, spatially and socially just democracy. In the light of student protests in the UK, resistance against mega-projects and uprisings in the Arab world, this is a timely undertaking. The group adopted a non-authoritarian 'governance structure' to find a feasible ground between the highest common denominator of shared aims and the lowest level of abstraction of generalised agreement. This experiment in collective writing illustrates how the TINAG festivals are acting as catalyst of creative critical interaction.

2. For example, Raymond Aron, *La revolution introuvable: Reflexions sur les evenements de mai* (Paris: Fayard, 1968).

3. Wilhelm Frederik Wertheim, *Evolution and Revolution: The Rising Waves of Emancipation* (Harmondsworth: Penguin, 1974). See his pre-revolutionary conditions, economic, social, political, psychological, and the presence of accelerators (e.g. war deficient public finances).

4. David Harvey, *Social Justice and the City* (London: Edward Arnold, 1973); Edward W. Soja, *Seeking Spatial Justice* (Minneapolis: University of Minnesota Press, 2010).

5. Henri Lefebvre, *Writing on Cities* (Oxford: Blackwell Publishers, 2000).

6. David Harvey, *Spaces of Hope* (Berkeley: University of California Press, 2000).

7. Roberto Mangebeira Unger, *Democracy Realized: The Progressive Alternative* (New York: Verso, 2001).

8. Emma Goldman, 'Anarchism: What it Really Stands for', in Robert Hoffman (ed.), *Anarchism as Political Philosophy* (New Brunswick: Transaction Publishers, 2010).

9. Horacio Capel, *El Modelo Barcelona: un examen critico* (Barcelona: Ediciones del Serbal, 2005).

10. Manuel Delgado, *El Animal Público* (Barcelona: Anagrama, 1999); Manuel Delgado, *La Ciudad Mentirosa. Fraude y Miseria del Modelo Barcelona* (Madrid: Los Libros de la Catarata, 2007); Manuel Delgado, *Sociedades Movedizas* (Barcelona: Anagrama 2007); Maripaz Balibrea, 'Barcelona: del Modelo a la Marca', 2005, http://www.scribd.com/doc/32207546/Barcelona-de-Modelo-a-La-Marca-Mari-Paz-Balibrea.

11. Disculpen las Molestias / The City of the Spectacle, 2006, www.laciudadelespectaculo. blogspot.com.

12. Jesús Carrillo and Ignacio Estella Noriega (eds), Desacuerdos 3, 'Sobre Arte, Políticas y Esfera Pública en el Estado Español', 2005, http://ypsite.net/pdfs/barcelona_del_modelo_a_la_marca.pdf.

13. Discussed in Martin Slavin's presentation at the seminar 'Learning from Barcelona: Art, Real Estate and the Olympic City', Birkbeck College, London, January 2011.

14. Games Monitor, www.gamesmonitor.org.uk.

15. Richard Sennett, *The Uses of Disorder: Personal Identity and City Life* (New York: Norton, 1970).

16. *ibid.*, Edward W. Soja (2010); David Harvey, *The Enigma of Capital and the Crisis of Capitalism* (London: Profile Books, 2010).

17. Very funnily represented in the movie *Milou en Mai*, Louis Malle (1990).

18. John Rawls, *A Theory of Justice* (revised edition) (Cambridge, MA: Harvard University Press, 1999).

19. Guy Debord, *Society of the Spectacle* (New York: Zone Books, 1995).

20. Dominique LeCourt, *Mediocracy: French Philosophy since the Mid-1970s* (London: Verso, 2001).

21. Quotes from Marxist tract overlay from Jean Luc Godard, *British Sounds* (UK/France: Kestrel Productions, 1969).

22. http://news.bbc.co.uk/1/hi/2765041.stm.

23. Simon Sadler, *The Situationist City* (Cambridge, MA: MIT Press, 1999).

24. Jenny Diski, *The sixties* (London: Profile, 2009) pp. 69–95.
25. Dan Hancox (ed.), *Fight Back: A Reader on the Winter of Protest* (London: OpenDemocracy, 2011) http://www.scribd.com/doc/48950923/Fight-Back.
26. Aida Sánchez de Serdio Martin, 2010.
27. *ibid.*, Dan Hancox (2011).
28. Felix Guattari, *The Three Ecologies* (New Brunswick: Athlone, 2000).
29. *ibid.*, Roberto Mangebeira Unger (2001).
30. Andrew Mawson, *The Social Entrepreneur: Making Communities Work* (London: Atlantic Books, 2008).
31. For example, the female workers in the banana plantations in Costa Rica. See http://www.tescopoly.org/index.php?option=com_content&task=view&id=55&Itemid=176.
32. UK Minister for Universities and Science.
33. *ibid.*, Felix Guattari (2000). For example, Joseph Beuys conceived 'social sculpture' and co-founded innovative political institutions.
34. www.growingcommunities.org.
35. www.antiacademies.org.uk.
36. www.38degrees.org.uk.

East End Battleground

Defending Multicultural Spaces and Lives

DAVID ROSENBERG

The most surprising phenomenon in the growth of British fascism is the great popular support we have gained in East London ... It would be superficial merely to attribute our East End strength to the natural and healthy antisemitism which is always to be found in areas thickly populated by Jews ... the cause is to be found deep in the character and history of East London. The people there, not so well fed or well housed as are the inhabitants of more prosperous London, have yet a deeper patriotism, deeper loyalty to tradition than is to be found in the suburbs where the sickly enervating propaganda of so-called modern thought has softened the fibre of British youth ... We are winning wholehearted adherence because we have preached a cause and a system bringing hope and sunlight into lives darkened by long years of hunger, squalor and despair, because we have shown them a way to cast off the foreign yoke of a domineering, all pervading Yiddish culture, which strives to make East London take on the character of Odessa or Warsaw.

Clement Bruning, propagandist for the British Union of Fascists, October 1935 [1]

A year to the day from Bruning's gushing tribute to struggling East Londoners on the hinterland of what they contemptuously regarded as an "alien ghetto", the British Union of Fascists, led by Sir Oswald Mosley, assembled in the City of London and then attempted to invade and reclaim the East End in what became known as the "Battle of Cable Street". In 2011, as we mark the 75th anniversary of this encounter, arguments over territory, belonging and identity that the fascists fomented then, seem to have been given a new and menacing lease of life.

Mosley's *Blackshirt* newspaper promised both supporters and opponents "Four Great Meetings" that day. And trooping to these meetings, through the streets where 60,000 beleaguered Jews eked out a living, would be "Four Marching Columns" of uniformed fascists. The platforms, in Limehouse, Bow, Bethnal Green and Shoreditch, encircled the "Jewish East End". Mosley could have approached these platforms from Hackney in the north, from further east in Stratford, or from the south, across Tower Bridge. Instead he assembled his uniformed and jackbooted divisions on Royal Mint Street in the south-eastern edge of the City of London, beneath the architecture of imperial wealth. Wearing a peaked cap and black paramilitary uniform, Mosley duly arrived to inspect his 3,000 troops in a black open-top car. His desire to cross that boundary separating the City of riches from the depressed and dilapidated East End was replete with symbolism.

Mosley's movement, like those of his contemporaries in Italy, Germany and Spain, thrived on a sense of superiority and invincibility. That day it came unstuck as some 300,000 people came out to oppose them. A human wall, bolstered by deliberately abandoned trams, blocked "Gardiners Corner" at Aldgate – the gateway to the East End from the City. Several thousand police, including London's entire mounted regiment, repeatedly battered the front lines to clear a path. Heads were cracked open, people were bloodied and bruised, but the mass at Aldgate, Jew and non-Jew, women and men, young and old, chanting "They Shall Not Pass", was unmoveable. The focus eventually shifted south to a narrower route into the East End along Cable Street, which stretched from the City towards the docks, but three sets of improvised barricades and a constant showering of objects slung by incensed occupants of tenements above the street's shops ultimately prevented any incursion there.

Locals and the police fought furiously while the fascists, chanting "The Yids, the Yids, we've got to get rid of the Yids", waited to proceed. The fiercest battles took place at the City end of Cable Street, and many among the 84 individuals arrested that day (79 of them anti-fascists) were dragged to Leman Street police station from this combat zone. By late afternoon Police Commissioner Sir Philip Game acknowledged defeat and ordered Mosley to march his troops in the opposite direction and disperse them on the Embankment. Mosley accused the government of "surrendering to red violence and Jewish corruption" but absolved "the British people of East London" from any responsibility for this "riot": an "alien mob", he said, had turned "peaceful streets into a battleground".[2]

It was a spectacular victory by communities who stayed united despite crude and sustained efforts by fascists to divide them, and despite the state actively assisting Mosley's invasion in the name of free speech and movement. Earlier that week 100,000 local residents – Jewish and non-Jewish – had signed a petition drafted by the Jewish People's Council, a grassroots Jewish anti-fascist body, calling for Mosley's march to be banned. By ignoring their demand, though, the Home Secretary, Sir John Simon, unwittingly facilitated a greater victory of people's power over those who sought the "freedom" only to terrorise, abuse, and intimidate.

But why was this decrepit square mile of East London abutting the City so important to Mosley? His party claimed that in this area British sovereignty had been ceded to another culture, another "race". Fascist literature lamented how recently the local "cabinet-maker, polisher and tailor were Englishmen", whereas now, "the Englishman in East London is the slave of the Jewish master".[3] But Mosley's designation of certain areas as "ghettoes" or "alien territory", his party's insistence on distinguishing between their inhabitants (most of whom were actually born there) and fully fledged "British people", and his fervent desire to reclaim these districts for the national good, have an eerie modern-day resonance.

It was in February 2011, in Munich, that Prime Minister David Cameron railed against the "failure" of "multiculturalism" that induces "different cultures to live separate lives, apart from each other and apart from the mainstream".[4] He chose his words partly to ingratiate himself with his host, Angela Merkel, who herself had previously told young Christian Democrats that "this multi-kulti approach, saying that we simply live side by side and are happy about each other ... has failed, utterly failed", adding with chagrin, "we kidded ourselves ... [that] they won't stay, sometime they will be gone".[5]

Naming Muslims, but polite enough to distinguish moderate and extreme variants, Cameron reiterated how generous "mainstream Britain" has been to its recalcitrant minorities. "We've even tolerated these segregated communities behaving in ways that run counter to our values." He demanded that "the passive tolerance of recent years" be replaced by "a clear sense of national identity".[6] Cameron's "hard times" mantra may affirm "we are all in it together" but his arrogant sense of *"we"* and *"our"*, evinced in his Munich speech, seems far from inclusive. His notion of national identity is allegedly "open to everyone", but the hierarchies and barriers are as plain as day.

Even "toleration" is a step too far, yet toleration itself, as Georgie Wemyss has shown, is always something granted by the powerful to the powerless.[7] What Cameron cannot conceive of today, any more than Mosley could in the 1930s, is a genuinely pluralist society held together by different kinds of bonds between people, some stronger, some looser, that is *not* predicated on British nationalism. Cameron, Merkel, and the growth of the English Defence League, merely confirm that the issues highlighted by Mosley's 1930s encounter with the East End refuse to be confined to history.

Cameron's mainstream political opponents have been implicated too in recent years. In December 2001 New Labour's David Blunkett regretted that "over-tolerance" encouraged certain groups to "self-segregate".[8] In August 2006 his colleague Ruth Kelly instigated the Commission on Integration and Cohesion, whose central idea, according to Race Relations commentator Jenny Bourne, is that the nation had "a deficit of glue which would have to be artificially manufactured and injected into British institutions", while the very communities excluded through economic decline and discrimination, especially in housing, are themselves "blamed for their isolation".[9]

If Mosley were still alive and surveying the East End, he would surely be gratified that just 1,500–2,000 mainly poor, elderly Jews remain there, but the area would still give him nightmares. The borough of Tower Hamlets, which includes the East End, has the highest concentration of Bangladeshi families in Britain, a growing East and West African population, Caribbean, Chinese, Vietnamese and East European residents too, alongside white English and Irish populations. Mosley was no racially obsessed fascist fantasising a pure white world. In 1933, he wrote how Britain owed its "versatile genius" to being "composed of more different races than almost any other nation in the world", adding, "If we had been merely a pure race type of Nordic men, we should have achieved no more than Sweden or Norway".[10] But he firmly advocated white superiority and supremacy. The multiculturalism that actually flourishes in inner London boroughs, including Tower Hamlets, where people of different cultural origins, including British, live side by side in relative equality (often equality of poverty), would have been anathema to him.

In his party's formative years Mosley rejected charges of xenophobia, affirming that Jews or Gentiles who are loyal to Great Britain "will get a square deal from us". He dismissed crudely prejudiced attitudes as both unfair and ineffective, but insisted that any co-existence of cultures must be predicated on an *imbalance* of power and opportunity, the adaptation of minorities to the white majority, and, above all, a commitment to British nationalism. This arrogant worldview, which advances cultural and racial supremacy while commandeering the language of fairness, embodies a class–based conceit that echoes loudly today.

Mosley launched his movement nationally in October 1932 at the height of an economic depression. Unemployment had rocketed from 1.5 million to nearly 3 million since 1930. His appeal was cross–class: outside London it engaged the embattled working class – especially cotton workers in Lancashire and miners in the north east and Wales. In smaller towns it sought support from the self–employed; in Dorset it appealed mainly to farmers, and in many areas it appealed to former soldiers, sailors and airmen who had become unemployed. But in London it was a different story.

There, until late 1934, Mosley principally courted the rich and powerful. He derided "old gang" politicians as incapable of meeting the needs of "hungry England", but knew that the starving could not fill the party's coffers. Mosley cultivated well–fed establishment figures – business magnates, newspaper proprietors and leading professionals – through the innocuously named "January Club", a regular wining and dining event at exclusive hotels, chaired by Sir John Squire, editor of the *London Mercury* literary journal. As club members discussed the merits of the corporate state, Mosley gauged the support he might obtain from them for his radical economic ideas and his authoritarian political model. Regular attendees included: General Sir Hubert de la Poer Gough, a director of Siemens and of Caxton Electric Development; Vincent Vickers of Vickers Electronics and a director also of London Assurance; Colonel Middleton, director of Yorkshire Insurance; and J.F. Rennel Rodd, a partner in Morgan Grenfell merchant bank. For the first six months of 1934, Mosley had enthusiastic and powerful backing from Viscount Rothermere, whose *Daily Mail* newspaper published a spread in January that year entitled "Hurrah for the Blackshirts!"[11]

Mosley was comfortable in the West End but ambivalent about the City of London. He admired the City as a centre of power that built a great empire but despaired of its role in 1930s Britain, which he saw as profitable foreign lending which, he believed, had a predatory effect on Britain's home industries, fuelling unemployment. He derided the House of Commons (in which he served as a Tory from 1918, and on the Labour benches from 1926–31) as merely "debt collectors for the City of London" cringing before the vested interests of finance capitalism.[12] But it was in the shadows of the City's capitalist citadels that Mosley gathered his troops for their assault on the East End on 4 October 1936.

Determined to reclaim the "alien", "communist controlled" territory east of the City, he wanted equally to redeem the City of London from "alien financiers". After Mosley's establishment support ebbed away – finding fascist violence, if not their ideology, distasteful – his party concentrated its efforts on impoverished areas such as East London. The *Blackshirt's* report of its first East London branch's inaugural activity, in October 1934, revealed how they conceived the political and human landscape they would battle over.

The Blackshirts marched … from Bow … into Stepney Green, where a large crowd … had gathered which later increased to well over 1,500. The Blackshirts had a very noisy reception as the larger part of the audience were aliens who resented British people holding a meeting in what they considered to be their own territory … October 4th will go down in Blackshirt history as a memorable day when the seed of fascism was sown in another East London communist stronghold.[13]

While the City collected riches over generations, the East End amassed poverty. It was a land of plenty not in wealth but in people, especially waves of immigrants and refugees: Huguenots fleeing France in the late 1600s; the Irish in the late 18th and 19th centuries; the Jews at the turn of the 20th century. Other smaller communities settled too – Indian Lascars, Somalis, Chinese, Italians and Germans – but by the 1930s the East End was mostly identified with Jewish tailors, boot and shoe makers, and cabinet makers, and Irish dockers and labourers. Politically, the rich and powerful labelled it a "red" area where trade union and communist agitation dominated.

By 1936 the fascists had branches in Bow, Shoreditch, Bethnal Green and Limehouse, surrounding the "Jewish East End". In an era when political argument radiated from street-corner platforms, East London's fascist orators spewed vile populist antisemitism almost on the Jews' doorsteps, vilifying them as "rats and vermin from the gutters of Whitechapel", "an incredible species of sub-humanity", and "simians with prehensile toes". Speakers declared: "It is gentiles versus Jews, white man versus black man". They warned that "a dirty negroid Jewish culture is sweeping over the whole country", while they acclaimed their own supporters: "You English are blood of our blood, flesh of our flesh."[14]

They sought, especially, to win the East End's other large minority population – the Irish – to these perspectives. Though powerful bonds of solidarity existed between Jewish and Irish trade unionists from overlapping strikes among dockers and tailors in 1889 and 1912, there was often hostility at street level. Those struggling with economic hardship could easily be persuaded to blame other unfortunates for their situation. In this charged atmosphere, local Catholic preachers purveying traditional "Christ-killers" antisemitism were almost superfluous.

And yet, the crude antisemitism exuding from street-corner meetings in East London was absent from the fascists' early party statements. This "evolved" over several years, after the party initially identified Jews as a problematic minority presenting as a potentially disloyal group. Mosley urged them to put "British interests" before "Jewish interests". The fascists' newspaper distinguished "good" patriotic Jews, who had become "very British in outlook" from the "low type of foreign Jew" – internationalists who kept company with communists.[15] "Good Jews" were highly assimilated, wealthy industrialists or outstanding professionals, from earlier Spanish/Portuguese and German Jewish immigrations, who lived in areas such as Kensington or Mayfair, rather than recognisably "Jewish" districts. But, gradually, all Jews were squeezed under the umbrella of "Jewry" and charged equally with organising as a separate, antagonistic racial interest. Parallels with the attitudes towards Muslims of the right-wing press post-9/11, and those of the English Defence League, which claim to target Islamic fundamentalism but continually extend the net, are indeed stark.

Mosley eventually spelled out the consequences of "Jewry's" obstinate insistence on cultural integrity. Jews who had not become sufficiently British would be treated as aliens and denied civil rights. Thousands at an Albert Hall rally in March 1935 heard Mosley unmask and vilify "Jewish international finance" as the "nameless, homeless and all-powerful force which stretches its greedy fingers from the shelter of England to throttle the trade and menace the peace of the west ... grasping the puppets of Westminster, dominating every party of the state".[16] But, by 1936, as his party focused on building populist support in more working-class areas, especially the East End of London, a cruder street antisemitism came to the fore, complementing its anti-communist agitation. When the middle-class-led British National Party (BNP) adopted similar racist populism in recent years, it won council seats in impoverished areas such as Burnley, Stoke and Barking in East London, even though its economic policies would ultimately harm the interests of its voters.

In 1937, a perceptive journalist and author, William Zukerman, used the prism of class to analyse the deeper economic and political agendas lurking behind the fascists' antisemitic façade. He wrote:

> *To the British fascists and their middle-class sympathisers, the English 'Reds', Labourites and Communists of the 'lower classes' are a true 'alien nation' psychologically as well as socially. They know as little about them as they know about the Jews, and when these 'lower classes' become restive and even threatening, the fascist hostility to them becomes no less bitter and strong than against the Jews. But in these days of nationalism, it is bad form to show hostility to one's own 'alien nation'. The Jew provides a much more convenient outlet for the feeling ... Fundamentally the British Fascists' outburst against the Jews is an outburst against British Labour, 'Reds', Socialists and Communists. It is more political and economic than national and racial. Its antisemitism is a guise under which its profounder class feeling is hidden.*[17]

If this were true then perhaps the beleaguered Jews would be best advised to form class-based alliances to confront fascism. Against the wishes of the West End-based Jewish establishment, that's what East End Jews did. In July 1936 local Jewish trade unionists called a conference at ABSA House on Commercial Road where representatives from 87 local organisations created the Jewish People's Council Against Fascism and Antisemitism (JPC). Like Zukerman, the JPC characterised antisemitism as: "both a rallying cry and a smokescreen ... hiding from the British people as a whole the true purpose of fascism". It argued that although antisemitism primarily impacted on Jews, fascism threatened the democratic liberties of all. Its founding statement affirmed: "The struggle against antisemitism is as much a task for the British people as a whole as for the Jews; and the struggle against fascism is a task for Jews as much as for the British people as a whole."

When the Home Office decided to ignore the Jewish People's Council's mass petition and, instead, enshrine the fascists' right to "free speech", the JPC rallied its supporters to "bar the road to fascism". This call was backed by radical political organisations that were winning adherents across the East End's different communities, such as the Communist Party, the Independent

Labour Party and the Labour League of Youth. Local trade union branches, bringing together Jewish and non-Jewish workers, mobilised too. Many Jewish veterans of the Battle of Cable Street recall with a mixture of surprise and local pride how Irish dockers helped Jews repel the fascists.

Jack Dash, who led dock strikes after the war recalls the activity the night before 4 October:

> ... *dockers, stevedores, tailors, engineers, ship repairers, council workers, busmen, railwaymen ... with their wives and kids, were busy lugging and hauling old furniture, bed springs, tables and chests of drawers out on to the streets building barricades ... when Sunday dawned, Stepney was ready to prevent the fascist march.*[18]

As Jewish and non-Jewish anti-fascists erected barricades and fought off police charges, they were reinforced by dockers marching to their aid from the "Irish" end of Cable Street, many among them bringing pick-axe handles for lifting the paving stones to bolster the barricades.

Jewish member of the Labour League of Youth, Aubrey Morris, whose family ran a bakery at 86 Cable Street, and who helped build the barricades, remembers:

> *When the first wave of mounted police arrived to clear the way they were pelted from ground level with broken paving and cobble stones and from every window with missiles ranging from filled piss-pots to lumps of wood, rotten fruit and old bedding ... The timely arrival of a large number of dockworkers ... helped sustain the resistance.*[19]

Mosley's party had tried to frame the battle for the East End as "British" (albeit including Irish) versus "Jewish", but a *multicultural* class-based response, which defended East London as a multicultural space, defeated his forces that day. Victory on the streets was cemented through determined joint struggles on housing estates.[20] Jewish and non-Jewish tenants united against unscrupulous private landlords through the Stepney Tenants' Defence League, a militant grassroots federation that owed much to the organisational skills of local communists. Typically it fought for demands such as getting repairs and decorations done, replacing old lavatory seats and scullery sinks, repairing drains and defects in drinking water supplies, replacing old refuse chutes, tackling vermin, improving lighting, demanding rent controls and seeking to get rents lowered. Through these joint activities, not only did economically disadvantaged non–Jews understand that their Jewish neighbours faced similar problems, and vice versa, but joint campaigning against bad landlords, whether Jewish or not, emphasised the point, especially to those of Irish Catholic descent whom Mosley felt would warm to his antisemitic themes, that it was the practices of bad landlordism, not the ethnic origins or religious beliefs of the landlord, that were significant.

The tenants' movement's crowning anti–fascist moment was a successful defence of two families in rent arrears from eviction – one with five children, the other with six – in Paragon Mansions near Stepney Green in June 1937. This estate had experienced sporadic rent strikes since 1935, and tenant activists geared themselves up for a further battle. In this instance, though, the families directly affected stayed aloof from the left–wing inspired tenants' committee. They were members of the British Union of Fascists. Phil Piratin, a leading Jewish communist and local tenants' activist records: "One family would have nothing to do with us whatsoever that evening. The other was prepared to listen. The only way to stop the eviction was to fight." The families had received no help from their party. Whatever feelings of anger and resentment Jewish tenant activists may have had against families attached to a political party trading in vicious antisemitism were put aside, and a defence was organised. After a battle with the bailiffs and the police, the notice to quit was withdrawn. Soon afterwards, Piratin adds triumphantly, their fascist membership cards "were destroyed voluntarily and in disgust".[21]

Mosley's last throw of the dice in the East End was the 1937 local elections. Six fascist candidates contested seats in their three strongest districts. They talked up their prospects in the *Blackshirt* – "Great Election Rallies … The March to Victory Begins" – but had to settle for returns ranging from 14.8% to 23%, and did not win any seats. Mosley was left perplexed that more Eastenders did not embrace a politics of ethnic rivalry and hatred, but probably concluded inwardly that the masses knew no better.

The East End suffered greatly from war bombing. Some of the newer estates, which replaced crumbling tenements, house very mixed communities; others remain more ethnically segregated. But Ken Leech, a veteran commentator on British race relations who worked in the East End over several decades, notes that nationally, Jews and Sikhs are more segregated geographically than Muslims, while in Scotland Roman Catholics are more segregated geographically than any other minority groups. Allan Brimicombe's research for the University of East London in 2006 showed high levels of voluntary segregation by Sikhs, Hindus and Jews in better-off areas of London, on the basis of religious identity, but noted that the most segregated Muslim communities occupied areas with social and economic deprivation.[22]

Professor Danny Dorling argues that "[i]ncreasingly, Britain is segregated by inequality, poverty, wealth and opportunity, not by race and area", as successive governments allow inequality to grow and social mobility to decline.[23] The most aggressive move towards geographical ghettoisation today comes from mainly white people within the predominantly middle and upper income bracket increasingly housing themselves within gated communities. On the pretext of security from crime, they guard their wealth and power by limiting their physical contact with people from less privileged classes. Britain today has more than 1,000 gated communities – some in the East End. The City of London, of course, remains a fortress as segregated from its surrounding communities as it ever was.

David Cameron returned to the themes of fragmented communities and segregation in April 2011, accusing immigrants of creating "discomfort and disjointedness" in communities.[24] Aside from rich inhabitants of gated ghettoes claiming territory and services for exclusive use, in the East End today it is surely increasing gentrification that causes problems of disjointedness and discomfort. Low-income families are discomforted by rising rents for private landlords, reduced access to housing stock, and inflated prices for everyday goods as shops adapt to more affluent sectors settling their streets. Cameron chose to ignore a report from Manchester University based on a survey sample of 25,000 people, released at the end of March 2011, which confirmed that deprivation rather than "multiculturalism" fragments communities, while more diverse neighbourhoods actually display greater social cohesion.[25]

The massive strides forward that we have made as a fully-fledged multicultural society since Mosley's day, and the ways that most people actually live multicultural lives in Britain's cities today, are in danger of being reversed in an era of drastic cuts in jobs, services and housing benefits. How can we ensure that we challenge cutbacks as united communities, defending and strengthening our multicultural reality? And, can we simultaneously put forward a vision of sustainable regeneration that promotes the highest expectations for the material as well as the social fabric of the built environment in which we live our culturally intertwined lives?

Our Battle of Cable Street 75 years on, in inner–city areas such as the East End, is to prevent the invasion of more inequality, more neglect and more hopelessness in our communities and to resist any attempts by the powerful to link inequality to our cultural diversity.

1. *Blackshirt*, 4 October 1935.
2. *Blackshirt*, 10 October 1936.
3. E.G. Clarke, *The British Union and the Jews* (London: Abbey Press, 1937).
4. David Cameron, speech to security conference in Munich, 5 February 2011.
5. Angela Merkel, speech in Potsdam, 16 October 2010.
6. David Cameron, *op.cit.*
7. G. Wemyss, *The Invisible Empire: White Discourse, Tolerance and Belonging* (Farnham: Ashgate, 2009) pp. 124–133.
8. "If we want social cohesion we need a sense of identity", interview with David Blunkett by Colin Brown, *Independent on Sunday*, 9 December 2001.
9. J. Bourne, *In Defence of Multiculturalism*, IRR Briefing Paper No 2 (London: Institute of Race Relations, 2007).
10. *Blackshirt*, 30 September 1933.
11. *Daily Mail*, 15 January 1934.
12. Mosley won the seat of Harrow West for the Tories in 1918 and held it again as an independent until 1924. In 1926 he won the seat of Smethwick for Labour.
13. *Blackshirt*, 19 October 1934.
14. *Jewish Chronicle*, 31 July 1936. The crudest examples of biological antisemitism were associated with a local street–corner speaker, E.G. "Mick" Clarke from Bethnal Green, and the fascists' national director of propaganda, William Joyce, who stood as a council candidate in Shoreditch in 1937.
15. See *Blackshirt*, 16 September 1933, 18 October 1933 and 30 November 1933.
16. *Blackshirt*, 29 March 1935.
17. W. Zuckerman, *The Jew in Revolt* (London: Secker, 1937) p. 75.
18. J. Dash, *Good Morning Brothers*, (London: Lawrence & Wishart, 1969) p. 39.
19. A. Morris, *Unfinished Journey* (London: Artery Publications, 2006) pp. 52–53.
20. Anti–fascists also carried through a deliberate strategy of undermining fascist arguments through contact on neutral ground, especially in boxing clubs and other sports facilities.
21. P. Piratin, *Our Flag Stays Red* (London: Lawrence & Wishart, 1948).
22. A. Brimicombe, 'Ethnicity, religion, and residential segregation in London: evidence from a computational typology of minority communities', *Environment and Planning B: Planning and Design*, 34(5), 2007, pp. 884–904.
23. 'Why Trevor is wrong about race ghettoes', *The Observer*, 25 September 2005.
24. Speech by David Cameron in Southampton, 14 April 2011.
25. Report based on research led by Dr Laia Becares, Manchester University, http://www.manchester.ac.uk/aboutus/news/display/?id=6866.

We Write the Story of Our Town

A Folk Tale of 21st Century Tottenham

RUTH ALLEN *&* MITAL PATEL

A fairytale beginning

There is a place called Wards Corner, above Seven Sisters tube station in Tottenham, North London. She has shops, houses and an indoor market full of food and produce and music of the world. She is the heroine of our little fairytale. She has a heart full of memories and she is a place where people now live, work and meet their friends. To them – and to many of those who live nearby – she represents continuity from past to present. This is imbued in her bricks and mortar, in her architecture and in the hard work of the people from all over the world who create her rich ecology.

But Wards Corner has become like a wayward daughter of the local council, Lord Haringey. This exasperated patriarch is desperate to tame her. She has been going her own way far too long, keeping 'exotic', unruly and bohemian company. With her tatty appearance and ragtag associates, she has become a disgrace, bringing shame upon the borough.

Wards Corner had a scheming stepmother: the Bridge New Deal for Communities regeneration project. She told wicked tales of Wards Corner's depravity to the local people and tried to turn them against our heroine. Lady Bridge wanted rid of this embarrassing stepdaughter. Together, Lord Haringey and Lady Bridge plotted to find a husband for this disgraceful daughter – a knight in a shining city suit who would transform her.

And so they secretly chose Sir Grainger (plc) of Newcastle. He and his entourage rode into town with a gaudy show of riches and many, many

promises. Father and stepmother swooned in gratitude. (And handed over a goodly
part of their daughter's dowry before the wedding date was even discussed!)

    Sir Grainger promised to redeem not only Wards Corner and the tarnished
reputation of Lord Haringey, but also to save the poor people of the parish
from their apparent refusal to become more ... well ... middle class! And he
planned to do this by subjugating and breaking Wards Corner completely.
The people, the buildings, the life and activity – they would be destroyed
and replaced by a sanitised, privatised, perfect bride. This Stepford–style
replacement would be packaged and sold back to the people of Tottenham as
the Wards Corner daughter they have always really, secretly desired. Through
her, the people would realise their love of all things corporate and their desire to
consume, consume, consume from the globalised market place of the chain store.

    BUT ... our heroine, Wards Corner, has other ideas. She loves her life
and all her friends and she believes a different future – a different end to this
story – is possible. She is in love with a different dream.

Setting the scene

This is a story about story making within a community resistance campaign in
Tottenham, North London. 'We' are the Wards Corner Community Coalition
(WCC) – a group of shopkeepers, market traders, local residents, community
activists and allies from further afield, campaigning to save homes, small
businesses, social amenities and historic buildings at the Wards Corner site
above Seven Sisters tube station.

In July 2007, over 60 small businesses and the residents of Wards Corner
and wider Tottenham found out from a local press article that the residential
developer Grainger plc proposed to demolish all the buildings and businesses
on the two–hectare site. These proposals were made in collaboration with
Haringey Council, the (now defunct) Bridge New Deal for Communities
(NDC) and Transport for London (TFL). While 'development' of this site had
been proposed over many years, these 'finalised' proposals came as a shock.

The plans involved creating a high–rise, gated, residential block of nearly
200 entirely private flats above retail outlets. There was consternation at the
scale of demolition, horror at the massing, height and embedded carbon of
the replacement buildings, outcry over the demolition of our history, outrage
at the lack of consideration of those directly affected, and disbelief that the

developer might get permission for a development without any affordable or social housing. While there have been some minor changes to the exterior design of the Grainger architecture since 2007, the fundamental paradigm has remained exactly the same.

This is a familiar 'slash and burn' tale in contemporary British urban planning orthodoxy – and a familiar 'community' response. But the pain and sense of disempowerment for the human subjects involved is not diminished through retelling, and so it has been at Wards Corner.

Many parts of the Wards Corner site do need physical repair. Some parts of it are unoccupied including the iconic Edwardian corner building that was once the main entrance to the locally fabled Wards department store. There is a burnt-out building on the High Street frontage and, at the back of the site, houses are variously falling into disrepair or are concreted up. These buildings speak of neglect, as though no one cares what happens here.

And yet there is a different story to be told of this place. For 30 years, Haringey Council and TFL, intending to rebuild this site, have blocked efforts for piecemeal, natural improvement and investment. Over the years, shopkeepers have applied to make improvements to their buildings and ironically have been prevented by planning and conservation area regulations. Many people have expressed an interest in moving into the empty Wards Stores building on the corner and have not been allowed to pursue their interest. And now Grainger plc is playing its part in promoting physical deterioration and blight by concreting shut the housing it has already bought on the site.

Despite all this, lively trade and habitation have persisted and taken root. Most recently, an international foods supermarket has transformed itself in part into a whole foods store selling organic and fair-trade goods. In many ways, the self-defined, small-scale industries at Wards Corner – and the organised campaign of the WCC – fit with ideas being packaged by the current British government (albeit loosely and confusedly) as the Big Society[1]. Yet the potential for longstanding, small-scale investors on this site to further improve and grow is dismissed by those determined to raze it to the ground.

In June 2010 WCC had a victory in a precedent-setting High Court ruling.[2] This overturned Grainger plc's planning permission to demolish and rebuild, on the grounds of breach of equalities legislation by the council. While the developer and the council still seem determined to carry on with their plans largely unaltered, WCC is just as determined to challenge their orthodoxies of urban planning and

Wards Corner: Contested space, contested story,
2009, WCC

regeneration, and the corporatisation of space and place. And we are using human rights and equalities narratives within legislation to underpin our resistance.

WCC has identified some key 'myths' about the people and the place of Wards Corner and Tottenham which have been used by Haringey Council, Grainger and the NDC to underpin their discourse and decisions. Myths are historically defined as widely believed, often religious stories that organise the thinking and actions of the population around axiomatic ideas and values. In more colloquial, modern definition, 'myth' tends to describe an enduring version or story of events, or the inherent qualities of a thing that cannot be linked definitively to any coherent argument or empirical evidence. These modern myths tend to be part of the 'taken for granted' culture promulgated in dominant, hegemonic discourse – from politicians, the press, corporate businesses, state authorities – and serve to maintain the status quo.

Three myths explored in this essay are:

(1) 'The people of Tottenham don't have the social and cultural capital to really participate in planning for their area.'

(2) 'Wards Corner is a place of crime, transient, unimportant trade and habitation that no one cares about.'

(3) 'The businesses on this site cannot innovate and provide the foundation for its rejuvenation.'

WCC recognises these myths about Wards Corner as subsets of common negative myths about Tottenham more generally. The stigmatisation of the latter is the stigmatisation of us all.

... it's the story, stupid!

Stories are what people use all over the world to communicate meaning and belief. If we can change the story that is shared and believed, we can start to change what happens in the world and we have the chance to author our own futures.

Stories are the basis of the enormous global power of corporate advertising and media. Advertisers sell us a story about ourselves that captures our imagination and, in response, we act (we spend) because we believe. Or rather we temporarily and willingly suspend our disbelief to pursue the advertised dream – that we will look younger, seem more successful, be more attractive, feel more secure.

In WCC we use this process of story making and telling for reasons of social justice and resistance. This is not to *manipulate* people's perceptions as in the corporate mode, but to *represent* the voices of those rendered vulnerable by corporate and political attack and the conventions of urban planning in the UK, and to *persuade* people to listen, believe and act to support those under attack. As Selbin suggests, recognising the power of stories does not diminish the importance of analytic social science and other ways of 'knowing' but "the critical point is that stories offer us a way in; they are another tool of the trade which can be turned to building a better understanding of who we are and where we are going".[3]

One of the reasons the corporations are successful in selling us consumerist dreams (including the dream of corporate regeneration) is because they develop and then offer to cure our internalised negative views of ourselves and our communities. We are 'not good enough', 'not affluent enough'. Tottenham has been relentlessly fed this sort of view of itself for too long, by the press, by politicians, by officers of the council. It is demoralising and inhibits action. We become vulnerable to almost *colonial* intrusion from outside forces as our confidence and our ability to tell our own story is diminished.

This underpins the myth (1) that 'the people of Tottenham don't have the social and cultural capital to really participate in planning for their area'. Restrictive myths about the limits of people's abilities to really influence the planning process help to maintain the social, political and economic 'norm'.

The political status quo of Haringey is characterised by the materially poorer and apparently socially more 'disorganised' east of the borough, which has traditionally voted for the paternalistic Labour politicians who have held civic power continuously since the 1960s, and a much more affluent, differently voting west. Arguably, the politicians in charge have a vested interest in keeping the people of Tottenham in a subjugated state – recognising only their disadvantage and vulnerability and not tapping into their potential to take control of their own futures – because this might change their voting patterns.

This observation is not made to suggest that this is a necessary characteristic of the British Labour Party or to suggest any other party in their position in Haringey would have behaved differently. It is merely an observation made by WCC about the culture of civic power in the borough.

Professor Bryan Fanning's research into the council's planning 'real politick' supports this view, showing that: "in the affluent west, organised networks of amenity and single issue groups forced levels of institutional accountability that contrasted with indifference by the local political elite to community views on planning issues in Tottenham and other deprived areas to the east of the borough ... the Council treated west and east differently when it came to development proposals."[4]

Creating alternative community stories of the possible

WCC has always wanted to build a coherent group that could represent the voice of Wards Corner and wider Tottenham over time. But we needed first to create a coherent narrative amongst ourselves. Could WCC hold together (and be seen to hold together) the interests of a Columbian market stallholder, an East African Guajarati newsagent, a British retired history teacher, a radical green activist, an advertising creative, the proprietor of an off-licence on the site and a health–activist optometrist, among others? Often campaigns that start with such a diversity of interests falter. The story fragments. How could this diversity become a rich source of unity?

From the outset, we explicitly created internal and external stories of ourselves as a meaningful, coherent and *capable* entity with a shared, positive history that was entirely our own. We were explicitly not aligned to any political party or other major activist group, but would transparently relate to any group or individual that would support our key aims. We quickly adopted a name, a slogan ('Plan for the Community'), a memorable visual image (a brand), a rhythm to our regular meetings, a website, a high standard of written and visual artifacts including posters, photographs and films. We created events, large community parties, happenings and stunts that could engage people from many perspectives and also had high 'production values' at no or low financial cost. Our very identifiable imagery and slogans became 'memes' for the campaign, "self replicating units of cultural information that spread virally from person to person ... with a life of their own".[5]

Crucial to the identity and growing strength of the WCC are our many relationships with other similar campaigns in London and beyond, and our links with urban planning, sustainability and human rights activists. We have also been invited to contribute to formal, London–wide, civic processes, such as the Greater London Authority's consultation on the London Plan. The specific, local story of WCC has become part of a much wider and growing story of discontent and solidarity. Through our campaign we can tell not only our own story, but the stories of others. Stories of the threats to markets across London. Stories of the disregard for particular ethnic minority groups within civic life. Stories of how ordinary people striving to take control of urban space and their means of production can align with notions of environmental sustainability and new sustainable economics. In creating the holistic story of Wards Corner, we have contributed to wide networks of people seeking similar ends and have been part of finding the bridges between specific stories and underlying themes.

It is a truism that you can't be a prophet in your own land. Despite the growing visibility of, and respect for, WCC amongst other activists and some formal civic authorities outside our immediate area, communications with the Haringey Council officers and members and the developers have continued to be characterised by the myth of our – or certainly our wider community's – inadequacy. Our opponents continue to labour under this myth, but we approach and disarm this position by treating it at all times as useful information. WCC's understanding of the "battle of the story"[6] means that every use of negative hegemonic stereotypes by our opponents – often revealed in dismissive or patronising attitudes and arrogance – has been turned into rich material for our self-scripted next chapter. We understand that the ineptitude of the public relations campaign by the developer, NDC and council about their proposals has been underpinned by the myth that we, the WCC and the people of Tottenham 'wouldn't expect or know any better' in planning terms. Their belief system is revealed in actions such as:

- the absence of any consultation process with local people about the fundamental paradigm underpinning the redevelopment
- the subsequent publication of images in the press of proposed buildings that were immediately derided by all as unacceptable, unattractive and out of date
- being told by the architect directly in a public meeting that local people "don't understand my plan"
- people at real and imminent risk of losing their homes and businesses through demolition being told by an officer of the NDC that "sometimes I think people are more interested in buildings than people".

Every time our opponents act in ways that reveal their disregard for our capabilities and our humanity, we openly turn this back on them and reveal it as the story of *their* inadequacy and disrespectful behaviour. This becomes a story to tell others but also to tell ourselves, to build our cohesion.

As Brian Fanning found, the council had no experience in collaborating in an authentic way with community organisations in the east of the borough – outside of a heavily paternalistic (patriarchal) framework of state–funded regeneration institutions. It has become very apparent to us in the WCC that the council has no language, no means of discourse to use to communicate with us on level terms, to enter into our authentic, relationship–rich discourse. When we communicate with civic authority figures, they are usually discombobulated by, for instance, our lack of a single 'leader' through which to funnel their communications. In the absence of such an individual we have been described as leaderless. Yet the reality is that we have many leaders – and developing us all into leaders is part of how the WCC has retained its hydra-like, surprising energy.

One notable episode that contrasted WCC and council approaches to communication, power and hierarchy was a meeting that turned into an enacted psychodrama in the main chamber of the Town Hall in 2009. We had approached the then leader of the council for a meeting on equal, collaborative terms, in a neutral place. In conversations with the leader's office, our approach to them was quickly and unashamedly transformed into the expectation that *we* would be attending the *leader's* meeting – in council offices.

We finally agreed to meet in the Civic Centre and ended up in the main chamber with its hierarchical layout. There is a raised platform at the front where senior figures sit during council meetings with rows of chairs and tables below. We started to move chairs into a circle to create a space for equal discussion on the level below the platform – only to find the leader of the council making his way directly to one of the raised seats of power and declaring his intention of sitting there. So some of us placed seats at his level and joined him, along with the local MP. He was obdurate and we would not be subjugated by the trappings of power – although joining the elevated podium was a theatrical not an ethical move on our part. We wanted equal human communication, not power games.

The leader and the MP had no language, no discourse for equal, human collaboration. They could not even create a temporary space to suspend the formal power relations they relied upon to display their authority. In a discussion circle, they would of course still have had the authority vested in their civic offices but they could have let a different, inclusive form of human discourse emerge. It was as if they didn't know how.

I am here, now ... hear me

Wards Corner is the site where the livelihoods of over 60 people and their families are made. Some people have lived and/or worked there for 25 years or more. The indoor market is a social as well as a commercial space for all comers and has been providing a meeting place in particular for the Latin American community across London and beyond for ten years. Yet the council, NDC and developers all along have treated Wards Corner like a virtual brownfield site, as if occupied by a few unwelcome and somehow 'illegitimate', temporary occupants.

When Grainger plc first unveiled its plans, it and the council and NDC made apparent their intention to use the myth (2) that 'this is a place of crime, transient, unimportant activity and habitation that no one cares about'. This belief was revealed in myriad ways:

- the chairman of the planning committee spoke about the 'fact' that the market is full of drugs and crime
- the market traders received no notification of the plans to demolish and rebuild at all and the street shopkeepers only received general notices
- the two 'business support seminars' organised for the businesses that were required to move had seating for 20 when over 60 were affected (and turned up) – and provided no Spanish and Portuguese translation for the many Latin Americans affected
- at the planning committee meeting for the Grainger plan, a senior officer of the planning department stated that "these market traders have moved before, they can move again"
- a councillor in support of Grainger's plans at the planning committee said: "it's a dump, it's always been a dump" – and received no admonishment from the chairman.

The story of crime at Wards Corner has been particularly important for the council, NDC and developers, playing on primal fears. WCC has been informed repeatedly by the local police that there is virtually no crime reported in the indoor market and that crime around the site is certainly no higher than in the surrounding areas and is lower than in some areas which have types of commercial development similar to that proposed by Grainger, such as at Wood Green. Indeed, the indoor market is most characterised by safety for the many young children that run around and as a safe meeting place for teenagers and adults of all ages. And yet the elision of 'neglect' and 'crime' has been important in the developer's and council's attempts to create a public story that only demolition and replacement will make us all feel safer.

The fact that many of the market traders and some shopkeepers don't use English fluently makes silencing their stories all the more easy. Authorities can get away with, for instance, erroneously merging 'Latin American' with 'Colombian', and 'Colombian' with 'drugs' in hostile discourse about the market. One of the primary tasks of WCC has been to ensure that people who cannot tell their story in English are heard. Coverage in the local and London–wide press (including *Time Out*) and a short BBC film for the Inside Out series have started to reveal the life of this site to the outside world. Using imagery, actions and feelings, including in our own films, WCC can create communications with the wider public and with civic authorities that transcend verbal or written national languages.

A street action that perhaps captured most vividly the sense of Wards Corner being a place with life, to be preserved and nourished, was the Hug, in which 500 people held hands to form a circle around the site. This warm gesture told many stories – to passers–by and to the press on the day – which have since been retold many times in words and pictures: a story of care, of unity, of defence, of human diversity, of the power of visible, organised resistance.

How will we create the future of our town?

The point has been made already that this is a site that is currently, properly inhabited and used – richly and densely and persistently. The point has also been made that, while the fabric of the site is falling into disrepair, the current custodians of it want to be part of its growth and change. During the campaign, despite all the uncertainty and threat, many people recommitted to the site through diversifying their business, offering more fair–trade and organic goods, improving the fabric of their buildings, even investing in freehold interest. This investment of heart and money seems invisible to the council, which remains committed to its myth (3) that 'the businesses on this site cannot innovate and provide the foundation for its rejuvenation'.

From the outset in 2007, people from Pueblito Paisa, a market traders' association on the Wards Corner site, showed their ability to promote a different vision of the future by commissioning an alternative architectural plan for Wards Corner (the 'Community Plan'). The existence of this plan – and the positive interest and enthusiasm it garnered – was an immediate challenge to the lie that people in the area could not organise to contribute to the future of their area. The plan was embraced by the wider WCC. We held what several longstanding residents and activists called 'the largest public meeting in Tottenham for 40 years' to discuss our ideas for stopping Grainger and building on the Community Plan. One participant wrote at the end of the meeting: "This is astonishing and fantastic. It's how democracy works." The gathering of over 300 people, all talking with enthusiasm and intelligence about what they wanted, set a precedent. The press reported it and it soon became an important moment in Tottenham folklore.

The Community Plan is being further refined as WCC organises to capture further community views and ideas and aspirations.[7] WCC has spoken to thousands of people at summer fairs, street parties, political hustings, within the market, and during our own street actions and community parties. We have held community planning events and substantial discussions with potential funders and designers. We have logged and recorded and filmed hundreds of people's views. The overriding characteristic of these interactions, mostly with people from Tottenham or wider Haringey, is their dismay at being silenced by public authorities in the planning and development process. But what comes over even more strongly is the richness of their imagination and articulacy.

Telling a different story of Wards Corner won't in itself save homes, histories, livelihoods and valued social spaces. It may not be sufficient, but it is almost certainly necessary. Without belief in a different future in which the human rights of ordinary people are not at the mercy of corporate interests and unaccountable civic power, urban space will increasingly be colonised and made less diverse, less controlled by the people who use it, less interesting. Perhaps the greatest success of the WCC to date has been its contribution to enabling local people to communicate, to talk and find their voice, to contribute something distinctive to the wider story of urban planning and sustainability activism.

And finally ... billboard wars

Perhaps the most graphic display of how WCC has been creating and using story to campaign, to communicate and to debunk myth is the story of 'billboard wars'. In 2009, for two weeks WCC legitimately hired a billboard – that most emblematic tool of consumerism – at the front of Seven Sisters. On it we pasted a professional poster saying: "If Haringey Council approves the plan to demolish these buildings, it would completely wreck a thriving local community." After three days, in the middle of the night, the poster on the billboard was professionally obliterated. The police investigated for us. Looking through CCTV, they spotted a van that may have been involved but could not see the culprits. They got away. But we had a replacement poster ... because we already knew how this story was likely to go. And two days later, almost on cue, that too was professionally pasted over, and again those responsible could not be traced. We had no more professional posters, but we had something much, much better: a fabulous tale of a sneaky and ignominious foe, and a billboard on which to tell the story.

*The authors would like to give special thanks to Sara Hall and Karolina Maroszek for their fairytales.

1. Samuel Middleton, 'The Big Society's Biggest Problem. What can the Big Society offer Seven Sisters Market?', *ResPublica*, 16 February 2010, http://www.respublica.org.uk/blog/2011/02/big-society%E2%80%99s-biggest-problem.
2. See a short explanation of the High Court ruling on the Equalities and Human Rights Commission website at http://www.equalityhumanrights.com/news/2010/june/court-issues-a-reprieve-to-residents-of-wards-corner/, or find the whole ruling at www.wardscornercommunity.com.
3. Eric Selbin, *Revolution, Rebellion, Resistance: The Power of Story* (London & New York: Zed Books, 2010) p. 29.
4. Brian Fanning, '*Community Planning Elites and Spatial Inequality*', abstract of presentation at Birkbeck College, University of London, November 2010.
5. Patrick Reinsborough and Doyle Channing, *Re-imagining change* (Oakland: PM Press, 2010) p. 32.
6. *ibid.*, Reinsborough and Channing (2010).
7. See IDEAs page, www.wardscornercommunity.com.

William Morris, the Practical Utopian

HASSAN MAHAMDALLIE

When the famous artist and infamous revolutionary, William Morris, died in 1896 at the age of 63, Robert Blatchford, the editor of the northern mass working–class newspaper, the *Clarion*, wrote:

> *I cannot help thinking that it does not matter what goes in the Clarion this week, because Morris is dead. He was our best man, and he is dead. How can we think of the movement today but as a thing struck motionless? I have just been reading some of the obituary notices in some of the Labour papers, and I feel sick and sorry. The fine phrases, the elaborate compliments, the ostentatious parade of their own erudition, and the little covert smears at the socialism Morris loved; all the tawdry upholsteries of these journalistic undertakers seems like desecration … Morris was not only a genius, he was a man. Strike at him where you would, he rang true.*[1]

My experience in writing and talking about William Morris is that the influence of this remarkable 19th–century figure still rings true, and has at least partially escaped being consigned to a dusty corner of Victoriana. I like to think that his uncompromising radical politics has stymied attempts by avowed 'fans', such as Tony Blair, to put him in the 'harmless Victorian icon' box.

Modern affinities

Morris's present–day admirers continue to flow from unexpected quarters. One of the most interesting projects I have taken part in was a BBC Radio programme *Morris and the Muslims*[2] in which the producer talked to a number of Muslims about their admiration for William Morris and what he meant to them. Principally Morris connected to them through his art – it is easy to see the Muslim connection in Morris's fruit blossom wallpaper patterns which repeat to geometric infinity, in the simplicity and beauty of his Morris Chair, and in his emphasis on the medieval guild system of manufacture which equates to a similar historic mode of production in the Middle East.

But some of those interviewed had clearly been struck by a deeper affinity – one which I expressed in the programme as "Morris's jihad", by which I mean his predisposition to 'struggle' on every level: his art and craftsmanship, his business dealings, his politics and his personal life. That Morris was non-religious does not matter to those Muslims who relate to him today. Like many others before, it is Morris in his entirety that has somehow touched them. For me, the Muslims who took part in that radio programme have a much better understanding of Morris than those who love his art but decry his political life.

His achievements certainly deserve to be rediscovered by a new generation of artists, urban radicals, anti–capitalists and socialists, because if you could sum up Morris's message to the Victorian working class it would surely be: 'Another world is possible.' We should look at him not so much as an interesting historical figure, but as a voice with contemporary relevance and as an inspiration.

His declarations against the age he was forced to live in and endure come through to us today with perfect clarity:

> *All wars now waged, under whatever pretences, are really wars for the great prizes in the world market.[3]*

> *It is profit which draws men into enormous unmanageable aggregations called towns, for instance; profit which crowds them up when they are there into quarters without gardens or open spaces; profit which won't take the most ordinary precautions against wrapping a whole district in a cloud of sulphurous smoke; which turns beautiful rivers into filthy sewers, which condemns all but the rich to live in houses idiotically cramped and confined at the best, and at the worst in houses for whose wretchedness there is no name.[4]*

> *That system, which I have called competitive commerce, is distinctly a system of war; that is of waste and destruction ... the point of it being that under it whatever a man gains he gains at the expense of some other man's loss. Such a*

*system cannot heed whether those who make them are degraded by their work:
it heeds one thing and only one, namely, what is called making a profit ... the
plunder of the weak by the strong.[5]*

*The misery of those who are sweated, whether by the drill of factory or the
many links of the sweated chain, is the high price to pay for the glory of sus-
taining a class of idle, rich men. Is the gain worth the price?[6]*

Integrity and integration

Many commentators have tried to separate off the bit of Morris they find
uncomfortable. They are missing the point: what is fascinating about Morris's
art is that it expressed precisely the conditions and contradictions of the
period he lived through and in it one can trace the trajectory of his political
career. For William Morris the artist was also William Morris the revolutionary
socialist. In 1884, at the age of 49, this feted and respected son of the establishment set himself against the establishment; he crossed what he described as
the "river of fire"[7]. He joined the 200 or so Marxist revolutionaries in Britain
at that time, and worked unceasingly until his death in 1896 for the cause of
socialism. In the declaration for the Socialist League, the revolutionary party
he founded in 1885, Morris wrote: "Fellow citizens, we come before you as a
body advocating the principles of revolutionary international socialism; that
is, we seek a change in the basis of society – a change which would destroy the
distinctions of classes and nationalities."[8]

Morris fused his love and deep knowledge of art and the artistic process
with the processes that bring about revolutionary change, to give us a unique
insight into the potential of humanity and to show that, under socialism, work
and play, art and manufacture, urban planning and the people who inhabit
our cities, would no longer be divided but fused into one.

During his lifetime Morris talked to many thousands of workers,
from those in the East End of London fighting for free speech to striking
miners in Northumberland, on subjects as varied as the Paris Commune,
art under socialism, and the Marxist theory of labour. Morris had
around him such figures as Marx's daughter Eleanor and her partner
Edward Aveling, George Bernard Shaw before he went over to the Fabians,
H.G. Wells, the science–fiction writer whose work was undoubtedly

influenced by Morris's visions of the future, and working–class leaders Tom Mann and John Burns.

Morris was central to the launch of the arts and crafts movement, combining a rejection of the ornate and grotesque Victorian design and architecture with its primary purpose of showing how rich and powerful the owner was, with the conviction that the working class should have access to the best art.

Morris's enduring political contribution was to the worker, who would have Morris's great utopian work *News from Nowhere* that science–fictioned a post–revolutionary London, or his stirring tale about the Peasants' Revolt, *A Dream of John Bull,* on their shelves. His visions of the future have inspired successive generations in Britain, turning them on to radical thought, precisely because he attempts to provide a positive and rich answer to the question: what would you replace capitalism with, and what would such a society be like?

Morris represents an unbroken thread of practical dreamers, extending back to early utopian visionaries like Thomas More, those who organised the Peasants' Revolt, the Diggers, the Levellers and the radical wing of the English Revolution, through figures like William Blake, the Chartists and the abolition movement against slavery, to the later 19th century of Morris's life and onwards. This story is well told by the Communist Party historian A.L. Morton in his book, *The English Utopia.*[9] This tradition, once an integral presence in the historical consciousness of the British and international left, found its modern expression in the 1990s in the visionary demands of the anti–capitalist movement.

A wider historical perspective places Morris in the ranks of those of the disenfranchised and the dissenting, including the few questioning individuals from the ruling elite, who struggled to project an alternative vision to the development of British capitalism. That's why he deserves rescuing for posterity – and that link with our history thereby restored to us all.

Becoming socialist

William Morris was born in 1834 in Walthamstow, north London, into a wealthy middle–class family. When he was ten his stockbroker father acquired 272 £1 shares in a new Devonshire copper mining company. Within six months, when the mines were found to be richer than first believed, the shares were worth £200,000, a fortune for those times. Of course, one consequence was that William and the rest of the family didn't have to worry about money, but the mining venture is also an indication of the economic and political changes that were being wrought in society. While the young William was growing up, British society was changing rapidly. The political watershed was 1848 – the year the British working class, in the form of the Chartists, suffered a historic defeat at the hands of a fast maturing British state.

The Chartists were the first mass workers' movement. They agitated and fought for a 'People's Charter' of universal suffrage, no property qualifications for voters, annual parliaments, worker's pay for MPs and vote by the ballot box. Political action during the Chartist period spanned parliamentary pressure, monster petitions that were millions strong, a general strike (1842), riots, uprisings, armed struggle and revolutionary plots. Their agitation was a radical challenge to the (corrupt) order of things, but at the end of the day, the ruling class faced down the Chartists, proving itself more ruthless than its democratic opponents. If there was a single turning point, it was the face–off that took place on 10 April 1842. A mass Chartist demonstration assembled at Kennington Common, south London, with just a short march to Westminster. The would–be demonstrators were met by a ban, 85,000 special constables armed with staves, mounted police and troops equipped with field–guns, all under the command of the Duke of Wellington. The Chartist leaders, faced with the prospect of a massacre, backed down, allowing the state to go on the offensive, and thereafter the movement began to decline.

The period that followed was marked by what historian John Saville has persuasively defined as "the consolidation of the capitalist state".[10] This enforced political stability brought British capitalism a period of continuous economic expansion between 1848 and 1874, shaping the world in which Morris was to grow to maturity.

The economic expansion and increasing industrialisation sucked labour into the cities, creating rapid unplanned urbanisation. The slums and smokestacks that marked Victorian prosperity were a symbol of, as Morris himself put it, "all the incredible filth, disorder and degradation of modern civilisation"[11]. After repeated epidemics of cholera, typhus and smallpox demonstrated to the ruling class that certain reforms in sanitation and sewerage systems were desirable from their point of view, the worst aspects of these slums were dealt with, beginning in the 1840s. However, that did not mean that the working–class people in the cities were lifted in some philanthropic way out of the degradation imposed on them. It was rather that, as Frederick

Engels put it, "the bourgeoisie have made further progress in the art of hiding the distress of the working class".[12]

It is worth quoting at length Morris's description of his feeling of hopelessness and suffocation in his 1894 article 'How I Became a Socialist':

> *The immediate future seemed to me likely to intensify all the present evils by sweeping away the last survivals of the days before the dull squalor of civilisation had settled down on the world ... Think of it! Was it all to end in a counting house on the top of a cinder-heap, with Podsnap's drawing room in the offing and a Whig committee dealing out champagne to the rich and margarine to the poor in such convenient proportions as would make all men contented together ... Yet believe me, in my heart, when I really forced myself to look towards the future, that is what I saw in it, and, as far as I could tell, scarce anyone seemed to think it worthwhile to struggle against such a consummation of civilisation.*[13]

Morris was a product of the society in which he lived, but he was no little Englander. He was an internationalist, which was very much a minority position at the time of the heyday of imperialism. He was inspired by the struggle of revolutionaries in Russia. He defended to the hilt the Paris Commune of 1873. He broke from the dead-end liberalism of Gladstone (a lesson some are painfully re-learning today) and allied himself with the working-class movement rather than with Gladstone's imperialist adventures abroad. Morris condemned colonial expansion, questioning how Britain could play the role of spreading so called "civilisation" when "it is necessary to kill a man in order to make him accept it".[14] At a time when Marxism was considered by most in the movement as a 'foreign import', Morris defended it.

As a young man at Oxford University, William Morris fell in with a group of idealists and set up a quasi religious 'brotherhood' – a mock monastic order "for a Crusade and holy warfare against the age and the heartless coldness of the times".[15] He steeped himself in the anti-capitalist literature of the time, especially the work of Thomas Carlyle and John Ruskin. It is easy to see why. Carlyle's *Past and Present* was a blistering attack on the "cash nexus" and the degradation of the individual under Victorian capitalism. In its place, he idealised 12th-century monastic life. Ruskin's *The Nature of the*

Gothic compared 19th-century capitalism with medieval society through the medium of architecture and condemned the way in which the craftsmanship of the small producers of the Middle Ages had been replaced by the alienation of the factory system. He said, quite rightly, that human beings were being turned into machines.

Guided by these critiques, Morris rebelled against the stifling world he lived in. He was inspired by the romantic notion of a purer, more dignified mediaeval past, particularly the guild system. In 1861 Morris set up a factory called The Firm and based its processes on the methods of medieval manufacture. The individual work of the carpenter or the weaver, with their simple decorations and lines, was a revolt against the gaudy, over-the-top fussiness of Victorian design. Morris researched natural dyeing techniques and his famous wallpaper was hand printed (with blocks now owned by Sanderson).

During this period (roughly 1856–84), Morris increasingly came up against a contradiction that eventually drove him into political action. This was the contradiction between the past he revered and the actual society he lived in. There was no real escape and nowhere to hide. It would be wrong to say that Morris wanted to slavishly recreate Gothic art and architecture. What was important was embodied in the process of mastering past skills, whether that be in book binding, glass firing, engraving or weaving. It was the manner of the work – bringing out the creativity of the worker – that was central to his medievalism. This meant that the processes he used for manufacturing his furnishings cost a lot of money. He was forced to build up a clientele among the very rich, the very people who symbolised everything he detested. But to make his handicraft cheaper and thus more widely available would mean surrendering to mass production – separating the worker from his or her work. This, too, went against Morris's philosophy.

So he was caught. He expressed this contradiction in typically rebellious and impatient fashion. He lost a contract to provide a silk and gold altar cross for a church after he included the following comment with the estimate: "Note: In consideration of the fact that the above item is a wholly unnecessary and inexcusable extravagance at a time when thousands of poor people in this so-called Christian country are in want of food – additional charge to that set forth above, ten pounds."[16]

Morris must have been infuriated when his contempt for his clients only served to make him even more fashionable with the rich.

Street fighting days

Morris became a socialist just as the working–class movement revived and shifted to the left. Suddenly the missing part of the formula, an active agent of change, the working class, thrust him out of his brooding about the past and into trying to build the future. In July 1883 he was received as a Fellow of Exeter College, and just four months later, when he returned to Oxford to give a lecture on politics to liberal and radical–minded undergraduates, Morris delivered a storming critique of capitalism, including an extraordinary denunciation of war:

I tell you that the very essence of competitive commerce is waste; the waste that comes of the anarchy of war. Do not be deceived by the outside appearance of order ... how clean the polished cannon; neat as a new pin are the storehouses of murder ... the very orders for destruction and plunder are given with the quiet precision which seems the very token of a good conscience; this is the mask that lies before the ruined cornfield and the burning cottage, the mangled bodies, the untimely death of worthy men, the desolated home.[17]

At the end of the lecture, there was a 'deathly hush'. Morris's imminent investiture as poet laureate (he was a prodigious poet) was suddenly cancelled.

When the Social Democratic Federation he had joined split, in December 1884, Morris and Eleanor Marx went to Friedrich Engels for advice on how to form a new party, and then created the Socialist League. It launched a paper, *Commonweal,* edited by Morris and with a list of contributors that included Engels, French socialist Paul Lafargue, and George Bernard Shaw, playwright and scholar of Marxism.

This small band of comrades was soon plunged into the struggles taking place. Increasingly through the 1880s, the London police harassed the small groups of socialists and radicals, no doubt fearing the kind of solidarity they expressed with the Paris Commune of 1871. In the summer of 1885 the harassment was stepped up in the East End of London with socialists arrested every weekend. A protest demonstration was held. This was attacked by the police, the socialist banner was seized and eight people were arrested. Then Morris himself was arrested when protests erupted outside the court after the crowd heard that harsh sentences of hard labour had been handed down against the eight accused. Morris was hauled off the pavement and into the dock. Accused of assaulting a police officer (pulling his helmet off – he was probably 'guilty'), he was charged with a public order offence. The magistrate had the sense to drop the charges, but only after this priceless courtroom exchange[18] had been played out:

Mr Saunders: *What are you?*
Prisoner: *I am an artist, and a literary man, pretty well known, I think, throughout Europe.*
Mr Saunders: *I suppose you did not intend to do this [strike the officer].*
Prisoner: *I never struck him at all*
Mr Saunders: *Well, I will let you go.*
Prisoner: *But I have not done anything.*
Mr Saunders: *Well, you can stay if you like.*
Prisoner: *I don't want to stay.*

He was then liberated and on getting into the street was loudly cheered by the crowd.

This episode scandalised Morris's respectable contemporaries. The then fashionable writer George Gissing moaned in piteous 'art for art's sake' mode: "It is painful to me beyond expression. Why cannot he write poetry in the shade? ... Keep apart, keep apart, and preserve one's soul alive – that is the teaching for the day. It is ill to have been born in these times, but one can make a world within a world."[19]

The police, out to crush the movement, came back for more, and notoriously on 13 November 1887, which became known as Bloody Sunday, they attacked a peaceful demonstration in Trafalgar Square. Morris was shocked and disgusted at the brutality of the police. Two hundred demonstrators were hospitalised, two men dying shortly after as a result of their injuries. Three hundred were arrested, and 160 people sent to jail. The hundred-odd police injuries were a testament to the courage with which the demonstrators attempted to fight back. The following Sunday a 40,000-strong meeting in Hyde Park demanded the release of those arrested and the right to assembly in the capital. Later, back in Trafalgar Square, an innocent law clerk, Alfred Linnell, was killed by mounted police. The working class of London turned out to mourn and vent their anger. A huge demonstration, 120,000 strong, marched the miles from central London to Bow cemetery in the East End singing 'A Death Song', the poem Morris had written and which had been set to music. Here is the opening verse:

What cometh from west to east a-wending?
And who are these, the marchers stern and slow?
We bear the message that the rich are sending
Aback to those who bade them wake and know.
Not one, not one, nor thousands must they slay,
But one and all if they would dusk the day.

The Socialist League printed the poem as a penny pamphlet to be sold during the march to raise money for Linnell's bereaved family. In a passionate speech at the graveside, Morris said: "Our friend who lies here has had a hard life and met with a hard death, and if life had been differently constituted his life might have been delightful, a beautiful and a happy one. It is our business to begin to organise for the purpose of seeing that such things shall not happen; to try and make this Earth a beautiful and happy place."[20]

Between 1884 and 1890, a space of six years, Morris published no less than 500 signed articles, including poetry, prose, sketches, lectures, essays and columns. His creative energies were reawakened and fully engaged. Amongst this output were three highly significant works: the novel, *News From Nowhere*, and two extended poems.

The Pilgrims of Hope is a 70-page poem that merges Morris's early days as a socialist with a defence of the Paris Commune. In *The Dream of John Bull*, which takes the Peasants Revolt of 1381 as its subject, Morris draws on his knowledge of medievalism to deliver a modern lesson. Following a classic device (which he also uses in *News From Nowhere*), the narrator falls asleep and is transported back to 14th-century England where he is able to give John Bull a glimpse of the future before he is killed by the king's men. Through this fictional strategy, Morris explores the nature of the role of the individual in history, expanding on an earlier statement: "The past is not dead, it is living with us, and will be alive in the future which we are now helping to make."[21]

Garden cities

News from Nowhere, as well as being a futuristic novel of a post–revolutionary epoch, explored ecological issues. This is significant. Socialists have often been criticised for adhering to a system of thought that has nothing to say about the environment, and socialism is indeed founded on the notion that humanity's needs are dependent on the continued expansion of industrial development and so necessarily come above ecological considerations. However, this view is being increasingly challenged, for example by John Bellamy Foster in his book *Marx's Ecology – Materialism and Nature*.[22] Foster argues that "although there is a long history of denouncing Marx for a lack of ecological concern, it is now abundantly clear, after decades of debate, that this view does not at all fit with the evidence ... From the start, Marx's notion of the alienation of human labour was connected to an understanding of the alienation of human beings from nature."[23] He points out that "the close connection between Marx's vision of communism and ecological sustainability is evident in the utopian conceptions of the acclaimed 19th–century English artist, master craftsperson, designer, poet, and socialist activist William Morris ... who was not only a firm advocate of Marxian socialism but also one of the formative Green thinkers in the English context."[24] Singling out *News from Nowhere* as an exposition of how a socialist society would reverse human beings' "alienation from the earth: the ultimate foundation/precondition for capitalism", Foster finds that Morris writes "in the spirit of Marx". He cites the passage in the novel where the character Hammond explains that, after the revolution, those who previously packed the conurbations "flocked into the country villages, and so to say, flung themselves upon the freed land like a wild beast upon his prey". Hammond then recounts that after a while the invaders "yielded to the influence of their surroundings". Morris sketches out how the division between town and country "grew less and less", and in this he echoed Marx's conviction that there would, in a world free of capitalist alienation, be a 'restoration' of "the metabolic relation between human beings and the earth".[25]

Morris's vision of a broken and polluted landscape was not his alone. The growing environmental nightmare had previously been conjured up in 1845 by the then 24–year–old Friedrich Engels. In the superb reportage that is his book *The Condition of the Working Class in England*, Engels describes a district of Manchester close by the present site of Manchester University:

> *The most horrible spot … is known as Little Ireland. In a rather deep hole, in a curve of the Medlock and surrounded on all four sides by tall factories and high embankments, covered with buildings, stand two groups of about 200 cottages, built chiefly back to back, in which live about 4,000 human beings, most of them Irish. The cottages are old, dirty, and of the smallest sort, the streets uneven, fallen into ruts and in part without drains or pavements; masses of refuse, offal, and sickening filth lie among standing pools in all directions; the atmosphere is poisoned by the effluvia from these, and laden and darkened by the smoke of a dozen tall factory chimneys.*[26]

For the contemporary reader, Engels and Morris do not only speak of 19th-century Britain. They speak directly to the despoliation of the environment that is accompanying modern industrialisation in the global south. Witness this contemporary description of the southern Malaysian industrialised city of Johor Baru:

> *Through the heart of this sore afflicted town flows the Sungei Seggat, a river by only the most extravagant leap of the imagination. To say it 'flows' is to do hideous injustice to the word; the Sungei Seggat is a rank, black, stagnant, noisome ditch, filling the town centre of Johor Baru with the aroma of raw sewage and rotting carcasses. At the first sight and smell of the Sungei Seggat, it is no longer difficult to imagine the river that must flow through hell.*[27]

Time and again Morris returned to critique and re-envision the urban slums that were the reservoirs of the industrial revolution. He wanted the natural world to be reflected in town planning. "We must turn this land from the grimy backyard of the workshop into a garden."[28] Town architecture should "to a certain extent make up to town dwellers for their loss of field, and river, and mountain".[29] He wanted housing to be built around existing trees instead of levelling everything until it was "as bare as a pavement".[30] "Every child should be able to play in a garden close to the place where his parents live."[31] Morris also advocated that housing should be social and that there should be a harmonious interplay between public and private spaces. In his 1884 article 'The Housing of the Poor',[32] he imagined that good housing could be built:

> ... *in tall blocks, in what might be called vertical streets, but that need not prevent ample room in each lodging, so as to include such comforts of space, air and privacy as every moderately living middle–class family considers itself entitled to ... Inside the houses, beside such obvious conveniences as common laundries and kitchens, a very little arrangement would give the dwellers in them ample and airy public rooms in addition to their private ones; the top storey of each block might well be utilised for such purposes, the great hall for dining in, and for social gathering, being the chief feature of it.*

Morris's aesthetic reflected his attitude to the world outside the door of his workshop. His famous wallpaper patterns were a radical statement: *Jasmine*, *Marigold*, *Apple* and *Vine* were created to indicate the natural world outside the conurbations. Above all, Morris wanted his designs to be enjoyed as a symbol of nature, clothing "our daily and domestic walls with ornament that reminds us of the outward face of the earth, of the innocent love of animals, or of man passing his days between work and rest".[33]

Such vivid, seductive visions run throughout William Morris's writings and speeches. His artistic output was intertwined with his revolutionary views on art and with his radical vision for society. As one of the contributors to the *Morris and the Muslims* radio programme pointed out, it was Morris's conviction that "beauty is everyone's birthright" that drove him towards radicalism.

All the ugly aspects of the modern world were identified by Morris in their nascent forms and their causes analysed. He expounded views deemed by the authorities so extreme that they earned him the attentions of the security services of the time. Glance back at the group of quotes in the first section of this article: imperialism, war and the control of resources, people forced to live in slums, the triumph of profit over need, sweatshop labour. It's all there, and much more. There is something very contemporary about both the restlessness of Morris's critique of capitalism and the egalitarian alternatives he conjured up. It is easy to feel a link between Morris, resisting the brutal manifestations of rising global capitalism, and our lives today, as we struggle against being corrupted and dragged down by that same system's ruinous disintegration.

1. Quoted in E.P. Thompson, *William Morris: Romantic to Revolutionary* (London: Merlin Press, 1976) p. 638.
2. Aired on 7 July 2009 on BBC Radio 4.
3. Nicholas Salmon (ed.), William Morris, *Political Writings: Contributions to Justice and Commonweal 1883–1890* (Bristol: Thoemmes Press, 1994) p. 225.
4. A.L. Morton, *Political Writings of William Morris* (London: Lawrence & Wishart, 1979) p. 153.
5. *ibid.*, Morton (1979) p. 123.
6. *ibid.*, Salmon (1994) p. 382.
7. *ibid.*, Thompson (1976).
8. *ibid.*, Thompson (1976) p. 732.
9. A.L. Morton, *The English Utopia* (London: Lawrence & Wishart, 1952). The whole book is an exposition on various utopian tracts.
10. John Saville, *The Consolidation of the Capitalist State, 1800–50* (London: Pluto Press, 1994).
11. William Morris, 'How We Live And How We Might Live', 1884, lecture, http://www.marxists.org/archive/morris/works/1884/hwl/hwl.htm.
12. Friedrich Engels, *The Condition of the Working Class in England*, first published 1845, http://www.marxists.org/archive/marx/works/1845/condition-working-class/.
13. *ibid.*, Salmon (1994) p. 551.
14. William Morris, 1880, lecture, quoted in *ibid.*, Thompson (1976).
15. *ibid.*, Thompson (1976) p. 25.
16. *ibid.*, Thompson (1976) p. 249.
17. *ibid.*, Salmon (1994) p. 244.
18. *ibid.*, Thompson (1976) p. 394.
19. Fiona MacCarthy, *William Morris: A Life For Our Time* (London: Faber & Faber, 1994) p. 528.
20. *ibid.*, Thompson (1976) p. 494.
21. William Morris, 'The Prospects of Architecture in Civilisation', lecture delivered at the London Institution, 1880, http://www.readbookonline.net/readOnLine/24603/.
22. John Bellamy Foster, *Marx's Ecology: Materialism and Nature* (New York: Monthly Review Press, 2000).
23. *ibid.*, Bellamy Foster (2000) p. 9.
24. *ibid.*, Bellamy Foster (2000) p.176
25. *ibid.*, Bellamy Foster (2000) p.176
26. Friedrich Engels, *The Condition of the Working Class in England* (Oxford: OUP, 1993) p. 72.
27. Victor Mallet, *The Trouble With Tigers: The Rise and Fall of South East Asia* (New York: HarperCollins Business, 2000) p. 168.
28. *ibid.*, Thompson (1976) p. 105.
29. William Morris, 'Making the Best Of It', 1870s, http://www.readbookonline.net/readOnLine/24605/.
30. William Morris, *Hopes and Fears For Art*, 1882,http://www.ebooktakeaway.com/hopes_and_fears_for_art_william_morris p. 38.
31. William Morris, 'How We Live and How We Might Live', 1884, http://www.marxists.org/archive/morris/works/1884/hwl/hwl.htm.
32. William Morris, 'The Housing of the Poor', *Justice*, 19 July 1884, pp. 4–5, http://www.marxists.org/archive/morris/works/1884/justice/15hous.htm.
33. William Morris, 'Some Hints on Pattern–Designing', 1881, http://www.marxists.org/archive/morris/works/1881/hints.htm.

STRATIFICATION

5

Introduction

DEEPA NAIK *&* TRENTON OLDFIELD

The Urban Industry[1] makes much–ado about cities as unrivalled centres of creativity, trade, efficiency and financial might, and also as 'natural' centres for democracy and somehow therefore centres of freedom and prosperity. Citizens are strongly encouraged by governments as well as through popular culture to move from rural areas to cities. Sometimes, as in the case of the UK, people are forcibly removed from rural areas[2] leaving them little choice but to migrate to cities.

Today it is estimated Britain's 60 million+ population live in just 7% of the total land mass,[3] meaning life for the overwhelming majority of people is within clearly defined boundaries that are unnecessarily dense, dirty and over–crowded. In less than two centuries, while many of the most pleasant and productive areas have become the preserve and domain of the few, the majority of the British population has been ushered into increasingly smaller spaces. These conurbations are more heavily policed, controlled, monitored and seemingly bounded than ever before.[4] With reducing supply and increasing demand, property prices have risen by over 90% in just the last ten years.[5]

Throughout South America, North America and Australia, people, principally First Nations people, have been forcibly isolated into smaller and smaller areas. Four in five Australians live in just five cities, despite Australia being one of earth's largest continents.[6] Those Aboriginal Australians not slain by colonialism have, for the most part, been isolated to a few specific locations, leaving the overwhelming majority of the land under the ownership of 'the Crown'[7], a small handful of settler families, and corporations. Despite massive and ongoing clearances, a mythology has been perpetrated that much of the land of Australia is empty, unpopulated. The Crown is the main negotiator and beneficiary. Mining contracts, for example, are arranged with little scrutiny or accountability and are able to be communicated as 'victimless' due to the regularly presented story that the land is 'uninhabited'.[8]

Similar patterns of the emptying of people from 'rural areas' and their subsequent concentration in just a few conurbations can be witnessed right across the planet. Not only are more people living in cities than ever before, more people than ever are concentrated in the smallest amount of space than ever before.[9] Meanwhile the resource–rich areas have been appropriated by the elite, and as a result, urban citizens, isolated from rural, forested and agricultural land, have become more and more reliant on that elite to get basic necessities – food, water, fuel – from these now inaccessible areas. It is time for us to reconsider how cities are promoted and what they really will mean for future generations. Underneath the promises (and experience) of democracy, efficiency, creativity and endless 'possibilities' lie some worrying unintended consequences. It is some of these that the five essays in this chapter explore in detail, first in Bogota, then Beirut, Croatia and London.

Corabastos, the vast fruit and vegetable market in Bogota, Colombia, is one specific urban space where the territorialisation of rural areas, urban migration, and labour and food politics collide. It is here that those displaced from the countryside, mainly by war, agribusiness and drug production, often first find themselves. Currently un–mechanised, the largest fruit and vegetable market in South America commonly has opportunities for work – a life–saver for new migrants to the city. Those now working as market porters might have previously been doctors, farmers, truck drivers or researchers ... anyone. Often they are indigenous people who have been displaced from their lands. Corabastos is the focus of the first two contributions to this section.[10]

The socio–political backdrop to Corabastos is revealed in the opening conversation between artist Juan delGado and researcher Miriam Metliss. They get to the core of the post–colonial context quite quickly when they explain the city of Bogota is divided into clearly defined socio–economic zones: Estrata 1 the 'lowest' and Estrata 6 the 'highest'. Juan delGado details how the division originally came about as a way of enabling wealthier areas to subsidise the energy bills of the poorer areas. The outcome, perhaps unexpectedly, was the geographic solidifying of inequalities, class and stratification.

It is perhaps no surprise then that Juan delGado, a London–based Spanish artist talks of the city's elite minority living in secluded spaces he felt were along the lines of self imprisonment, isolation. He explains that many of the people he met and worked with were unaware of or chose to ignore the existence of markets like Corabastos. The strains of Social–Darwinian colonial logics and 'place denial' are, he suggests, as virulent as ever: "They don't want to go to markets due to the social implications. You are actually acknowledging the 'other' who is of lower class ... having an interaction, even if you are just buying food from them, you are acknowledging them."

Miriam Metliss and Juan delGado discuss how cities like Bogota are important sites for the ongoing struggles of European modernists in the pursuit of demonising 'the rural' and particularly the indigenous non-monotheists. The struggles are being played out through class biases, veiled agendas and incongruous partnerships. We learn the food market is itself at the centre of modernist struggles – it has been bought by a global conglomerate with plans to mechanise the operations, which will, inevitably, reduce work opportunities for migrants and increase unemployment and urban poverty.

The market workers of Corabastos are the subject of Jhon Arias's photographic essay. Jhon documented some of the 200,000 people who pass through the market each day, creating a series of individual portraits that tell an increasingly universal story about the conditions and complexities of labour and migration in 21st-century cities.

Despite the best endeavours of modernism and modernists, inequalities have progressively increased in most urban centres around the world. One of the outcomes of modernism in cities was the notion of zoning in western planning philosophy and policy.[11] In one of those unanticipated correlations, modernism also marshalled the arrival and reputation of management theory and practice.[12] Management theory seeks to remove pressure points and inconveniences while at the same time pre-emptively deterring real or perceived threats in order for the status quo to continue implementing its own ideas of efficiency and shield it from disruption or rebellion and overthrow. It will be no surprise then that the London 2012 Olympic Games was deemed a success, by the Prime Minister of Britain, because there were no problems: "Britain delivered".[13]With dissent firmly muted, the globalising neoliberal machine was able to roll across London without interruption or disturbance. The entire city was akin to an Olympic zone.

The next essay, 'Recognising the Invisible Monument: On the Politics of Memorialisation and Public Space in Post-war Beirut', is by Fadi Shayya, Fouad Asfour and Lana Salman. It problematises the zoning/ghettoisation of different religious and/or political communities exacerbated by the 1990 peace treaty, the Guccification of Beirut's ancient centre, and the recent proposal to 'thread the city together' along the civil–war demarcation line (the Green Line) while at the same time emptying it of any of the conflict signifiers. Known as the 'Soft Connection', this project aims to connect Horsh Al–Sanawbar, the substantial though closed–to–the–public park in the south, to the now exclusive space of downtown Beirut in the north by a landscaped pedestrian and cycle route. And, the authors suggest, it is probably also likely a method to fund more road building despite claiming the project aims to reduce traffic congestion.

What is particularly striking about this proposed grand metropolitan intervention is the seeming naivety of the authorities in regards to the production of space in an infinitely fragile post–war context. The authors point out that all but a few public spaces throughout the city remain unrepaired since the end of the civil war and could well do with the attention of funders and the government. We learn the Soft Connection project managers, Île–de–France, claim as outsiders they are unaware of the political sensitivities and are just choosing the best options based on their 'technical expertise'. Politics is somehow absent from 'the technical'.

The authors examine the role of memory in today's Beirut and suggest that "[i]n post–conflict societies, conflict never ends". "Everyone is talking about reconciliation but no one seems to reach a consensus on its definition or departure point. On the one hand people are still charged with animosity and blind loyalty to their confessional representatives in power; on the other hand, people's war memories have been suppressed by a hegemonic discourse that simplifies the post–war context into promises of utopian spaces." In attempting to ignore the past, the Soft Connection, rather than lessening the trauma of the citizens, will provide a 'glossy' new false cover, leaving conflicts unresolved and ready to erupt.

Zagreb, the capital city of the relatively new nation of Croatia, has also been re–constructed by contemporary warfare. The city's population is one of Europe's most ethnically and religiously homogenous, mainly as a result of the mid–1990s conflict. The performance of national unity along with an attempt to fix a new national identity (based largely on an interpretation of a distant and nostalgic past) has been critical to the reconfigured Republic of Croatia's establishment. This ambition has resulted in significant reductions in civil and political rights, such as the right to protest and rally near the parliament, government ministries, courts and a number of religious sites located mostly in the historic 'Upper Town'. And while a lot of effort has been expended on prominent sites, behind restored facades and out of sight many large buildings deteriorate and vast areas remain derelict. At the same time, a policy of charging the residents of the Upper Town a tax for the restoration of historic monuments is resulting in the area being emptied of its less financially affluent inhabitants. Of note, this urban condition is currently not the result of rapid transformation, but a result of the domination and ossification of the state and its institutions, "which subtly mask the privatisation of public space and common goods". In their essay '(Im)Possible Alternatives: Reclaiming the Public Spaces of Zagreb's Upper Town', Marijana Rimanic, Ivana Hanacek and Ana Kutlesa write: "It would seem that both these legal acts serve to represent the Croatian national identity, transforming the historic core of Zagreb into a kind of Potemkin village, a capital city with no social unrest, a town centre with nice facades, behind which lie rotten ..."

The authors are the organisers of UrbanFestival[14], an annual cultural event that examines different aspects of Zagreb's urban context. Intentionally antagonist and propositional, UrbanFestival's commissioned works happen in the public realm and the highly contentious and un-debated condition and symbolic culture of the Upper Town was the ideal focus for its tenth anniversary programme. The essay charts a controversial salon debate about the role of cultural institutions located in the Upper Town and considers the implications of the artists' interventions, which "... try to render visible the conflicts existing in public space and to suggest possible alternatives. They might instigate a different use and view of public space among its users; however, if this failed to happen, the micro-political gesture of opening up the problematic situation would remain relevant as a form of resistance and critique to dominant practices".

In one particularly dramatic intervention, *Marking*, performed by Sinisa Labrovic, the artist urinated in Marko's Square in the middle of the day, surrounded by a pre-arranged but unknowing audience. His artist's statement explains he was performing this act in order to "soften the exclusivity of the place" and problematise the Law on Public Gathering, otherwise known as Marko's Law. The festival organisers believe that artistic confrontations like this are needed to disrupt the status quo, make existing dissent apparent and highlighting the sites of conflict, particularly sites silenced as a result of attempts at post-war nationalism.

Towards the end of World War II, a parliamentary report was published in Britain introducing the concept of what became known as the 'Social Welfare State'.[15] Aware that it was social turmoil that led to the overthrow of numerous monarchies and empires at the end of World War I, the British establishment, while remaining resolutely unchanged itself, undertook measures to improve living conditions and increase civil rights. With more than a thousand years' experience in reading the moods of the British public, it was keenly aware of growing anger at the devastatingly enormous human losses, the terrible treatment of injured soldiers, the suppression of wages and the wholesale use free labour, particularly of women's labour. At the same time, hundreds of thousands of military personnel had experience of the conditions in which many 'colonial subjects' suffered, and were often sympathetic to their hopes of independence and shared their desire for equality and justice. Class, race and gender consciousness was extremely high.

The almost overnight invention of the British welfare state has been read by many as the deployment of a 'safety valve' on a metaphorical 'pressure cooker'. Anyone lucky enough to have experienced the first 30 years (1950–80) of this experiment might well have lived through the period of greatest social equality, prosperity and innovation known in Britain. Since the early 1980s there has been a step-by-step undoing and privatisation of the social welfare system and an increase in the authoritarianism of the state. In his essay '"I know thee not, old man": The Designated Public', Robin Bale sets out to interrogate one important aspect of the contemporary condition: the existence in recent years of 'the Designated Public'. Robin undertook a guided walk/drink-in during the TINAG festival in which fellow walkers/drinkers traversed lower Hackney's Designated Public Spaces – a masterstroke of tautology as these public spaces are in fact spaces of increased regulation. For example, drinking alcohol is prohibited – they have become Alcohol Control Zones. Penalties can be issued, convictions sought and people moved on – "giving the police the power to deal with them".

Robin Bale reflects on his performance/walk and reveals that in May 2010 Hackney Council formalised the entire borough, not just isolated gentrifying hot spots, as a Designated Public Place. The process was undertaken without consultation, and without publicity. When faced with criticism, the council defended its obtuse actions by conflating 'anti-social behaviour' with 'unhealthiness' and individuals meeting to drink together. As police comment makes apparent they also see it as a class concern: "We wouldn't want to take alcohol from people having a picnic and some wine in Shoreditch Park, for instance." Robin Bale argues the current neoliberal obsession with management means there is an unrelenting momentum towards flattening spontaneity and forestalling the unpredictable – even if it means removing people from 'the public'. Modernism demands it.

There is, of course, something appealing about the possibility of much of the planet's population coming together in well–organised, highly responsive cities. Ideally, proximity could translate into efficient housing, transport and energy use, quick access to health care and higher education, and unprecedented sociability and networks … a realisation, perhaps, of one version of the modernist utopia? However, as this chapter shows, urgent questions arise from the demographic and spatial transformation of rural areas resulting from the emptying of the countryside. If these patterns of rural to urban migration continue, will much of the earth be very lightly populated while billions live in a small number of massive conurbations? With already existing problems of high urban unemployment and lack of affordable housing and services, how can cities cope with continually increasing density and population? Will cities have to become yet more 'managed', more bureaucratically 'organised', and urban lives still more regimented and surveilled, in order to accommodate the vast numbers and complexities? Of prime concern, who will own these massive cities, and equally importantly, who will own the countryside with its essential resources, and what would this mean for both urban and rural dwellers? It is suggested we are seeing the implementation of the largest and longest 'kettle'[16] and the latest iniquitous attempt to remove 'the commons' from the people. The disconnection of the urban and the rural is a strategic neoliberal tactic; the 'land grabs' and struggles in rural areas are umbilically linked to struggles in urban areas. How can we turn this situation into a determined reclaiming of 'the commons', so that rather than corporations and a few 'colonising' families, the people own, manage and distribute the natural resources needed to sustain the billions in cities?

These essays highlight some potent though largely camouflaged strategies at work in 21st–century class conflict – many of them hangovers from European colonialism and now reborn in American and/or neoliberal imperialism. We learn that despite proclaimed civil rights, declarations of human rights and promulgation of anti–discrimination laws, abominable ideas of human classification and stratification remain embedded in the logic of many establishment institutions and are being employed in the conception, construction and management of today's cities. What can we draw from the experiences and current protests of people in cities around the world to devise more effective tactics? What role can greater global awareness and solidarity play? Is it possible that we actually have what we need – the impetus and means to achieve mutual respect and equality, to overcome the divisions created by bigotry, racism and other imposed forms of classification and stratification, to break free from debt and economic slavery – in the combined agency of urban populations?

1. For more information see our introduction to *Critical Cities: Volume 2* titled 'The Urban Industry and its Post–Critical Condition' (Myrdle Court Press: London, 2010) pp. 3–27, which analyses how the fields of architecture, property development, real estate investment, planning, design, urban regeneration, conservation management, the creative industries and visual cultures (along with their related foundations, festivals, media, PR and academia) have assisted in attempts to assemble the many in subservience to capitalist interests.

2. See for example, Peter Linebaugh, *The Manifesto of the Magna Carta: Liberties and Commons for All* (University of California Press: Berkeley, 2008).

3. Mark Easton, 'The great myth of urban Britain', BBC, 28 June 2012. http://www.bbc.co.uk/news/uk–18623096 (accessed 30/08/12).

4. Stephen Graham, *Cities Under Siege: The New Military Urbanism* (Verso: London, 2010).

5. 'The Premier League housing boom', 18 August 2012, http://www.lloydsbankinggroup.com/media1/press_releases/2012_press_release_brands/halifax/1808_housing.asp (accessed 30/08/12).

6. Susan Thompson, *Planning Australia: An Overview of Urban and Regional Planning* (Cambridge University Press: Cambridge, 2007).

7. Kevin Cahill, *Who Owns the World: The Hidden Facts Behind Landownership* (Mainstream Publishing: Edinburgh, 2006).

8. See for example, Anne M. Fitzgerald, *Mining agreements: negotiated frameworks in the Australian minerals sector* (Prospect Media: Chatswood, 2002); Central Land Council, 'Making agreements on Aboriginal land', http://www.clc.org.au/articles/info/mining–and–development (accessed 31/08/12).

9. 'The Growing Urbanization of the World', http://www.earth.columbia.edu/news/2005/story03–07–05.html (accessed 31/08/12).

10. At the TINAG festival, Juan delGado exhibited his three–screen installation *The Flickering Darkness* and Jhon Arias exhibited 13 portraits titled *People of Corabastos*.

11. Anthony Alofsin, *The Struggle for Modernism: Architecture, Landscape Architecture and City Planning at Harvard* (WW Norton & Co: New York, 2002).

12. Richard Thorpe and Robin Holt, *Dictionary of Qualitative Management Research* (Sage Publications: Leeds, 2008).

13. 'London Olympics 2012: "Britain delivered", says David Cameron', http://www.guardian.

co.uk/sport/video/2012/aug/12/london-olympics-britain-delivered-cameron-video (accessed 31/08/12).

14. BLOK (Local Base for Cultural Refreshment) Urban Festival has been investigating and commissioning new works that question notions and uses of public space for over a decade. For more see, http://www.blok.hr/.

15. William Beveridge, Report of the Inter-Departmental Committee on Social Insurance and Allied Services (HMSO: London, 1942).

16. Kettling is a police tactic used to control crowds during protests and demonstrations. Police wearing riot gear use their bodies and vehicles to encircle and contain a group of protesters. Protesters are forcibly held inside the kettle for several hours during which time they are not given food, drink or access to toilets. The word is based on the German word 'kessel' – a cauldron, which has been used for a long time to refer to a military surrounding. "Kessel describes an encircled army about to be annihilated by a superior force." http://www.bbc.co.uk/news/uk-11963274.

The Flickering Darkness

Urban Bogota and its Food Flow

JUAN DELGADO *&* MIRIAM METLISS IN CONVERSATION

This exchange took place following the screening of Juan delGado's film, *The Flickering Darkness*, and started as we watched a YouTube video of the Samper Mendoza herb market of Bogota.

JdG: Cecilia! Señora Cecilia! This woman owns a very humble café in one of the corners of Samper Mendoza. Ah, Señora Cecilia!

MM: Is Cecilia one of the many individuals that you met on your journey through Bogota?

JdG: Yes. Cecilia's perception was clear and extraordinary. She said that Samper Mendoza market was the most beautiful place on earth.

MM: The 'urban imaginary' is often talked about as a city of multiple perspectives and languages. It depends on how the city dwellers themselves imagine their own city as the place of everyday life.[1] Your experience of Bogota became a very personal one, a journey of individuals guiding you through a densely populated city.

JdG: Hal Foster notes certain practices in contemporary art where the artist is faced with the 'other' and somehow has to act as an ethnographer.[2] Within my practice, I intend to be open and aware in this encounter in which what I am searching for will appear. The plan and results of my project changed through the personal experiences I shared with individuals and the film crew I worked with.

MM: And you developed your project in Bogota, which is a city of complex identities and histories …

JdG: Yes, even from the city's origins. Bogota is, of course, a colonial city with an indigenous past. The Muisca people were living in Bogota, at the time when the Spanish arrived, and apparently they called the city "Bacata", which means 'planting fields'.

MM: That name immediately highlights both the indigenous origins and also the vision of the city, even in pre–colonial times, as a source of agricultural production. The politics of food production, of course, was just as important then as it is today.[3]

JdG: Yes, a sophisticated system of trading salt for wild fish and cotton was in place before the Spanish arrived. Nowadays, the geostrategic position of the city within the 'capitalist world system' boasts enviable competitive conditions. When you consider the travel times by various possible ways and means, such as roads, railways, airports, river and sea ports, Bogota has an invaluable position. It is located in what might be called the 'new star

cardinal–market' in the heart of the Andes mountain range, with geographical linkages to the Amazon, the Orinoco, the Caribbean and the Pacific Ocean. This position allows fast and equidistant distribution of commodities, environmental and energy resources, information and financial resources, to different regions of the world.

MM: So would you consider Bogota a city of progress and development like other Latin American cities?

JdG: To me, the city is like a living organism, with the highways as the veins of nutrition. The urban layout of Santa Fe de Bogota grew out of the Law of the Indies: straight streets forming blocks intended to be inhabited by the new residents. In the centre, an open space for the Main Square or *plaza* from where a gridlock structure, made of traverse streets (east–west) and *carreras* (north–south), would grow into what we know as the Latin American city.

MM: The metropolis has indeed been said to descend on its geography, rejecting nature and creating an alternative landscape.

It creates a new plan, as if the city becomes a new world in itself.[4] Do you think the particular organisation of the city also refers to the human social divisions?

JdG: Yes. You see, the city is divided into *estratas* (zones) for water and energy supply. Energy and sewer bills are stratified based on the location of the owner's residence and income, the intended purpose being that wealthier sections of society subsidise the energy bills of the poorer. Bogota is divided into six socio–economic *estratas*, from Estrata 1 the lowest to Estrata 6 the highest. Normally in Europe you're lower class, middle class or high class depending on your income and the money you have. In Bogota, it's different. It depends on where you are actually based.

MM: And are the class divisions very apparent?

JdG: It is interesting to look at the way Bogota is divided into the rich north districts of Usaquen and Chapinero and the poor south districts of Usme and Bolivar City, which mirrors somehow the social class division or stratification. The wealth of neighbourhoods changes too. The aristocratic people who used to live in the Candelaria, the old city centre and previously the colonial headquarters, have now moved to the more modern north of the city. The Candelaria has now been emptied out of those wealthy people.

MM: And what are the 'richer' areas in the north of the city like?

JdG: If you go to the north, it is much more luxurious, the kind of thing you might find in the suburbia of a European city. I have a friend, Andres, who lives on the eastern side of the city, very near the mountains, with a wonderful view of the city. The red brick blocks of apartments are located in a private road all surrounded by an electric fence and monitored by security guards. For me, it was like visiting someone in a prison.

MM: And this is a trend in a number of Latin American cities, such as the *condominios* (condominiums) in Brazil. The *condominios* have been considered one of the oppositions to the ideal modernist utopia of the Latin American progressive city.[5] Despite economic progress and development, social inequalities and the threat of crime often dominate.[6]

JdG: Yes, well, it is about protection. I've never had my portrait taken so much as when I did my residency at the Universidad de los Andes. Every time I was in the university the security guard would take a picture of me and put it on a label that I would have to wear. That was the only way to get through security everyday, even though they knew who I was and they knew I was doing my artist's residency there. It was really quite a shock. Another thing that was shocking was the number of armed police throughout the city. I remember going often to the Ministry of Culture and every time I went in I would be stopped and my bag searched. It was shocking how often you were asked to disclose your identity.

MM: Of course, Bogota is the capital city of a country that has experienced many years of political, economic and social turmoil. Perhaps this justifies the need for protection and surveillance?[7]

JdG: Well actually, in the UK there are CCTV cameras everywhere, and from the moment you walk outside your house you are constantly monitored. We have accepted as natural that a camera constantly records our movements. In Bogota it is either the police or the army that monitors the public space.

MM: The Latin American city, such as Mexico City or Sao Paulo, is often associated with threatening crime, but it has almost been the reverse in Colombia. It is considered safer in the city of Bogota than in the countryside. Is this due to the degree of surveillance?

JdG: Yes, well a few years ago, I have been told, people were afraid of driving outside the city. The rural roads were dangerous due to guerrilla activity or military blockades, whereas Bogota is kind of protected by the army and the police. It was strange having the military around you but this is something quite common. When we first went to do filming in the Corabastos [the market that is the main location of *The Flickering Darkness*], there was a visible police presence. Although now they are having problems due to fewer police in the Corabastos; people feel threatened; they don't feel so protected anymore.

MM: So even within the city, there is a sense of 'safer' neighbourhoods?

JdG: Many people warned me not to go to certain places in the city. I can't say exactly how dangerous they were, but I can say that many of them were very poor. That I saw with my own eyes. I mean, extremely poor, like nothing I had ever seen before in my life.

MM: Is this limited to different zones?

JdG: There is a division in the city with Calle 7 (Road 7). I remember, even before going, I was told that Bogota is as dangerous as any other city in the world, think of London, Los Angeles, but that I should *not* go beyond Calle 7. I lived not far from there though, so I decided to explore it. And I walked down, expecting to be anxious and full of fear, but instead I could just see that I was entering an extremely poor neighbourhood. The pavements disappeared suddenly. Some of the houses had no roofs. There were people lying on the ground, drunk or sleeping. You could see a very sudden difference in the standard of living. El Palacio Narino, the prime minister's residence, was only about 100 metres away.

MM: Often travellers to the city are considered as the central protagonists of urban imaginaries and histories.[8] Tell me about your exploration of the different zones of Bogota in terms of the markets you visited.

JdD: Well, many local people didn't even know where the Corabastos was. They would know the Mercado de Abastos of the north, but they would not know about the Plaza de Mercado Paloquemao. With the artist Juan Fernando Herran, I went down to Restrepo market, all the way south, through Caracas Avenue all the way down to San Cristobal. Restrepo is on the border. It is still not considered a dangerous neighbourhood, but San Cristobal is considered already a no–go place. But I was taken to Restrepo market. It was the first market in Bogota that I had been to and I loved it. It was a market selling animals and the intensity of noise was unbelievable, an extraordinary auditory sensation. You had birds, pigeons, dogs, everything. I never did any filming there in Restrepo but I would have liked to. That was my first impression, and then my friend Lorena mentioned Samper Mendoza to me.

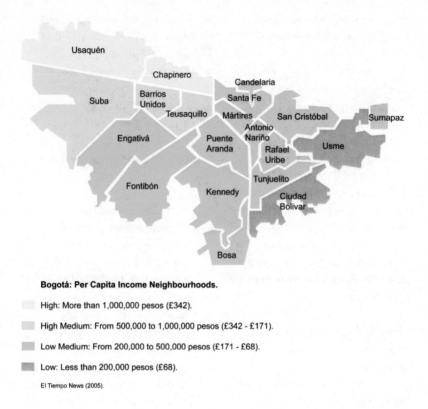

Bogotá: Per Capita Income Neighbourhoods.

High: More than 1,000,000 pesos (£342).

High Medium: From 500,000 to 1,000,000 pesos (£342 - £171).

Low Medium: From 200,000 to 500,000 pesos (£171 - £68).

Low: Less than 200,000 pesos (£68).

El Tiempo News (2005).

Map of Bogota and its main highways, 2005, El Tiempo News

MM: And how was your journey there?

JdD: Samper Mendoza is commonly known as one of the most dangerous places in the city of Bogota. As a foreigner arriving in Bogota though, I was not aware of this imaginary of fear. I have to say that I never had any fear, or that feeling of being in danger. But as you enter the dusty streets punctuated by demolished houses and the emptiness of wasted land, and you pass groups of people lighting fires to warm themselves, the scene reminded me of Goya's etchings: the flames projected a phantasmagorical flickering of shadows on the ruined walls.

MM: Is Samper Mendoza the biggest herb market in Bogota?

JdG: I think it is the biggest herb market in the country. It takes place at night. It is an extraordinary place. It was when I was there I decided I wanted to make a project about food and what food implies. As I had wandered around Bogota, I was struck by how much food there was everywhere. I wanted to use food as a metaphor, and food would allow me to move around the city and explore different levels of social strata.

MM: And what were the initial contrasts that this exploration highlighted?

JdG: I had some lunches with very wealthy families. The choreography was extraordinary, when the servant comes to serve you, like in a restaurant. I found it very intimidating; it was something I wasn't used to. So I decided I wanted to consider food as the object of social division. In contrast, when you walk inside Samper Mendoza, the building is in an indoor, communal square, where you see all these people, very humble, selling bunches of all kinds of herbs. You immediately realise that they have dark skin and are indigenous *campesinos*. With Cecilia we talked about how people there would bring their herbs from Tolima, Meta, Boyacá, all around the country.

MM: And how did you first go to the Corabastos?

JdG: Well, I went to some supermarkets in the city and the person I went with was complaining about the prices. So I said, "Well don't you have any markets nearby?" And she said, "Yes, well, we have the Corabastos but it is very very far." So I suggested that she take me to Corabastos one Sunday morning, and that was the first time. My first impression was that Corabastos was just a huge, immeasurable place. Corabastos is apparently the largest food market in the entire Latin American continent. It is an extraordinary place. It overwhelms you. Everything there seems immeasurable. The hectic influx of bodies, machines and food swirling through the otherwise dormant city hits your sleepy eyes as if you were dragged into another time. The 'flickering darkness' of the film's title refers to the blinking effect of the fluorescent lights that punctuates Corabastos.

MM: It seems unbelievable that people don't know that such a place exists. Or do people choose not to know?

JdG: Some people have heard of it but they are just not interested in it. They are accustomed to buying in supermarkets. They don't want to go to markets due to the social implications. You are actually acknowledging the 'other' who is of a lower class. The people that work in the market are of a lower class and by having an interaction, even if you are just buying food from them, you are acknowledging them.

MM: There is an interesting suggestion here of the rural and the urban mixing. Nestor Canclini Garcia mentions how the 'urban' has historically been considered in opposition to the 'rural'.[9] However, such a strong presence of the rural markets within the city disrupts such a clear opposition.

JdG: Yes, it is almost an invasion by the countryside and the rural. The rural merges with and almost penetrates the city, bringing products from the countryside, such as the Savannah, the Amazon, from Mesta … many places alien to the people of Bogota. Every night 11,000 tons of food are delivered from every corner of the country.

MM: Do you think, then, that the 'urban' continues to be associated with the idea of modernity and industrialisation in Bogota, as opposed to the 'rural'? Perhaps there is anxiety that the city has not completely 'developed' or not been modernised as they might have hoped? Do you think it is for this reason that people don't want to associate themselves with the rural?

JdG: I think so, I think people are conflicted and do not acknowledge their connection to nature, to the Amazon, to the mountains. Generally speaking, people want to look European, and this is perhaps the idea of modernity.

MM: So people still look to Europe as a model of modernity? You could even go back to when the British were in Bogota, for example, over 100 years ago, which has influenced the style of some buildings in the city.

JdG: My feeling is that people had quite a conflict, an internal struggle. People are very proud to be *colombiano* or *colombiana*, although this perhaps does not consider the indigenous as also part of the nation they are so proud of. They still don't consider the Amazon, it is something completely alien to many, more before than today. I believe this is something particularly noticeable in Bogota.

MM: It is an idea of the city as nation, as a whole.[10] You block out the rest.

JdG: Antonio Ruiz, the owner of the restaurant next to my house and a long-time resident in La Candelaria, used to say we Colombians are very confused. We have a conflictual emotion of loving our country but at the same time denying what our country consists of. So what kind of a Colombia do we want, do we recognise as ours? When I lived there I was thinking of that quite often. How would people acknowledge that Colombia is not just Bogota, and that Bogota is not just Calle 65 to 180 but is also San Cristobal, Kennedy City, Corabastos ...? Why do people think that way? What are they afraid of?

MM: The migration of many people from the rural countryside to the urban metropolis is, of course, a complex historical process that still continues today in Bogota.

JdG: As in the rest of the country, the acceleration of urban development in Bogota is not only due to industrialisation, since there are convoluted political and social reasons, such as poverty and violence, which have led to the exodus from the rural to the urban areas. This has resulted in an exponential growth of population in urban areas and belts of misery in their surroundings, mostly in the south part of the city. In terms of migration affecting the physical development of the city such as architecture, land value and property, *los barrios de invasion* (shantytowns) are something that defines the structure of the Latin American city, such as Caracas and La Paz. Often the major cities of the Cono Sur (Argentina, Chile, Bolivia, Peru) are situated in valleys, and they then grow and grow until they can't grow any more, and this is when they create the so-called *barrios de invasión*. In Bogota, the closer you get to a *barrio de invasión*, the less the grid structure of the city works. The grid just disappears. And often the *barrios de invasión* are right next to high *estratas*, so the attempt to classify the city in terms of regions doesn't work.

MM: And the *barrios de invasión* in Bogota are a direct consequence of wider social problems?

JdG: People come to the city and have no income. It is a consequence of poverty. They come to the city with nothing, perhaps displaced, so they build what they can to live in. In fact, it is a direct consequence of the violent conflict in the rural areas. Many people I spoke to had their farms confiscated by the guerrillas or were threatened by the paramilitary army; they fled their hometowns as they feared their children were going to be captured and recruited to the violent groups.

MM: When we consider it in this sense, growth and urbanisation do not necessarily represent progress and forward-thinking but instead the struggles of peoples, both prior to coming to the city and also current when living there.

JdG: Yes, which leads on to a major challenge of urbanisation: how to control the chaos. The slums grow in a very organic way, due to the sheer quantity of immigrants and the city's lack of resources to host them. Latin America is often considered chaotic, the Latin American mind unpredictable. These are stereotypes of course, like the Latin American considered as a cannibal in the European imaginary, just ideas, which keep being fed and keep reproducing themselves. But I am interested in the idea of the chaotic Latin American city as a reflection of the frenzied mind of the Latin American people. The chaotic *barrios de invasión* are a consequence of this. They are completely against the idea of order.

MM: These *barrios* become almost cities within themselves, just as the areas surrounding Mexico City do.[11]

JdG: Yes, but the people coming from the countryside often bring their ideas of rural living with them, so they almost live a rural life within a city. The presence of the iconic Virgin within the market of Samper Mendoza that is shown in *The Flickering Darkness* is representative of this. The city is even becoming more rural. The displaced people are changing the city. In my project I wanted to represent the difficult conditions experienced by many people who, after going through a traumatic experience, have been displaced from their rural towns to the city.

MM: And what can we consider to be a 'displaced person' in Bogota? This term is often quite loaded and ambiguous.

JdG: When you go to certain regions of Bogota and talk to people like Nubia and Octavio, they will tell you that a little while ago they lived in the countryside, farming in the province of Neiva, and how one day they left after being threatened by the paramilitary, leaving everything behind, and found themselves in a city they didn't know, and how they started a long journey to get heard by the institutions. According to the Consultancy for Human Rights, in the period 1999–2005, more than 260,000 people arrived in Bogota as a result of displacement. One of the consequences is the high percentage of people with no access to a basic healthy diet. Many children suffer from malnutrition and it was found that most of these children come from displaced families. To lessen this problem, 123 community dining halls have been funded by the Local Development Fund

within the framework of the Bogota without Hunger programme.[12] A high percentage of the manual labourers in the Corabastos belong to the 'displaced' community. These people work mainly at night and are therefore invisible to the city. I found it interesting that they are precisely the ones who help the metropolis to function.

MM: And this leads us back to the politics of food, and how it reflects the broader social reality.

JdG: Corabastos is almost like a mafia zone. It is the major supplier of food to Bogota and the traders have the power to determine the price of food. The farmers provide the food at the Corabastos, and they barter between themselves to trade products. These products are then sold to buyers, who will sell the food on, at a higher price, in other markets, for example, Samper Mendoza or Paloquemao, a co-operative. These buyers change the value of the food, they classify the foods and determine the prices. The prices aren't regulated. Although, if you look on the Corabastos website, you will see that a price comes up for the price of fruit for the day.[13] The food must be sold immediately, early in the morning, so it enters the chain of buying and selling. The Corabastos sells to 44 other markets in total, 19 owned by Distrito Capital.

MM: It is almost a mini economy in itself, but one that is central to the day-to-day functioning of the city.

JdG: I looked at the building of the Corabastos as a monstrous stomach waiting to be fed, somehow a metaphor of the city as a living organism. All food from all the states goes to the Corabastos, and sometimes it comes from all these states, arrives in the Corabastos, and is then bought and distributed back to the different states, such as Tolima. 55% of the food that enters the city goes through the Corabastos. The figures on Corabastos commercial transactions are phenomenal: 6,500 traders, 12,500 vehicles, 200,000 passing people and a money flow around CO$ 6,000,000,000 (£2,000 million approximately).[14]

MM: That is a huge amount. And I imagine the people selling there are not benefiting from it?

JdG: The *campesinos* are the agents and producers that bring the food

into the city. The irony is that in the wider economy the price of basic things such as milk, corn, etc., puts many people under the poverty line.

MM: Are there structures in place to try to defend the rights of the *campesinos* selling in the Corabastos, for example?

JdG: There is this PMAAB which stands for *Plan Maestro de Abastecimiento de Alimentos de Bogota* (Principal Plan for Food Markets of Bogota). It is linked with the *Bogota sin Hambre* (Bogota without Hunger) programme designed by Mockus, the mayor of Bogota in 2001–03. Both systems have the final goal of reducing the food prices in the capital.[15] However, PMAAB is based on a prejudice that "the informal economy is inefficient". This prejudice overtakes the previous analysis about the functioning of thousands of economic agents that assume diverse functions in the food supply of Bogota. We are talking of the rural–urban intermediaries, the *mayoristas* in the Corabastos, the storekeepers. PMAAB plans a system in which all these agents are replaced by modern operators, formalised in supermarket style. The mayor's office and the co-ordinators of the *Bogota sin Hambre* programme both acknowledge that their system of supply doesn't exclude 'informal' agents. On the contrary, their policy is to improve what it calls "popular economy". I guess it is here that a conflict between the two different plans exists.

MM: So is there a plan to upgrade the market places in line with the city's 'modernisation'?

JdG: It has been said that "the modernisation of the market places is an important step for the reduction of intermediaries in the marketing of food products and crafts that will allow the benefit of farmers and consumers, that generates some relief to prices of products that are purchased in them, and to some extent may represent relief for poorer classes as they are presented a more accessible opportunity both to have a viable economic outlet for their crops and products, such as being able to get food and meet certain needs in an easy manner and according to their capabilities."[16] This is something that vanished in Europe a long time ago.

MM: Yes, that is interesting, especially because now Spanish companies are interested in buying the market places. So, although they have vanished in Europe, do you think Spanish companies, for example, see the markets as an economic opportunity?

JdG: They can see the potential. Many people are now thinking in the short term. 'Gold' is no longer oil but food. Many big corporations know this and are already investing in this sector. According to the manager of Corabastos, the corporation could be sold to Spanish investors after a process of modernisation.

MM: And do you think this will change the city?

JdG: It will change the way food prices are regulated.

MM: It has also been said that this represents a 're-colonisation' or a repeat of the conquest of four centuries ago. After all, the Spanish used to view the produce of Latin America not only as a curiosity but as a flowing supply of wealth and prosperity that the colonisers in the Old World could own.[17]

JdG: Yes, and as a Spanish artist in Bogota I experienced mixed reactions to my nationality. I was called the *español* (Spanish man) on many occasions, both positively and negatively. Henri Lefebvre mentions the city as a place of conflictual energy.[18] Bogota seems to be a city of conflicting energies on many levels and this is due to continue into the future. The idea of darkness in my film mirrors the actual situation of not knowing how to sort out the problems of injustice and violence in the country's social and political system.

1. Andreas Huyssen, *Other Cities, Other Worlds: Urban Imaginaries in a Globalizing Age* (Durham and London: Duke University Press, 2008) p. 3.
2. Hal Foster, *The Return of the Real: The Avant-Garde at the End of the Century* (Cambridge, MA: MIT Press, 1996) p. 186.
3. John C. Super, *Food, Conquest and Colonization in Sixteenth-Century Spanish America* (Albuquerque: University of New Mexico Press, 1988) p. 39.
4. Arturo Almandoz, *Ensayos de cultura urbana* (Caracas: Fundarte, 2000) p. 6.
5. *ibid.*, Huyssen (2008) p. 5.
6. *ibid.*, Almandoz (2008) p. 8.
7. This theme of course is suggestive of Foucault's Panopticon, his exploration of different systems of social control, and the concept of gaining power and knowledge by watching others.
8. *ibid.*, Almandoz (2008) p. 8.
9. Nestor García Canclini, *Imaginarios Urbanos* (Buenos Aires: Universidad de Buenos Aires, 1999) p. 69.
10. *ibid.*, Almandoz (2008) p. 10.
11. *ibid.*, García Canclini (1999) p. 76.
12. http://www.codhes.org/ (accessed 03/06/11).
13. Corabastos, www.corabastos.com.co (accessed 04/03/11).
14. Caracol TV, http://www.caracoltv.com/noticias/informe-especial/video-217348-esta-pasando-corabastos (accessed 03/05/11).
15. Jaime Forero Alvarez, *Autonomía agroalimentaria: diálogos y controversias / organizaciones comunales y campesinas* (Bogota: Planeta Paz, 2006) p. 45.
16. Ministry of Culture, Bogota, http://www.mincultura.gov.co/ (accessed 04/0311).
17. *ibid.*, Super (1988) p. 39.
18. *ibid.*, García Canclini (1999) p. 77

People of Corabastos

Gente de Corabastos

JHON ARIAS

These images document the two main components of Corabastos – people and food – that engage in a reciprocal relationship, in which they interact every day, and where they pass the hours, as the food changes hands, moving from those who planted it to those who have to eat as a fact of survival and enjoyment.

Each person photographed is a story of Corabastos that shows the particular in the universal, an ephemeral universe that is built day by day between accumulations of food and the proud people who work there.

All images from the series People of Corabastos, 2010, JHON ARIAS

Recognising the Invisible Monument

On the Politics of Memorialisation and Public Space in Post-war Beirut

FADI SHAYYA, FOUAD ASFOUR & LANA SALMAN

Can public space remain neutral to conflict and emptied of political meaning in a neoliberal socio-spatial context that promotes formal aesthetics while society strives to transcend the post-colonial and post-modern conditions in the most brutal way: civil war? The war in Lebanon never ended. Probably, wars never do.

Twenty-one years after the ceasefire in 1990, the trauma persists in post-war Lebanon and the Lebanese do not seem to agree on country building but continue their power struggles over identity and resources. Their struggle is deeply reflected in a geopolitically divided spatiality of sectarian geography; if you live in Beirut long enough, you can clearly distinguish neighbourhoods/ spaces of dominant communities: Sunni Muslims, Shia Muslims, Maronite Christians, Greek Orthodox Christians, Roman Orthodox Christians, Druze and 12 other sects. Confessional politics frame and guide political life, social organisation and physical development, including planning and designing the supposed spatial social collector: Beirut's public space.

An urban park is renovated but still closed for over 15 years. Public gardens, pedestrian areas and plazas are created in the downtown area but exclusionary governance prevails. A pilot project for a pedestrian/bicycle link, the "Soft Connection", is proposed to link the park and the downtown, but the project seems farfetched. However, what strikes one's attention is the fact that those three spaces – park, connection, downtown – are superimposed on the demarcation line of the Lebanese civil war, the 'no man's land' of warring Beirut. Probably the most symbolic space in Beirut's modern history, the demarcation line is thus emptied of all references to conflict and purged of all traces of war, to provide instead a technically well-carved landscape of modern neoliberal consumption.

So, why do the main public space projects overlap the civil war's demarcation line? What was the discourse that brought those three spaces together? Where do cultural production and spatial planning meet or diverge? How do the mechanics of collective memory and memorialisation work in favour of constructing public space? Where is the tension limit between the technical and the political in public spatial discourse? And ultimately, what is public space in Beirut?

Answers to these questions are crucial to provide a platform for a critical reading of public space in post-war Beirut, taking into consideration the constant state of conflict in a confessional power politics society. Through discourse analysis and based on an anthropological approach to urbanism, and through one theoretical perspective and another more involved and activist angle, we aim to provide a critical reading of public space discourse in Beirut and the influential actors shaping it. Our case study focuses on municipal Beirut in order to situate the social, political and spatial condition within the limits of municipal governance of the city – although greater Beirut is a much more complex socio-economic and spatial organism.

We would argue that exclusive representations of authority and exclusionary politics resituate the spatial significance and programmatic identity of public space from spaces of democratic political engagement to places of totalitarian formal values of hegemonic semiosis like national reconciliation. Beyond critique, we want this text to contest the mechanisms of power and neoliberal economics inscribed in current projects of public space in Beirut and to reassert that the public has the right to access and to participate in planning this same public space and that authorities (municipality and planners) should take their voices into consideration.[1]

Public space and public domain in Beirut

In post-war Beirut not much has been done regarding upgrading existing public places or creating new ones except for the spaces discussed in this essay. It is clear to many people that the main spatial development projects have been infrastructural upgrading of the road network. The seaside Corniche, public gardens and sidewalks have received little attention, some refurbishing

Beirut's Park, Horsh Al-Sanawbar, still empty in the aftermath
of the war, 2010, FADI SHAYYA

The Fouad Shehab Bridge: physical infrastructure as boundary by politics/8 March
political camp, 2007, FADI SHAYYA
OVER: Crowded checkpoints of the Green Line during the war, 1986, NABIL ISMAIL

with new tiling and some landscaping; road medians got a greater share of landscape decoration. So the city's existing public spaces continued to function properly, with or without new tiling. Only the public places of the downtown have been totally redesigned within the reconstruction project of the city centre and the urban park has been renovated as part of the redevelopment in the city. The Soft Connection is the newest proposed addition to the public space project in Beirut.

If you go to Beirut, everyone will tell you to visit its downtown. As in many cities around the globe, Beirut's downtown[2] is the latest and biggest real-estate development project in Lebanon, which acquired its significance when promoted as the prime post-war rebuilding project of the "Heart of Beirut".[3] The downtown is the historic centre of Beirut and its current financial/business hub. It lies at the northern edge of the city, opening up to the sea with a reclaimed land addition. To 'facilitate' the process of reconstruction, the private real-estate company Solidere[4] transformed all private property ownership into shares and acquired government approval to supervise and manage the public domain. Today, the downtown is an island of offices of multinational corporations and their support services such as banks, luxury shopping outlets, restaurants, hotels and other recreational facilities mainly dedicated to affluent city dwellers. Burdened by claims about the fairness/unfairness of compensation given to the original property owners, and imprinted with the neoliberal policies common to many large-scale urban development projects in world capitals, exclusionary governance tops the headlines of discourse about downtown's public space.

At the opposite end, Beirut's urban park, Horsh Al-Sanawbar, lies on the southern edge of municipal Beirut, occupying what is left of historic pine woods.[5] Horsh is a public property of 330,000 square metres (≈1.8% of the city's area), owned by Beirut municipality since 1878 and officially designated as an urban park in the early 1960s. The park was burned to the ground during the Israeli Defense Forces' invasion of 1982 and the 15-year civil war (1975–1990). It was renovated with French funding[6] in the 1990s as part of rebuilding post-war Beirut and with an interest to facilitate communal reconciliation. Up till this day, more than 75% of the park is still closed to the public – with restricted access to permit holders. Several official excuses justify this closure, such as letting the trees grow, saving the park from litter, and the lack of a proper fire-fighting system.

Today, a new major public space project emerges on the horizon: the Soft Connection. The project proposes to connect downtown's public space to the urban park via a green landscaped route designed for pedestrians and cyclists. The project runs along the civil war's demarcation line – commonly known as the Green Line – and occupies the public domain, specifically the Rue de Damas and its sidewalks. The Soft Connection is a pilot experiment for upgrading pedestrian connectivity and reducing vehicular traffic in Beirut, funded by Beirut municipality and technically co-ordinated by Île-de-France. The project is still in the competition design phase and its connection to the north and south nodes is still under question as the southern node (the park) is still closed and the northern node (the downtown) is still an exclusionary space.

The discursive comfort zone of spatial planning

What is common between those spaces of Beirut – the park, the downtown, and the Soft Connection – and what instigates a critical interest in their production is the fact that they all once constituted the Green Line. Observed separately, each project has its own context, objectives and timeline; however, a deeper and critical observation reveals a common discourse in understanding and planning the public space of the post-war city.

Back in the early 1990s, the reconstruction of Beirut's downtown was presented as the national symbol of immediate rising from the ashes of war.[7] Despite what many might claim as a neoliberal plot to win the bid for reconstruction, the discourse of presenting the salvation of a single space as synonymous with the emancipation of an entire country proved effective when many Lebanese – inside or outside power circles – looked for a way out of their post-traumatic condition. As such, post-war spatial planning was highly influenced by a socio-political discourse that favoured a symbolically common yet neutral space among the Lebanese. Everyone can relate to the renowned city, the historic core and once bustling commercial and residential area during the first half of the last century.

In his paper 'Laying Claim to Beirut', Saree Makdisi argues that the reconstruction project "not only confuses public and private interests but that it represents the colonisation of the former by the latter" and the hijacking of the city centre's public space and broader "public sphere ... by capital".[8] Vital to understanding the pervasiveness of this discourse until today is the exclusion of city residents – even those who owned properties in the city centre – from all the discussions and debates about reconstruction plans. In fact, the reconstruction project was presented as "the only option ... (overlooking) how it came to be the only option, how other options were foreclosed long before the reconstruction effort officially began".[9] The reconstruction project kicked off and continued under the same symbolic veil and produced an exclusionary public space whose exclusion is a reflection of private powers and their interconnectedness to authority, politics and capital.

We would argue that the process of renovating the park adopted the same socio–political discourse, only this time away from public debate and media exposure. The competition brief and report clearly states Île–de–France's interest in funding the renovation of Horsh as a green space that can facilitate the spatial meeting and social reconciliation of Beiruti/Lebanese citizens.[10] The French donor was (and probably still is) interested in the fact that this park is an edge and a space for potential meetings between different communities: Muslim Sunnis to its west, Muslim Shia to its south and southeast, and Maronite and Greek Catholic Christians to its northeast. The fact that the park is an edge is true; actually, it constituted the southern node of the Green Line that separated space between geopolitically divided sectarian communities. One can understand choosing to renovate the park for reasons of increasing green space and revitalising a dilapidated area. However, the discourse of reconciliatory value attributed to this space is not innocent of a naïve view of post–war conditions where authority (be it the donor, the municipality, the politicians or the planners/designers in this case) attempts to demonstrate its understanding of the situation's gravity and to force its view of what is required to better it. Again, the choice falls on a space that is large enough to be worthy of a development project, that is symbolically beneficial to everyone, and that is almost politically neutral. Consequently, discourse produces a space that has no alternative: one unique space that will integrate all conflicting parties in the centre, a geometric utopian ideal similar to vanished 19th–century communist fantasies.

The technical numbs the political

Contrary to what neoliberal ideologists would like us to believe, political questions are not mere technical issues to be solved by experts. Properly political questions always involve decisions which require making a choice between conflicting alternatives.[11]

Similar to the discursive condition of the downtown and the park, so too was the discourse of choosing the axis that would be transformed into the Soft Connection. "Instead of having it either on the eastern side, or the western side [of the city], and look as if we are favouring one community, and privileging it over the other ... the choice fell on this axis," stated Île-de-France[12] which is partnering Beirut municipality and the CGLU-BTVL[13] on this project. According to a former staff member of Île-de-France, the idea to connect the park to the downtown along the Green Line has been discussed within closed circles since the early 1990s.[14] However, the call for proposals was discreetly launched some months ago with an invitation-only design competition. The former staff member wondered why the municipality and Île-de-France would still invest in memorialising the demarcation line 21 years after the end of the civil war.

A counter argument may suggest that the claimed similarity is a mere coincidence, or merely a biased reading of the situation, making the comparison between the public spaces of the downtown, the park and the Soft Connection obsolete. From our critical stance, this would be an oversimplification of connecting the dots. For the production of space to transcend its physicality and monumental symbolism to achieve a more complex reading of power interplay, we believe that urbanism – and those engaged in shaping it – must dare to be critical. It must critique the hegemonic discourses that are producing spaces that serve only to cover up the incompetence of politics to formulate common grounds. It seems, however, that in Beirut since the end of the war nobody "dares wins urbanism"[15], a practice that has become obvious in the discursive conception of public space.

Île-de-France contends that the Soft Connection (*Le Liaision Douce*) is a pilot project to reinstate pedestrian space and encourage non-vehicular transport in the city. "Being French", Île-de-France is not able to grasp the complexities of inter-communal conflict in Lebanon and, as such, their contribution is restricted to technical expertise and the location of the Soft Connection axis is a matter of "local choice".[16] This challenging project entails dealing with different design constraints along the axis: cutting through infrastructure, difficult site slopes, major road junctions, narrow sidewalks, parking space on sidewalks, high–security areas, and fences. However, it is *how* the location of this public space project came to be chosen that is the crux of this discussion. A political decision had to be made about the location and Beirut municipality was the main actor in determining this issue as it includes representatives of the major political powers in the city, i.e. representatives of the confessional political system.[17]

The choice necessitated consensus among the different representatives so it fell on an edge space, a middle ground that is almost neutral to confessional politics: the civil war's demarcation line. A connection between the park at the southern end of the Green Line and the downtown at its northern end was a perfect geographical fit – a truly wonderful collage weaving together three spaces that represent and memorialise the Lebanese civil war. But who controls access to and regulates the shaping of cultural and collective memory? Who decides to bridge (or not) social spaces and cultural differences? Currently, the connection is obsolete since it is between two inaccessible nodes: an exclusive downtown and a closed park. What does such a choice really stand for, and what does this space of the demarcation line signify? Why did the municipality practice top–down spatial planning, and what happens when the Soft Connection is built without the participation of the people who live along it and in the city?

Collective spaces of memory and forms of memorialisation

It is important to examine in detail the tension between the symbolic and the functional planning dimensions of municipal urban policies and how these relate to the reality of communities living in affected spaces.

So far, post–war development in Beirut has been predominantly revenue driven. Solidere and its land reclaimed from the sea – where more and more offices are being built – are testimony of a policy that calculates the extension of land, first and foremost, as increase in profit. This dimension is not visible to new visitors to Beirut and tourists (including consumer citizens) are the main target consumers of this space. But how do local Beirutis, who know the old city centre and the evolution of its spaces, speak about these developments? The current role of city spaces as money generating vehicles does not escape the notice of the local public, and knowledge about these processes can be traced in popular discourse, specifically in cynical jokes that Beirutis create. In one anecdote, for example, some friends are driving through the downtown, shortly after its reconstruction, and the driver jokingly notes that one cannot jump all the red lights here like in other parts of the city … because it is a private development space with its own control and policing mechanisms.

In order to explore the significance of these spontaneous oral practices which undermine the official and corporate discourse of economic exploitation of public space, we need to consider different forms and media of cultural memory and memorialisation, which are inscribed in (or translated into) oral or written form and which condense in a number of different cultural processes in the built environment. One way is by understanding how memory and trauma are worked through in Lebanese contemporary artistic and cultural productions. This might help urban planning learn from such organic processes for drafting proposals in a minefield of public memory, opening up alternative routes rather than choosing between simply eradicating all traces of history and trauma or installing a publicly sanctioned reading imposed by municipal authorities.

At this point, we want to highlight that this text refuses to format the urban dimension of conflict in Beirut as a commodified, traumatised space.[18] Similar tendencies have been identified around the psycho–social interventions of international relief efforts and most prominently criticised by Vanessa Pupavac as "therapeutic governance", i.e. "a new form of international governance based on social risk management strategies" that undermines local strategies of coping.[19] Pupavac argues that such interventions result in "pathologising war–affected populations as emotionally dysfunctional … which explains the prevailing political, economic and social conditions … [thus] questioning [their] capacity for self–government".[20]

Our approach connects with a criticism of corporate practice that generates exclusive spaces for its users, i.e. tourists or shoppers, and questions its contamination of the politics of municipal urban planning in the case of the Soft Connection, which considers the upward moving middle class as the only constituency it serves. However, the greater population who (still) lives within the demarcation of "Beirut" needs to be considered, even if this will open up antagonistic positions. Through some examples from cultural production we intend to illustrate that in spite of all sectarian, economic and imaginary borders in contemporary and historical Lebanon, there still exists a common political dimension of this constituency which can be called 'society', a political dimension which shares an identity shaped by memory, by language, and

Lost between the real and imaginary, Claudia still awaits her disappeared husband, 2005, JOANA HADJITHOMAS & KHALIL JOREIGE

Lebanese society conditioned by division: security fence in Martyrs' Square between 8 March and 14 March political gatherings, 2007, FADI SHAYYA

not the least by the use of public space. We provide evidence for one of these shared public realms – invisible however omnipresent – which could be called 'collective memory', that can be traced in popular culture as well as in films and contemporary art works that deal with the traumatic experiences of the civil war, the haunting of disappeared family members and the persistence of invisible spatial borders.

The return of the dead

Since the end of the civil war, the memory of experienced violence has been addressed in many cultural festivals, such as the Ayloul Festival (1997–2001), the Home Works series (1995–2010) and the UMAM Hangar productions[21]. Most presented art works bear testimony that people in Beirut still carry with them the shadows and presences of disappeared husbands, sons, family members and friends, never knowing if, when or where they died, nor if they might come back one day. In Joana Hadjithomas and Khalil Joreige's film *A Perfect Day (Yawmon Akhar)*, the protagonist's mother stays at home every day, waiting for her husband, as she still has not accepted his disappearance after 15 years.[22]

Literary theorist Aleida Assmann argues that even something as fundamentally individual as a personal biography is already deeply social:

The difference between … the remembrance of the individual that gives a perspective on his life from old age and the commemoration of that life from the retrospective view of posterity makes clear the specifically cultural element of collective remembering. We say that the dead one 'lives on' in the memory of posterity as if this has to do with a natural continuation deriving from its own power. In truth, however, it is a matter of an act of resuscitation which the dead owes to the determined will of the group not to allow him to fade away but to persist as a member of the community by virtue of remembrance and to carry him forward into the on–going present.[23]

This affliction is part of Lebanese cultural memory and an essential dimension of the contemporary discourse about spatial realities. It is important to point out the 'material' dimension of these memories about people who have disappeared. Their absence could be formulated as an invisible memorial, as it afflicts the daily lives of large parts of the population in Beirut and Lebanon. Any consideration about how to plan the formal space of the Green Line has to include considerations about how this fluent form of cultural memory has been already – although invisibly – monumentalised.

During a post–screening discussion of Omar Amiralay's film *Par un Jour de Violence Ordinaire, Mon Ami Michel Seurat* ... (*On a Day of Ordinary Violence, My Friend Michel Seurat* ...)[24] at the Home Works IV festival in 2008, the audience voiced their deep concern about the continuing ambiguity surrounding the death and burial place of the French sociologist. Through the exchanges of the discussion, this lack of knowledge became manifest as a gap in the collective memory. The murderer (and/or kidnapper) of Michel Seurat was seen as the vessel of knowledge of the final stages of the biography of the disappeared. This knowledge about where and when someone was killed was acknowledged as an element of power, and thus another form of appropriation of someone else's life. Only the murderer knows the place where the dead are buried and the time of their death. At the same time, the lack of this knowledge keeps the family members in an eternal suspense, one that has material and visible consequences: they cannot continue their life; they cannot find ways to resume normality. The material reality of the public's participation in the formation of collective memory became clear when, at the end of the discussion, some of the audience called for a march to appeal to murderers to release knowledge on the whereabouts of missing family members in Lebanon.

Transforming repressed traumata into living cultural memory

Maybe the denial of this condition could be used as a metaphor for the lack of ability to deal with public spaces in post–war Beirut. Everywhere you step, each inch of space along the Green Line (and other spaces), is mined with memories, material traces of violent experiences. One can only wonder what the people who were exposed to traumatic experiences during the war feel when they walk along the Green Line. In the minds of people, invisible borders are still present – hidden points of access, divided sectors, and boundary crossing checkpoints. Lebanese contemporary art has become quite renowned for dealing with this condition, such as the works of the Atlas Group (established by Walid Raad), Lamia Joreige, Akram Zaatari, Rabih Mroué and Nadine Touma.

For Touma, oral sources are an important resource. At the Missing Links exhibition at Cairo's Townhouse Gallery in 2001, Touma created an installation piece entitled *Selkeh Emneh* (*Crossable and Safe*) in homage to the Lebanese radio anchor Sharif el-Akhawi. The work addresses collective memories by making use of recorded broadcasts of el-Akhawi who was a pioneer in reporting, writing and producing radio shows in Lebanon. At the onset of the Lebanese war in 1975, he started a morning radio programme, *Selkeh Emneh,* which mainly directed people towards safe roads to avoid snipers. One month after it started, people would not leave their homes or any place without listening to the show. Sometimes, el-Akhawi was on air for 48 hours non-stop. People of different social and sectarian affiliations in Lebanon relied on this radio show, and it still resounds in the memory of many because of the tremendous impact it had on people's lives.

Such histories illustrate that the space of the Green Line cannot easily be commodified into a bicycle lane for the enjoyment of the urban middle class. Just like when municipalities across the world involve artists to create art in public space. The attempts to establish an engagement with the space through commemorating traumatic experiences and transforming traumatic spaces do not allow for an easy way out through strategies of repression of cultural memory. Rather, they invite conflicts rooted in history to be opened up and brought into today's public discourse. In fact, the Green Line has already been monumentalised in Beiruti cultural memory, and the municipality owes a materialisation of this invisible monument to the public.

Grounded in discourse

In a country where conflict seems to become the norm, the relation between people and space has transcended typical structural dichotomies of public–private and open–closed, resulting in versions of territorial prevalence. The conflict is still there in all its different forms: political, sectarian and armed; new traumas seem to sustain the everyday, and the geopolitically divided spatiality of sectarian geography persists and increases. Public space as collective space only exists within cultural and sectarian homogeneous territories, and collective political engagement in a public project for public space is undermined by the "uncontested hegemony of liberalism".[25]

There are to be sure many liberalisms, some more progressive than others but save a few exceptions the dominant tendency in liberal thought is characterised by a rationalist and individualist approach which is unable to adequately grasp the pluralistic nature of the social world, with the conflicts that pluralism entails; conflicts for which no rational solution could ever exist, hence the dimension of antagonism that characterises human societies ... Indeed, one of the main tenets of this liberalism is the rationalist belief in the availability of a universal consensus based on reason. No wonder that the political constitutes its blind spot.[26]

The experiment of rehabilitating Beirut's public park to re-integrate conflicting social groups and facilitate post-war reconciliation has failed. The failure is twofold: first, the objective of reopening the park for social integration did not take place; and second, social integration in Lebanon proved to be fragile 21 years after the end of the civil war. The public spaces of the downtown and the park do not seem to integrate with the social fabric of the city: the downtown is a socio-economically exclusive island that is spatially isolated by major transportation infrastructure (roads, tunnels and bridges), while the park is an out-of-reach green haven that is spatially isolated by roads and closed to the public. If these spaces are not integrated with the rest of their social, economic and political context, what is the use of a unilateral spatial connection between them, other than inducing further consumption?

The politics of shaping and producing public space in Beirut is trying hard to mask its ineptitude in addressing the post-war condition. Everyone is talking about reconciliation but no one seems to reach a consensus on its definition or its departure point. On the one hand, people are still charged with animosity and blind loyalty to their confessional representatives in power; on the other hand, people's war memories have been suppressed by a hegemonic discourse that simplifies the post-war socio-cultural context into promises of utopian spaces. The authorities present contemporary formal urban interventions like design aesthetics (landscape to gaze at) and lifestyle etiquette (pedestrian activity and cultural consumption) as platforms for proper social interaction. Similarly, the politics of choosing the ex-demarcation line to implement projects of public space is masked by formalities – in the words of Don Mitchell – like literally being the 'middle ground' between the civil war's conflicting communities. Public space turns into a 'landscape', which "as a produced object … is like a commodity in which evident, temporarily stable, form masks the facts of its production, and its status as social relation".[27]

In post–conflict societies, conflict never ends. It becomes an integral part of the socio–cultural and politico–artistic values for generations to come. Conflict becomes a socio–political reality to be factored (not avoided or merely represented) in discourse, politics and space. If public authorities will always assume a repressive role through sectarian political legitimacy, the community's responsibility – from people, to professionals, to civil society – to harness collective and individual memories through proactive political engagement is a prerequisite. Only such political practice will push forward alternative participative models of shaping collective memory, memorialisation and public space. So, if aestheticising public space is the semiotic equivalent for hegemonising the collective,[28] then disengagement from the formal and engagement in the political is the sought–after deterritorialisation. The only way for a body to conquer hegemonic power is through the "deterritorialisation" of its physical presence regardless of the power framework or its *semiotic equivalent*, argues Jean Baudrillard in his response to Michel Foucault's *The Will to Knowledge*.[29]

1. Even though, we are aware that participatory processes of remembering will probably be recognised by the heritage and tourism industry as profitable and thus exploited in order to gain economic value.

2. Beirut's downtown is the Beirut Central District (BCD) popularised as 'Solidere', a discursive mistake between the downtown and the developing real–estate company's name.

3. Expression after: Samir Khalaf, *Heart of Beirut: Reclaiming the Bourj* (London: Saqi Books, 2006).

4. La Société Libanaise pour le Développement et la Reconstruction du District Central de Beyrouth (Lebanese Company for the Development and Reconstruction of Beirut Central District).

5. *Horsh Al–Sanawbar* is Arabic for 'Pine Woods', whose planting and invigoration is attributed to Lebanese Emir Fakhreddin II Maan in the first half of 17th century. See Taha Al–Wali, *Beirut: History, Culture, and Urbanism* (in Arabic) (Beirut: Dar al–Elem lil'Malayeen, 1993).

6. A design competition was co–organised by the Institut d'Aménagement et d'Urbanisme de la Région Île–de–France (IAURIF) and the Council for Development and Reconstruction (CDR) and funded by the Conseil Regional d'Île–de–France, with a financial contribution of €1,524,490 in 1998. See Christian Feuillet, 'Mandature 1998–2004: Bilan et Perspectives', March 2004 (Fédération des Élu–es Écologistes, Région d'Île–de–France, 2 December 2007).

7. E. Scott and Y. Dlugy, 'Reconstructing Beirut', Case KSG1601.0 (Cambridge, MA: John F. Kennedy School of Government, 2001)

8. S. Makdisi, 'Laying Claim to Beirut: Urban Narrative and Spatial Identity in the Age of Solidere', *Critical Inquiry*, 23(3), 1997, pp. 660–705(693).

9. *ibid.*, Makdisi (1997) p. 664.
10. Christian Thibault, 'A Competition for the Pine Wood (Un Concours pour le Bois des Pins)', trans. Mary Pardoe, *Cahiers de l'IAURIF*, no.106, pp. 167–177(168–170).
11. C. Mouffe, 'Artistic Activism and Agonistic Politics', http://www. monumenttotransformation.org/en/activities/texts/chantal–mouffe (accessed 05/02/11).
12. Anonymous, quoted in 'Planning the Soft Connection', 24/02/11 (L. Salman, interviewer).
13. CGLU–BTVL is Cités et Gouvernements Locaux Unis–Bureau Technique des Villes Libanaises.
14. Anonymous, quoted in 'Designing the Green Line', 16/03/11 (L. Salman, interviewer).
15. A concept introduced in *Critical Cities Volume 2* (London: Myrdle Court Press, 2010) to account for the opportunistic and realpolitik nature of contemporary production of the urban.
16. Anonymous, quoted in 'Planning the Soft Connection', 24/02/11 (L. Salman, interviewer).
17. Anonymous, stated in 'Planning the Soft Connection', 24/02/11 (L. Salman, interviewer).
18. Check out the work of the New Yugoslav art/theory group Grupa Spomenik (The Monument Group) whose work address public space in the Socialist Federative Republic of Yugoslavia through believing "that the genocide is fully speakable, but that politics and critique of ideology are the only proper languages in which it can be spoken", http://grupaspomenik. wordpress.com and http://milicatomic.wordpress.com/works/politics–of–memory.
19. V. Pupavac, 'Therapeutic Governance: Psycho–social Intervention and Trauma Risk Management', *Disasters*, 2001, 25(4), pp. 358–372.
20. V. Pupavac, 'War on the Couch: The Emotionology of the New International Security Paradigm', *European Journal of Social Theory*, 7(2), pp. 149–170.
21. These artistic and research productions are multidisciplinary platforms that periodically take place in Lebanon to promote and exchange cultural practices on contemporary Lebanese history and beyond.
22. J. Hadjithomas and K. Joreige (dirs), *A Perfect Day (Yawmon Akhar)*, 2005.
23. In Aleida Assman's seminal essay 'Fest und flüssig: Anmerkungen zu einer Denkfigur', in Aleida Assmann and Dietrich Harth (eds), *Kultur als Lebenswelt* (Frankfurt: Fischer, 1991) translated and published in English as A. Assmann, 'Memory, Individual and Collective', in R.E. Goodin and C. Tilly (eds), *The Oxford Handbook of Contextual Political Analysis* (Oxford: Oxford University Press, 2006) pp. 210–24.
24. O. Amiralay (dir), *Par un Jour de Violence Ordinaire, Mon Ami Michel Seurat ... (On a Day of Ordinary Violence, My Friend Michel Seurat ...)*, 1996.
25. *ibid.*, Mouffe.
26. *ibid.*, Mouffe.
27. Don Mitchell, *Cultural Geography: A Critical Introduction* (Malden, USA: Blackwell Publishing, 2000) pp. 139–140.
28. D. Mitchell and R. Van Deusen, 'Downsview Park: Open Space or Public Space?', in J. Czerniak (ed.), *Case: Downsview Park Toronto* (Munich: Prestel and Harvard GSD, 2001) pp. 102–115.
29. Sylvère Lotringer, 'Exterminating Angel', in Jean Baudrillard, *Forget Foucault*, translated by Nicole Dufresne (Los Angeles: Semiotexte, 2007) pp. 7–25.

(Im)Possible Alternatives

Reclaiming the Public Space of Zagreb's Upper Town

MARIJANA RIMANIC, IVANA HANACEK & ANA KUTLESA

UrbanFestival is an annual event of contemporary art in public spaces that has been held in Zagreb, Croatia, since 2001 with the intention to broaden the territory of art action outside the protective walls of galleries and theatres, and to animate public sites as spaces of co–existence, confrontation (of different views), as well as possible antagonism. The festival is conceived primarily as a platform, a place of experimentation, a structure ready to react to local needs and intervene in the immediate context. Its programme is based on collaborations with Croatian and international artists, designers, architects and theoreticians, who are invited to produce new projects based on research on a specific annual thematic focus. Alongside the artists' projects, the curatorial team organises lectures, discussions and workshops.

UrbanFestivalX, under the title "(im)possibilities", took place in the area of Upper Town, the historical centre of Zagreb, in October 2010. This paper presents the context and analyses two of the main strategies used within the 2010 programme.

Current situation in Upper Town, Zagreb[1]

The Upper Town, together with the so–called Lower Town – the latter comprising a network of city blocks that date from the late 19th and first half of the 20th century – forms the central, historical part of Zagreb. When compared in terms of public space usage, the Upper Town and the Lower Town are two separate units, the former being passive and derelict, while the latter is vital and active. In comparison with other European cities, the difference is best summarised in the title the Upper Town received in a local newspaper article in 2005: "the most derelict historical core in Europe"[2]. Another specific attribute, connected with the mentioned dereliction, is the fact that the headquarters of the state and local government institutions are located in the Upper Town.

Numerous façades and buildings have been renovated since 2005, but the Upper Town got the title of "most derelict historical core" primarily because of its desolate character and lack of active urban life. The Upper Town squares have lost their function as public spaces, either because they have been turned into parking areas or because the law prohibits public gatherings near the parliament and government buildings. The parks have been left untended and, following archaeological excavations, have remained as featureless expanses, with no function or substance. It is also possible to detect abandoned buildings in the Upper Town, which, although they were planned to be used for cultural purposes, are now closed. For instance, the Jelačić Palace, which until recently served as a kindergarten, was given to the City of Zagreb Museum to use and has been closed to the public. Rakovac Manor is also problematic, as the negligence of the City of Zagreb Museum has left it on the edge of ruin. This situation raises the issue of the revitalisation of the Upper Town, Zagreb's oldest historic area[3], opening up many antagonisms.

The city's political authorities are not interested in initiating a project for the revitalisation of the Upper Town, nor has there been any interest from large commercial companies to invest in the area in any way. Luckily, we may say, or with a measure of scepticism, for the moment. A recent experience of 'investment' and treatment of public space in the Lower Town area, the Varšavska Street and Cvjetni project[4], was seen as an example of reckless local gentrification, in the course of which private capital, closely co-operating with the city authorities, literally destroyed a site of great social and symbolic value, and in so doing displayed utter negligence towards the regeneration and maintaining of public space and protected cultural heritage.

Unfortunately, such misuse of space and structures for short-term goals is, in the words of art historian and activist Snješka Knežević, a result of the shortcomings of official urban politics, which flinches from long-term planning, a notoriously neoliberal trait.[5] In a context where city politics completely dominate the expert opinion of professionals at the City Institute for the Conservation of Cultural and Natural Heritage, the self-organised

Conservationists' Society has folded, and the protection of monuments and nature serves neocapitalist ideology, calling for a project to revitalise the historic city centre would be nothing short of requesting its explicit devastation, gentrification and commercialisation. However, the run–down state of the Upper Town is not exclusively the result of the recently introduced value system promoting and stimulating the privatisation of public space and the atomisation of society in the post–socialist reality.

The dormant state of Zagreb's historic core is also closely linked to the politics of state institutions and the cultural bodies they encompass. In the first case, it is direct politics with malice of forethought, which, during the past ten years, has developed various mechanisms of surveillance and social control that both literally and figuratively block the citizens' access to the Upper Town. The most radical example of this is in the framework of the justice–political system, more precisely, in a law prohibiting public gatherings on Marko's Square. This law was enacted during radical right–wing groups' protests and hunger strikes, and, although declared unconstitutional, has been in effect since 2005. The law also prohibits public gatherings within 100 metres of the parliament, government and constitutional court buildings that are situated nearby. Although Marko's Square is understood to be the oldest square in the city, a veritable agora linked to a long tradition of the expression of public opinion, in recent years all active protesters (in the struggle against the commercialisation of higher education, or in revolt against the government, etc.) have been physically prevented from entering the square by security fences and a police cordon placed in the so–called contact zone, i.e. the streets connecting the Upper and Lower Towns, which effectively expanded the prohibition of assembly to the whole Upper Town area. In addition, control is institutionalised through the CCTV cameras installed on almost every Upper Town building/institution.

Another instance of social control institutionalised in the justice–political system relates to the protection of cultural monuments. In the prescribed system, the inhabitants of the Upper Town are obliged to pay a monument annuity each month. Considering that the population here (viewed through the lens of social status) is exceptionally heterogeneous as a consequence of the socialist policy of nationalisation implemented after World War II,[6] this legislation enforces gentrification on the area since citizens with low social status are not, or soon will not be, capable of paying the monument annuity. The never–retracted statement made by the mayor of Zagreb, Milan Bandić, in 2008 after the prices of municipal services rose, that the citizen "who finds it too expensive should move out of Zagreb", serves as confirmation that this is not a mere assumption.

It would seem that both these legal acts serve to represent the Croatian national identity, transforming the historic core of Zagreb into a kind of Potemkin village, a capital city with no social unrest, a town centre with nice facades, behind which lie rot and utter social insensitivity towards not only the inhabitants of the historic centre but also all Croatian citizens.

It might at first seem surprising, and even sound contradictory, that the cultural institutions located in the Upper Town – not a negligible number – also contribute to the further ossification of the area. An explanation of this situation can be found in a critique of post–socialist cultural institutions, which suggests that institutions of this kind have preserved the inherited infrastructure of socialism and that the political transition did not influence them; their existence is inertial; their logic is that of utter passivity.[7] The Upper Town cultural institutions do not employ a large number of people, nor do they possess complex infrastructure, yet they are entirely dependent on public funds. These museums' and galleries' programmes do not attract particular attention; nor do their exhibitions, educational projects or critical inquiry into official historical narratives place them on the regional cultural map. Just the opposite, their programmes don't even interest the inhabitants of Zagreb; few people show interest in exhibitions that are open for nine months, or in permanent museum displays that have not changed for several decades.

Nevertheless, some changes regarding cultural programmes may be sensed, but, unfortunately, they follow the neoliberal paradigm and the commercialisation of the cultural sphere. Among examples that can be cited are the recently opened Museum of Broken Relationships, and also the programme of the Klovićevi Dvori Gallery, which frequently hosts travelling exhibitions marked by a popular approach and strong marketing. In such circumstances, cultural workers *de facto* cease to deal with culture, becoming funky businessmen and entertainers on the treadmill of neoliberal capitalism.[8]

Proposing alternatives and strategies

Aware of the multilayered nature of the issues we were raising, the organisers of UrbanFestivalX chose to situate it right inside the highly controlled space

Picnic by Group 4/Marija Galić, Branko Palić, Darko Šeparović, Andrea Šimić,
Vranicani Field, Zagreb, 3 October 2010, DAMIR ŽIŽIĆ

Marking by Siniša Labrović,
Marko's Square, Zagreb, 1 October 2010, DAMIR ŽIŽIĆ

of the Upper Town. The aim was not to emphasise and articulate only the problems confronting the residents of Upper Town, but also to point to particular mechanisms that numb the area and make it hostile for all its users, residents as well as other citizens and visitors. The practices realised within UrbanFestivalX would try to render visible the conflicts existing in public space and to suggest possible alternatives. They might instigate a different use and view of public space among its users; however, if this failed to happen, the micro–political gesture of opening up the problematic situation would remain relevant as a form of resistance and critique of dominant practices.

The programme for UrbanFestivalX consisted of seven new works, a documentary exhibition, a film programme and a roundtable discussion. Our intention was to react to the current conditions that had been identified through research and to open up a space for discussing and critically acting *in* and *about* the given conditions in order to create what Chantal Mouffe calls "agonistic public space"[9]. Rather than offering strategies for accomplishing consensus, our aim was to uncover different positions – those of power and those of weakness – and the conflicts they provoke, assuming that "critical art is art that foments dissensus, that makes visible what the dominant consensus tends to obscure and obliterate. It is constituted by a manifold of artistic practices aiming at giving a voice to all those who are silenced within the framework of the existing hegemony."[10]

Locating festival actions directly in the area of concern, and bearing in mind the array of antagonisms and ambivalences that the festival might open up, we approached the given context using two main strategies. The first is a strategy of acting on specific problematic public spaces, from which the public has somehow been excluded, with interventions that reaffirm them as spaces of collective participation through active audience involvement, thereby making visible the fact that they are not as public as they should be (since they were formed with that intention and are nominally defined as such). The second is the strategy of introducing the problematic aspects of public space in the Upper Town into the public discourse at various levels, considering public space not as a physical entity but as a set of power relations, and public discourse as a means to activate the participation of citizens and their general understanding of public space, creating a platform for public articulation on the problematic aspects.

Strategy 1: Collective participation

The first strategy will be analysed through two examples of interventions in public space by the group of architecture students called Group 4: *Picnic* and *Birthday party*, which both emerged in response to identified problematic public areas. In the case of *Picnic*, the area in question is Vranicani's Field, a parcel on the south part of the Upper Town, just above the promenade, on the ground of the former city walls. The field appeared at the beginning of the 20th century after the demolition of private housing and convent buildings that used to be nested in the city walls[11]. Lotrscak Tower, the only historic city tower that has not been incorporated in a new architectural construction, is located on one side of the field, and the building of the State Hydro–meteorological Institute dating from the late 19th century, on the other. The field was used on a day–to–day basis, till the beginning of 2000, as a public space for fun and leisure; archive photos show a variety of temporary content, from an aquarium to a flower market. In mid–2000, the Ministry of Culture of the Republic of Croatia began "systematic and protective digging"[12] of the remains of the city walls hidden underneath the surface of the field. When the works were completed, the field was covered with gravel; the surface was not greened or made appropriate in any way for further public use. Moreover, the newly covered terrain is very porous which causes slipping and puddles of mud after each rainfall. The results of the archaeological research, which is said to be finished, have never been presented to the broader public, neither at the site itself, nor in any of the institutions that would be appropriate for that purpose. We could say that the field has become a sort of a "terrain vague"[13], inappropriate for any usage.

Inspired by the question of how it is possible that the area has not been restored to its former state since the completion of the archaeological digging and in whose interest this annihilation of function could be, the Group 4 constructed a polygonal lawn around one of the existing puddles and organised a get–together and a picnic on a Sunday afternoon during the festival. The perfect lawn, obviously grown somewhere else and placed upon the gravel, with the muddy puddle in the middle, resulted in an absurd, wondrous and comical image, underlining the state of the space that people have got used to and that they have stopped perceiving Vranicani's Field as their space to be used on a daily basis. Furthermore, the fact that a functional area is in question, as shown by the picnic activity, opens up possibilities of concrete participation of citizens in this space. In this way, the installation not only draws attention to the problematic public space, but also takes a step further, suggesting that its use could be collective and participatory and not conditioned by commercial content. As this area used to be intended for temporary content, *Picnic* puts emphasis on providing only the minimal infrastructure necessary to make it suitable for basic use. The picnic itself is just one of the possible uses.

Similar logic is present in the action entitled *Birthday party*, held on Marković Square as the closing event of the festival: a get-together with balloons, birthday cake and live street music. Marković Square, close to Vranicani's Field and one of the oldest Zagreb squares, is small in surface and surrounded by neo-renaissance and classicist one-storied edifices.[14] Due to long-term neglect of the problem of parking in the Upper Town, it has been turned into a parking place, and most people perceived it only in that way. Just as the puddle that wants to be a water feature of landscape architecture is absurd, so too, in this case, is the balloon tied to a rear-view mirror. A party with drinks, cakes and music in between the parked cars underlines, first, that this social use of public space springs from the need for collective participation, and second, that the current situation is an inadequate alternative caused by the negligence of the governing bodies regarding the needs of the community.

Both *Picnic* and *Birthday party* aim to draw attention to the fact that tendencies to narrow the public space can be countered by an alternative of self-initiated and self-organised actions taking over/creating/returning the space for collective participation. In doing so, both interventions are temporary and minimal in terms of physical impact on the environment. Their intention is not to set out the specific way of using the space (picnic, party) as the one that is considered appropriate by the artists or festival organisers, but to affirm the possibility of perceiving the space in a different way, so that public space is being made, not taken away, and its consummation is not happening in terms of pleasing one's needs and financial profit, but under the premise that public space should be open to all under same conditions for any kind of use that is not restrictive towards the other. In short, public space should be inclusive and free.

Strategy 2: Activating public discourse

The work entitled *Marking* by Croatian performing artist Siniša Labrović and the roundtable on cultural strategies of the Upper Town cultural institutions organised by the curatorial team are examples of the second strategy used in the framework of UrbanFestivalX. Both projects aimed to make visible the complex structures of power through which public space is manipulated, not only the physical aspects of public space (as in the first strategy) but also, more particularly, the complex range of mechanisms (political, media, legal, cultural) for the articulation of questions of public interest.

The scenario of the performance by Siniša Labrović was as follows: at noon on the day of the festival opening, the artist arrived at Marko's Square, stood in the middle, took out his penis and urinated, turning around himself and leaving a wet trace on the ground. While other festival projects were described by short statements in the media and PR materials that preceded the festival, this performance was announced strictly with the title, artist's name, time and venue. Aside from the fact that the directness and austerity of the performance would lose their power if expected, the reason for keeping the content secret lies, of course, also in the fear of a legal ban of the performance by the police, i.e. censorship. However, the possibility that urinating in public space could be taken as an offence to the moral feelings of citizens and a threat to public peace and order (despite the fact that we're dealing with an artist's act, thus displaced ontologically from the realm of reality into the realm of art) and serve as the basis for an arrest was not the only reason to fear. Another, and from a legal perspective more justified, reason was the fact that Marko's Square is an area that falls under the terms of the law which prohibits public gathering within 100 metres of government buildings. According to the law, the gathering of Labrović's audience was not permitted and the organisers of such an event should be arrested and, if found guilty, pay a fine. To avoid this scenario, the organisers and the artist decided to officially report the gathering (which is obligatory for any gathering in public space, even exhibition openings) in the nearby Lotrscak Tower, where a gallery is located and where some of the festival programme was indeed taking place. This was also the official venue announced in all the media and PR materials. Labrović met the audience there and invited them to follow him to the square.

In a certain way, all this 'dramaturgy' became part of the work, given the fact that it was an outcome of the specific situation that caused the artist to choose the particular location in the first place. As mentioned, Marko's Square is the centre of state political power and has been transformed from a public square (and moreover, Zagreb's first civil square) to a sort of inner courtyard of the parliament and the government. Its public use has been completely appropriated by those institutions. And, as a consequence of the law on public gathering, the square is mostly empty, devoid of any content that is not connected to the governing institutions or the church in its centre, and without a single piece of urban furniture that would suggest the function of the square as public space *par excellence*. Aside from a practical means of avoiding the legal prevention of the work, for us as organisers and for the artist, this dramatic subversion of the law was also a way to turn attention to the idea that the law, which does not make any distinctions regarding the nature or cause of the gathering, should be implemented consistently, in the same way for everyone. Consequently, tourist groups should also undertake some kind of scheme to comply with the law. In reality, of course, they are ignored, just as breaking the law was ignored in a more serious situation when ex–US–president Bush visited Zagreb and the state held a public reception in Marko's Square.

As it happened, neither Siniša Labrović nor the organisers were arrested. The audience gathered around the artist was small enough not be perceived as a threat by the police officers, and big enough to surround the artist and block the view so that the policemen didn't even see what was going on. Labrović explained his piece in the following way:

This year's UrbanFestival 10 has Zagreb's Upper Town both as its topic and location. It is a space of great symbolic, cultural and political significance. It is also the space of the contemporary political power, the place where the legislative, executive and judicial power of the Republic of Croatia – the Parliament, the Government, and the Constitutional Court – are located. These institutions have a great impact on the life of every citizen of the Republic of Croatia. The strong presence of the police and the great number of surveillance cameras in Upper Town are understandable, as is the lack of urban events and everyday liveliness. The exclusivity of that space has been increased by the Law on Public Gathering which prohibits the citizens to gather within the distance of one hundred metres from the Parliament, Government, and Constitutional Court buildings, as well as the offices of the President. The Law is popularly known as the Marko's Square public gathering ban. Because of my good intention to soften the exclusivity of the place, because of the relentless hope that I will intensify the feeling and the awareness

that the mentioned institutions and power belong to each and every one of
us, that they are yours, mine, ours, and also because of the platonic love and
deep respect I feel for all the institutions situated on Marko's Square and in its
neighbourhood, as well as because of the tender desire to make UrbanFestival
feel at home in the space of Upper Town, I will do a performance called
Marking on the Marko's Square at the opening of UrbanFestival.[15]

This text, as well as photo documentation, was published on the festival's website immediately after the performance. Despite the fact that the media was not present at the performance in great numbers, the photos and news spread quickly through the media space. Although the police did not react by arresting Labrović at the scene of the event, a few days later he got a call to go for questioning at the police station, and in the end he faced a minor charge on which grounds he was declared guilty and paid a fine.

We could say that Siniša Labrović's performance intervened in three different ways in public space: physically, mediatically and legally. The signification of the physical intervention is symbolic (unlike the interventions in public space which use the first mentioned strategy) and gains its sense only through the perception of the audience, random passers-by, and even the police officers. All those groups, by interpreting Labrović's work, also interpret the set of power relations used by the state structures to control the public sphere. In addition, the media and legal interventions could exist only if there was a certain perception of the performance by the press and broader media audience, on the one hand, and by the structures of executive power, on the other.

During our research on the situation in the Upper Town, we detected, as mentioned previously, a wide range of mechanisms by which cultural institutions contribute to the apparent state of non-activity, and behind which the privatisation of public spaces and common goods is hidden. We also identified a chronic lack of communication among these institutions, as well as the lack of an overall perspective on their possibilities and on the ways the state and city governing bodies, which decide on the financial distribution of the public money intended for culture, function. The result of this absence of strategy are: illogical plans for the redistribution of spatial resources among the institutions, constant avoidance of solving the difficulties that institutions working in heritage protection face, spending a great deal of money on operating costs, and lack of unified and consistent criteria for evaluating programmes. Articulation of these issues in the public sphere mainly comes through media news on specific institutions and their particular problems, and through articles that appear from time to time dealing with the Upper Town's revitalisation plans and its "brighter" cultural–touristic future. No attention is paid to tendencies of commodification of culture and heritage, or to the social insensibility present in these plans, or to the current condition, the complexity of the situation and the real possibilities. Therefore our aim as organisers was to offer an alternative to such discourse and to make all identified problematic aspects into valid content for public discussion. UrbanFestivalX's roundtable gathered a large active audience. As well as the broad public and representatives of the cultural institutions located in Upper Town, we called on four experts to offer an overall view of the situation from their perspective. Snješka Knežević, an art historian specialised in the urban and architectural heritage of Zagreb, and Marijan Hržić, the architect of several public projects in the city of Zagreb and a resident of Upper Town, spoke on potential future uses of Upper Town's architectural heritage that would make it more accessible to the public and, at the same time, be as sensitive as possible regarding the preservation of its original characteristics. Professor Silvije Novak, the director of the City Institute for the Conservation of Cultural and Natural Heritage spoke on the history of conservation in Upper Town, but was very reluctant to answer any specific questions concerning the current situation. The fourth speaker, Professor Andrea Zlatar approached the situation from the perspective of cultural policy, providing a concrete analysis of the current programmatic strategies and missions of Upper Town cultural institutions.

The series of conflicts that emerged during the discussion, as well as in the media reactions afterwards, point to the fact that an approach that aims to reveal all the antagonisms and make them visible, rather than offering a consensus, is exactly what is needed to create a public field appropriate for the articulation of the manifold aspects of the problems in question. One of the critiques of us as organisers, which had a more positive or negative implication depending on the source, was that we were instigators from outside, i.e. from the so-called independent, non-institutional scene. While one section of the public perceived the fact that the critique was from outside the institutions as very negative for the institutions in question, the other section, mainly representatives of those institutions, resented the organisers calling for public discussion on their work and expecting them to answer criticism in public. This was yet another indicator of the lack of understanding within the Upper Town institutions of the notion of the public.

In both the roundtable and Labrović's work, the approach was that of a citizen/curator or citizen/artist. Indeed the citizen/artist, like the citizen/curator, is a public worker, and has a right and to some extent an obligation to articulate public issues through his/her actions. The format of the performance and the roundtable debate in public space was designed to activate a complex field of public mechanisms, and it is precisely the counter-action/response by the public – be it in the form of direct participation or through the media or law services – that gives meaning to the activities and points to the fact that the issues they are dealing with really are issues in need of better articulation.

Self-reflection and self-critique (instead of conclusion)

Projects such as Birthday party and Picnic deal with a certain problematic situation in a specific public space by offering a temporary social scenario as an alternative to its currently accepted form of use. What is their effect after the action has ended? Has the alternative scenario become at least a sporadic practice of the citizens? On the one hand, it is impossible to answer these questions completely as we cannot be sure whether the project changed the mind-set or practice of some of the users of the space. On the other hand, a year after the festival, Marko's Square is still a parking zone, and Vranicani's Field remains empty, even though the festival lawn is slowly spreading its roots. The ban on public gathering, challenged by Siniša Labrović's performance, also still remains in effect.

Keeping in mind Chantal Mouffe's definition of critical art as that which foments dissent, we could say that the projects realised within UrbanFestivalX aimed not so much to solve problems, but to reveal and articulate them in the public sphere, to render visible the different conflicted positions of the actors that use public space, and to point to the fact that the current use of the space is not based on a consensus of all, but is an effect of the exclusion and suppression of certain interests, needs and possibilities.

Although these artistic practices don't solve problematic social situations, they do interfere with a set of power relations contained within these situations, and do so from an artistic position that is not neutral. Intervention in public space that is designated as an artistic intervention functions according to a certain set of rules; it does not have the same logic of functioning as if it was conducted by a regular citizen. We can say that there are certain mechanisms that protect action marked as art. Specifically, it means that the artist Siniša Labrović can be legally protected from sanctions for disturbing public law and order on the basis that his act was artistic not civic; a group of architects can get permission to set up balloons, loudspeakers and musical instruments on a square that is really a parking place precisely because they do it as an action within an art festival. The reaction of other actors that are present in the given situation, not only the forces of law and order, is also different when something is labelled as art; not understanding is often accepted as the common reaction.

Although the position of the artist and curator is far from neutral, it would be misleading just to state that it is a protected position. It is protected, but at the same time exposed to a different set of 'threats' that emerge from the way the art world functions. It would also be incorrect to conclude that being somehow protected diminishes the significance of these or similar actions. Quite the contrary, it makes them possible, opening up a space for action that would be sanctioned in a non-artistic context, and which can and indeed desires to reveal conflicting positions and point to other options excluded by the current hegemony. What must be considered, in this regard, is the possibility of a self-critical position, where a curatorial/artistic position and strategy is revealed, discussed and criticised openly.

To present all the problems which emerge during the production and performance of an art work, as well as the mechanisms that enable its realisation and the ways in which the audience and the so-called participants are included, and to make all that a part of the work itself, can be a way of revealing one's own position. By putting an emphasis on the process, and connecting the presentation of the produced art through formats such as discussions, essays and exhibitions, we try to create a self-critical representational space within UrbanFestival.

To conclude, what we find important and valuable in our work as organisers is, on the one hand, to bear in mind the character and boundaries of artistic practices – paraphrasing Chantal Mouffe, to abandon the modernist illusion that art should provide a radical change and to take into account the necessity of traditional forms of political intervention in the fight against neoliberal hegemony[16] – and, on the other hand, to recognise the limits of our own position, aware that artistic agency is no less burdened with the mechanisms of exclusion, power relations and hegemonies than any other field of public agency.

1. The overview of the current social and urban situation in the Upper Town is based on extensive research done before the festival by the curatorial team, i.e. the authors of this paper.
2. Nina Ožegović, 'Upper Town: Out with the Government and Parliament!' ('*Vladu i Sabor van iz Gornjeg grada*'), *Nacional*, 512, 2005, http://www.nacional.hr/clanak/20256/vladu-i-sabor-van-iz-gornjeg-grada.
3. The Upper Town is the modern name for Gradec, the small medieval town of craftsmen and traders, which was located on a small hill, and which forms the nucleus of the city of Zagreb along with the neighbouring small town, Kaptol.
4. The Cvjetni project is an instance of the gentrification of the downtown centre and its pedestrian zone, which spurred the largest civic protests in the past few decades in Zagreb. The investor managed to buy a residential block within a protected cultural monument, razed it to the ground and constructed a shopping centre and large private garage. The city authorities and 'experts' from the Office for the Strategy Planning of the City of Zagreb, as well as the Institute for the Conservation of Cultural and Natural Heritage gave such support to the project that they in fact gifted part of Varšavska Street in the pedestrian zone to the investor to build an access ramp for his garage.
5. Snješka Knežević, 'Heritage, communication and culture last on the list' ('*Baština, komunikacija i kultura u zadnjem planu*'), *Zarez*, 292, 2010, 20.
6. Nationalisation, that is, the conversion of private into social/state property, took place immediately after World War II, in 1945. Part of the rural population that moved into Zagreb in the course of nationalisation settled in the Upper Town in palaces and tall buildings, which had till then been privately owned by the well-off citizenry and gentry.
7. Vesna Vukovic, Leonardo Kovacevic, 'The Landscape of Post-transformation Institutions in Zagreb and their Political Impact', 2011, http://eipcp.net/transversal/0208/kovacevic-vukovic/en.
8. Dušan Grlja and Jelena Vesić, 'The Neo-liberal Institution of Culture', 2011, http://eipcp. net/transversal/0208/prelom/en.
9. Chantal Mouffe, 'Artistic activism and agonistic spaces', *Art & Research*, 1(2), 2007, http://www.artandresearch.org.uk/v1n2/mouffe.html; Croatian edition: 'Umjetnički aktivizam i agonistički prostori', in *Operation: City*, L. Kovacevic et al. (eds) (Zagreb: Prosinac, 2008).
10. *ibid.*, Mouffe (2007).
11. Lelja Dobronic, *Zagrebacki Kapitol i Gornji Grad – Nekad i Danas* (Zagreb Kaptol and Upper Town – before and today) (Zagreb: Školska Knjiga, 1986).
12. Ministry of Culture of the Republic of Croatia, http://www.min-kulture.hr/default.aspx?id=30.
13. James P. Cramer and Jennifer Evans Yankopolous (eds), *Almanac of Architecture & Design 2006* (Atlanta: Greenway Communications, 2006).
14. *ibid.*, Dobronic (1986).
15. http://www.urbanfestival.hr/2010/en/artists/sinisa-labrovic-en/.
16. *ibid.*, Mouffe (2007).

"I know thee not, old man"

The Designated Public

ROBIN BALE

Aesthetics can be understood ... as the system of a priori forms determining what presents itself to sense experience. It is a delimitation of spaces and times, of the visible and the invisible, of speech and noise, that simultaneously determines the place and the stakes of politics as a form of experience.[1]

Public space is the space of the visible, the arena in which the questions of who has the right to be visible in that space are played out. To be public is to be visible, to be visible is to be the public.

The present system, whose philosophical basis could be accurately described as market individualism[2], has given rise in recent decades to the dominant model of subjectivity – *Homo economicus*. That fabled entity's rational choices, as voter and consumer, underwrite that system. Voters choose a party, consumers buy things – and, more recently, also run public services efficiently in their spare time. Because 'choice' is the mantra and justification of the system, the old liberal welfare state, with its universalism in terms of provision, is now obsolete. We must all, as a previous prime minister told us, "modernise or die".[3] It is the nature of *Homo economicus*, focused on improvement, calculating his striving ('aspiring' would be the current buzz word), to consider the present as merely a vestibule to the future when his investments, of time, energy and capital, come to fruition. This temporality affects spaces, individuals and practices, consigning some of them to an unredeemable past.

There are some problems, however, with atomised choice and the pursuit of advantage. If all our collective and individual welfare amounts to is making choices, what are we to say to those who, like Dostoyevsky's underground man, respond to this headlong rush into a bright and shiny future with: "And why are you so firmly, so triumphantly convinced that only the normal and the positive – in other words, only what is conducive to welfare – is for the advantage of man? Does not man, perhaps, love something besides well-being?"[4] Valorising the

We Are Bad, poster, 2007

choices of autonomous agents, because they are their choices, can lead some benighted souls to think they have the right to do what they want; resulting in an 'epidemic' (a nicely medicalised term) of what has come to be called anti-social behaviour. The contemporary response to this willed difference seems to be therapy and the law.

It is from therapy that we get a concept which seems to have become common currency within public discourse, that of 'dependency' – on benefits, public housing – used as both something reprehensible in itself and morally harmful to the dependents. They must be weaned off, *for their own good.* Thus, we can have government ministers speaking of "dependency culture"[5] in reference to claimants of state benefits, as if the sick or unemployed constitute a separate group within society. Dependency is projected as a euphemism for addiction, something that clouds the lucid self-presence of the choosing subject, breaks the hermetic seal that protects that core from the contingency of need and undermines the legitimating function of choice.

An illustrative example: "We have created and are perpetuating a vicious circle of dependency. The challenge is to recognise the individual household's need and to support this through income subsidies allowing people to make choices for themselves in the market."[6]

On 24 October 2010, I led four people on a walk from Curtain Road, on the fringes of the City of London, to Shoreditch Park. As an integral part of the piece, I drank alcohol throughout as we walked, and encouraged the other participants to do likewise. The skewed perspective this gave, both in the effects of the alcohol on the participants and the effect of the knowledge that they were performing as street drinkers, was necessary, as I hope will become clear.

The impetus for my first conceiving this event was the imposition, by Hackney Council, of Alcohol Control Zones in several discrete areas along my planned route. These zones, otherwise known as Designated Public Places (DPP), are areas where, in the words of the 2001 Criminal Justice and Police Act, one can legally be ordered: "(a) not to consume in that place anything which is, or which the constable reasonably believes to be, alcohol; (b) to surrender anything in his possession which is, or which the constable reasonably believes to be, alcohol or a container for alcohol ..."[7] Refusal to comply with the demand is an offence and, as the Act says, will render the offender "liable on summary conviction to a fine". The fine can be a fixed penalty notice of £50 up to a maximum of £500.

The original plan was to take a group to circumnavigate these discrete DPPs and observe what, in the environment, might have given rise to the measure. Like any other resident of the borough, I was aware of the tide of gentrification that has swept across it, as in large swathes of the rest of London. Locally, this has been exacerbated by the recent improvement of public transport links and, arguably, the fact that the 2012 Olympic Games are to be held here.

The wording of the original orders was detailed about the areas they covered, down to which side of Hoxton Street was included (west rather than east), for example. One such zone was tiny, simply enclosing the churchyard of St Leonard's Shoreditch, a long-standing resort of street drinkers. I had an idea of what we would find; my assumption was that the imposition of the orders was partly there to assuage the fears of the newly arrived and relatively wealthy about their neighbours, the poor – who, after all, cannot afford the newly refurbished pubs in the borough. Therefore, constellations of tarted-up pubs serving food and Belgian lagers, 'specialist' shops and expensive delicatessens, new-build private developments, recently owner-occupied terraces and parks undergoing regeneration would all have been evident.

However, in May 2010, six months after the creation of the separate zones, Hackney Council, without any fanfare and little publicity, declared the entire borough a DPP. This was surprising, especially in light of the council's protestations that nothing had changed. In the online comments to a piece in the *Hackney Post*, Councillor Alan Laing insists: "this is not a ban on public drinking. This point has been made throughout the process and through the consultation. The council and the local police have expressly stated that it is not a ban on public drinking ..."[8] In fact, as the comments on the page where it is archived make clear, the headline of the piece was amended by the addition of the qualifier 'anti-social' to the original 'Public drinking banned in Hackney'. It seems that council and police were falling over themselves to make clear that the ban was only aimed at *other people*.

A report on the council's move contained the following:

> *Councillor Karen Alcock, Hackney's Deputy Mayor said: 'It doesn't stop people from sitting on their own and having a beer – that's not what the powers are there to do. It's for the persistent drinkers who're shouting and intimidating people, and giving police the power to deal with them'.[9]* (emphasis added)

Alcock's statement gives a clearer indication of the intent of the ban. She differentiates solitary drinkers from intimidating ones. It looks like drinking in public is not a problem as long as it is solitary – one is tempted to point out that this would surely be anti-social drinking, the opposite of the social variety. The worry seems to be more about people congregating together. We are not informed how large a group of drinkers would need to be to intimidate the councillor.

> *Sergeant Matt Devereau, from Hoxton's safer neighbourhood team, said the police would not be 'rushing out' to confiscate drinks. 'We wouldn't want to take alcohol from people having a picnic and some wine in Shoreditch Park, for instance. We would only do it if it was anti-social and unhealthy'.[10]*

Devereau insists that the measure is directed, not against wine-drinking picnic-goers, but the "anti-social *and* unhealthy" (note the conflation of the two terms). Who could possibly be against health? Only the anti-social, who probably need treatment. So it is not in fact groups of drinkers, as such, that are the problem. He does not specify who is at risk from this unhealthy behaviour; whether it is those who are consuming the alcohol (in an insufficiently social manner) or those who might come into contact with them. It may also seem strange that behaviour that is unhealthy to the person doing it, but left others unharmed, should require the intervention of the law.

The largest concern of those against was on ensuring that street drinkers had access to treatment, something we are committed to providing and this will make it easier for them to so access.[11]

This was from Councillor Laing, describing the substance of objections to the creation of the DPP. As with Devereau's statement, it purports a therapeutic motivation for the measure that exists as a complement to the punitive. Why a control order should make it easier for "support workers to access problem street drinkers and help them into treatment options", as he claims, is rather mysterious. Support workers would surely already know where to look. However it is presented, this remains an action intended to clear drinkers – of the wrong kind – off the streets and out of the parks; getting them into rehab would be a means to the same end.

Tim Shields, Chief Executive of Hackney Council and Chair of the Hackney Drug and Alcohol Action Team, said: "This is just one of a number of measures that we will be using to combat alcohol–related anti–social behaviour. We don't want to stop those drinking alcohol responsibly but we want to ensure that people can enjoy our public spaces safely."[12] There have been laws against assault, threatening behaviour and public urination for generations, so why is there suddenly a need for extra measures to ensure people's safe enjoyment of 'our' public spaces? We shall also return to the question of who 'responsible' drinkers are responsible to shortly.

But first, it is worthwhile at this point to reconsider the nomenclature: DPP, a Designated Public Place. These places – streets, parks, benches – were public beforehand. However, that is the point. The tautology is necessary, and will seem less nonsensical, if we take the time to question what is being designated. One of the defining joys of city life has always been a certain contingency and heterogeneity in the population of its public spaces. Streets, parks or squares are simply used by whoever happens to be there. And anyone has the right to be there. One never knows who one will meet. It seems that this very fact has been viewed with increasing suspicion in recent years. If what is being specified is a 'Designated Public', meaning the users of the place, rather than a 'Designated Place', what motivates this legislation might become clearer.

The 'Public' is not the same entity as that public which means, in terms of space, open to all, and in terms of entities, contingency – whoever happens to be there. The creation of the zones is a speech act, which like all the most effective ones ("I sentence you to life imprisonment", or "You are under arrest", or "I hereby pronounce you man and wife") describes a change in state, and has a police and court system to back it. The 'Public' who will use these transfigured spaces (the DPP) are being willed into being by that very act of designation. The spaces that they will inhabit are already demarcated and shaped by the law. These are the sober, law–abiding, hard–working subjects, whom politicians and columnists never tire of conscripting (as Stefan Collini[13] has pointed out, official uncertainties towards the market individualist position are betrayed by the uneasy shifting from individuals to families in invocations of the basic unit of society). These people who we must become are already pictured for us, larger than life and in glossy colour, on the hoardings that conceal the construction of the new–build apartments that are being prepared for them.

Building site hoarding, Packington Estate, 2010

On responsible drinking: "... the era of the long boozy lunch is now coming to an end ... many of us are too busy to fit in anything more than a sandwich at our desks. These days it seems that you're more likely to find your colleagues down the gym at lunch rather than the pub."[14]

What I find surprising in this gem (which is fairly representative of the whole site) is that the problem framed is not that of being too busy to eat lunch beyond a snatched sandwich. The problem, apparently, was lunchtime drinking, now thankfully consigned to the dustbin of history along with trade union membership.

Falstaff

"Falstaff: Now, Hal, what time of day is it, lad?
Prince Henry: Thou art so fat-witted, with drinking of old sack and unbuttoning thee after supper and sleeping upon benches after noon, that thou hast forgotten to demand that truly which thou wouldst truly know. *What a devil hast thou to do with the time of the day?*" (emphasis added) *Henry IV, Part 1*, Act 1 Scene 2

So – after a preamble that, I hope, has marked out the territory – to the walk as it actually happened. The premise of the walk had to change. It would no longer be enough to map out the discrete zones, look at whatever pockets of gentrification and poverty were existing cheek by jowl. This was not a matter of localised incursions, the semi–privatisation or pseudo–privatisation of a public area. The entire borough was now existing as a zone. It was not that discrete gated communities had suddenly sprung up, closing everyone else out; more that we find ourselves within a gated community with strict requirements for membership and no way to get out.

As the whole of Hackney was now under the sign of the new Designated Public, an invocation of the same, one could start anywhere, go anywhere, and find it; the eternal and brightly lit present of the gym, where the machines are equipped with mirrors facing them so its clientele can observe their own endless becoming. There was a necessity to find a fracture, to insert difference. How to thread these spaces together, whilst pushing them apart; how to consider time and untimeliness?

The reasons for the recently legislated antipathy to street drinkers are probably many; dislike of the poor is part of it, but it is the visibility of this particular section of the poor that might be a major factor. They are outside, we have to see them. It is, to a large extent, a matter of theatre. They parade what might be their dependency, or is quite possibly their choice – but must be the wrong one. As the user of any drug will confirm, drug time is not normal time. They appear to live in a different time to everyone else; evidenced not just in the clumsy movements and slurred speech of the drunk. They are not just passing through, hurrying to get somewhere else, they stay. They drink in the day, when others have to work, they have been assumed to be unemployed, or under–employed, avatars of a benefits culture that is outmoded, an obsolete temporality. They hoard time, so there is less of it for decent people.

The first stop on our way, after the off–licence, was a small brown plaque, halfway up the side of a Victorian building on Hewett Street, off Curtain Road. It reads: "Near this site stood The Curtain Theatre 1577 – c.1627 Second English public playhouse ..." It was speculation (though not entirely unfounded) on my part but, for the sake of poetic clarity, I claimed that there was a strong possibility that this unremarkable street with the van depot at the end of it was where the character of Sir John Falstaff first appeared.

Falstaff was my link, the trope that could tie the differing times and subjectivities together through opposition. A quick Google search for his name comes up with three hotels, a brewery, a type of apple, cigars and something called the "Falstaff Experience", home of Tudor World, an edutainment tourist trap in Stratford–on–Avon. Falstaff has become a sort of trademark for "merrie olde Englande", a place of bawdy pleasures and healthy lusts, symbol of an organic social wholeness that never existed. That was not the Falstaff that I wanted to use. I was thinking of Falstaff the untimely, Falstaff the unappeased ghost.

Within the two history plays (*Henry IV*, Parts 1 and 2) of which he is a part, he is a much more troubling character than the ribald heritage drunk. He is an obese and unrepentant (in both profane and religious senses) layabout, a thief, sponger and drunk. The plays make clear that he is a remnant of a previous order, a corrupt feudalism he has outstayed. Throughout the plays he is reminded that he has lived too long. His lover asks him when he will "begin to patch up thine old body for heaven?"[15] The Lord Chief Justice cruelly reminds him: "You are as a candle, the better part burnt out."[16] He is often exhorted to reform, repent, 'modernise'.

Germaine Greer points out that the early theatres were:

> ... the only places where all the denizens of London ... could foregather and actually experience their membership of a community. Even the largest churches did not afford the same spectacular possibilities, for the pulpit was raised above the congregation who stood all on one plane. In the theatre the audience could see itself ...[17]

It was this public who would watch Falstaff verbally spar with Prince Hal in the Henry plays. It may also have been that they knew, even while watching the first play of the pair, that Hal, as heir to the throne, would have to eventually repudiate his fat friend and surrogate father. The moment comes at the end of Part 2, after Falstaff has spent five acts extorting money, drinking, making jokes, having one drunken brawl and being maudlin a couple of times. Hal has become king:

> *"I know thee not, old man: fall to thy prayers;*
>
> *How ill white hairs become a fool and jester!*
> *I have long dream'd of such a kind of man,*
> *So surfeit-swell'd, so old and so profane;*
> *But, being awaked, I do despise my dream.*
> *Make less thy body hence, and more thy grace;*
> *Leave gormandizing; know the grave doth gape*
> *For thee thrice wider than for other men.*
> *Reply not to me with a fool-born jest:*
> *Presume not that I am the thing I was;*
> *For God doth know, so shall the world perceive,*
> *That I have turn'd away my former self ..."*[18]

The cold brutality with which Hal – now King Henry V – consigns Falstaff to the past is shocking. It is a public judgement, witnessed both by the characters onstage and by the audience. It is framed – though not without a great deal of ambiguity – as a necessary symbolic act if Hal is to renew "broken Britain". It lends greater shine to Hal's apotheosis as the chivalric hero of a re-born nation at the battle of Agincourt in the next play. It is part of that theatre's attempt to forge a self-conscious (patriotic) public via the medium of the history play. It is through Falstaff the exile's eyes that I wished the walk to be seen.

We pass architectural models sitting on top of packing cases in a window on Curtain Road, a series of proposed futures waiting to be realised.

At the top end of Hoxton Street Market we passed through the Arden Estate. In a fanciful mood, and perhaps as a nod to local history, its blocks all have Shakespearian names. Or it might have been an assumption on the part of the council that ordinary people have as much right to the ownership of high culture, or what is now known as 'Heritage', as anyone else. Just off the street we find Falstaff House. It is fitting that Falstaff's last home is in the name of a denigrated form of housing.

> *The current social housing is warehousing poverty in the core of our great cities – cities which need to be the very engines of economic growth.*[19]

The assumed teleology is clear here; "warehousing" is the thickened time of stasis. Engines and growth are dynamic, future orientated.

On the roundabout at the top of Hoxton Street, a brightly coloured sculpture of three figures, two children and a long–haired youth, who points urgently away from the estates back down the road, stagger drunkenly in crocodile formation towards the market. One of the children has a fat chain around its ankle, perhaps the only trace left of a long–stolen bike.

Arden Estate Board, 2010   I *Love Hoxton*, 2011, KEVIN HARRISON

We ended in Shoreditch Park, next to John Frankland's sculpture *Boulder* (2009), a piece of Cornish granite weighing near 100 tons and around 12 foot high. It is an enormous presence, a miniature mountain in a relatively flat and featureless expanse of green. Its closed form seems to bend the space around it with the gravity of its age and weight. Unlike so much public sculpture, especially that which is part of 'regeneration' schemes, it does not make so much as a nod to context – local communities, anodyne versions of local history. It insists on its dumb presence and visibility.

Boulder, 2009, JOHN FRANKLAND

In terms of contemporary discourse around art and urban regeneration, this does create a 'place', a recognisable landmark, but it is worlds away from the inclusive and upbeat rhetoric:

> *Through aesthetic re-enchantment ... revival and recovery are abetted ... inhabitants are empowered by the reclaimed environment ... In so doing, the conversion of space to place builds the self-esteem of the locale, revitalising all that it touches.*[20]

Frankland, a rock climber himself, has claimed that it is intended to be climbed on and that this will 'activate' the piece, but this looks like a sop to those who would demand some sort of utilitarian inclusivity. The Shoreditch Trust, under whose aegis this work was created, say that this is "a way of playfully debunking the notion of those sculptures in park settings, which are often fenced off or prominently labelled as 'not to be touched'".[21] I would say that it debunks the notion of public art as it stands today. It contains its own time, millions of years of it, in its unknowable interior, oblivious to the attempts to gentrify – or 'modernise' – its surroundings. It is immovable and gives nothing. One can only look at it, sense its gravity, or walk past. I poured beer on it, the most honest homage I could do, and walked away.

*All photographs by Robin Bale

1. Jacques Rancière (trans. Gabriel Rockhill), *The Politics of Aesthetics* (New York: Continuum, 2006) p. 13.
2. Stefan Collini, 'Blahspeak', *London Review of Books*, 32(7), 2010, pp. 29–34.
3. Sara Helm, 'Modernise or die, Blair tells partners', *The Independent*, 6 June 1997, http://www.independent.co.uk/news/world/modernise-or-die-blair-tells-partners-1254375.html (accessed 27/02/11).
4. Fyodor Dostoyevsky (trans. Constance Garnett), 'Notes from the Underground', in Deborah A. Martinsen (ed.), *Notes from the Underground, The Double and other stories* (New York: Barnes & Noble, 2003) p. 261.
5. 'Benefits culture is a national crisis that must end, says Iain Duncan Smith', *Daily Telegraph*, 12 November 2010, http://www.telegraph.co.uk/news/newstopics/politics/8127923/Benefits-culture-is-a-national-crisis-that-must-end-says-Iain-Duncan-Smith.html (accessed 25/02/11).
6. Stephen Greenhalgh and John Moss, 'Principles for Social Housing Reform', Localis, 15 April 2009, http://www.localis.org.uk/images/Localis%20Principles%20for%20Social%20Housing%20Reform%20WEB.pdf (accessed 22/02/11).
7. *Criminal Justice and Police Act 2001, section 12*, HM Government, 2001, http://www.legislation.gov.uk/ukpga/2001/16/section/12#commentary-c1772955 (accessed 25/02/11).
8. Gregor Hunter, 'Anti-social public drinking banned in Hackney', *Hackney Post*, 23 March 2010, http://hackneypost.co.uk/?p=3784 (accessed 22/02/11).
9. *ibid.*, Gregor Hunter (2010).
10. Chris Kay and Arj Singh, 'Anti-social drinkers face fines or arrest', *Hackney Post*, 18 March 2010, http://hackneypost.co.uk/?p=3668 (accessed 22/02/11).
11. *ibid.*, Gregor Hunter (2010).
12. Team Hackney, *Safer Dalston* newsletter, May 2010, http://www.teamhackney.org/may2010-ward-dalston (accessed 20/02/11).
13. *ibid.*, Stefan Collini (2010).
14. 'Last orders for the boozy lunch', Drinkaware, 19 May 2010, http://www.drinkaware.co.uk/alcohol-and-you/work-and-study/last-orders-for-the-boozy-lunch (accessed 26/02/11).
15. William Shakespeare, *Henry IV, Part 2*, Act 2 Scene 4.
16. William Shakespeare, *Henry IV, Part 2*, Act 1 Scene 2.
17. Germaine Greer, *Shakespeare: A Very Short Introduction* (London: Oxford University Press, 2002) p. 24.
18. William Shakespeare, *Henry IV, Part 2*, Act 5 Scene 5.
19. *ibid.*, Stephen Greenhalgh and John Moss (2009).
20. Luca M. Visconti *et al.*, 'Street Art, Sweet Art? Reclaiming the "Public" in Public Place', *Journal of Consumer Research*, 2010, 36 (October), pp. 511–529.
21. *Boulder*, The Shoreditch Trust, 2009, http://www.shoreditchtrust.org.uk/Physical-Regeneration/Peer/John-Frankland-s-Boulder (accessed 22/02/11).

About Myrdle Court Press

Myrdle Court Press (MCP) advances critical, independent and rigorous inter-disciplinary work that interrogates contemporary notions and experience of 'cities'. It was established in 2009 to redress the incongruous situation that as the population, size and problems of cities are expanding, and despite the existence of many new cells of knowledge and urgent thinking, the spaces for critical public discourse are narrowing and the credibility of democracy rapidly declining.

An independent, not-for-profit organisation that straddles the spaces between the street and the academy, Myrdle Court Press commissions, collects and publishes work that tackles pressing and political concerns without restraint. It shares the experiences, astute insights and agitation of contributors from around the world including Beirut, Zagreb, Bogota, London, Hong Kong, Athens, Nicosia, Jerusalem, New York, Porto and Warsaw. Contributors come from the fields of visual arts, activism, education, property, architecture and planning, law, governmental policy, political economy, military strategy, filmmaking, philosophy and lived knowledge.

On Myrdle Court Press books:

"There is a dearth of critical commentaries examining the changes wrought by neo-liberalism. At last a multi-disciplinary collection of writing that brings together some of the best." Anna Minton, author of *Ground Control*

"This collection explicitly and honestly wears its politics on its sleeve. The exhilaration in the book lies in the stories told and in their transformative potential." Professor Jeremy Till, author of *Architecture Depends*

Select titles:

In Memory of Athiraman Kannan: Migration and Labour in the Early 21st Century, (2013)

Sign of the Times: An Alternative Reading of Collapse and Crisis in the City of London, (2012)

Common Enclosures and Great Escapes Vol.1, (2012)

Estate: Arts, Politics and Social Housing in Britain, (2010)

Critical Cities: Ideas, Knowledge and Agitation from Emerging Urbanists Vol.3, (2012)

Critical Cities: Ideas, Knowledge and Agitation from Emerging Urbanists Vol.2, (2010)

Critical Cities: Ideas, Knowledge and Agitation from Emerging Urbanists Vol.1, (2009)

Myrdle Court Press is based in London, UK and is the publishing arm of This Is Not A Gateway. It takes a back–to–fundamentals approach to book production using design for readability, high quality ethically sourced materials, local printers and independent distribution.

www.myrdlecourtpress.net